FREEDOM HAS A FACE

Carter G. Woodson Institute Series

Deborah E. McDowell, Editor

FREEDOM HAS A FACE

Race, Identity, and Community in Jefferson's Virginia

Kirt von Daacke

University of Virginia Press *Charlottesville and London*

University of Virginia Press

Printed in the United States of America on acid-free paper

First published 2012

1 3 5 7 9 8 6 4 2

LIBRARY OF CONGRESS CATALOGING-IN-PUBLICATION DATA

Von Daacke, Kirt, 1968–
Freedom has a face : race, identity, and community in Jefferson's Virginia / Kirt von Daacke.
p. cm. — (Carter G. Woodson Institute series)
Includes bibliographical references and index.
ISBN 978-0-8139-3309-2 (cloth : alk. paper) — ISBN 978-0-8139-3310-8 (e-book)
1. Free African Americans—Virginia—Albemarle County—History—19th century. 2. Free African Americans—Virginia—Albemarle County—Social conditions—19th century. 3. Albemarle County (Va.)—Race relations. 4. Albemarle County (Va.)—History—19th century. I. Title.
F232.A3V66 2012
305.896'0755482—dc23

2012008718

For my father,
who truly taught me that the love of learning
is indeed the key to a good life well lived.

Contents

Acknowledgments

Over the many years of working on this project, I have compiled a long list of people and organizations to whom I owe thanks. I could not have produced this book without all of their help—I am grateful beyond words for all of the assistance, love, and support they provided and doubt that their acknowledgment here truly repays them for their help.

I was blessed with two professors who were academic mentors of the highest order: Reginald D. Butler and Michael P. Johnson. I hope my book in some small way lives up to their great expectations. The kernel of inspiration for this project grew out of some classes I took as an undergraduate at the University of Virginia with Reginald D. Butler. His patient guidance, high standards, and trenchant criticisms changed the direction of my scholarly interests and prepared me for graduate school. I cannot thank him enough both for that start years ago and for his continuing advice long after I had left UVA.

Michael P. Johnson changed my life the day he called and invited me personally to come to The Johns Hopkins University to work with him as a graduate student. Ever since, I have been lucky to count him as a mentor and friend. While I was in graduate school, every meeting I had with him tore down and quietly helped reshape my scholarship but somehow sent me out the door feeling better and more confident. He has remained to this day a ceaseless supporter of my research and my professional ambitions and a model for how to treat students. In addition to a debt of gratitude for all that, I probably also owe him several meals out, preferably for ribs and beer.

At Hopkins, Ronald Walters's guidance and assistance—both in Baltimore and since—make me glad to be a historian. Philip Morgan, Toby Ditz,

Jane Dailey, and Jack Greene all deserve a huge thank you for their criticism and scholarly advice about my research. Outside of Baltimore, a number of other scholars offered excellent commentary and questions about parts of this project: Melvyn P. Ely, Peter Wallenstein, Tony Iaccarino, Laura Edwards, and Sabita Manian. Special thanks to Maurie McInnis for directing me to the image that appears on the cover—I never would have found it without her expert assistance.

I also had the good fortune of meeting Robert Vernon, a lay historian in Charlottesville, Virginia, who was then in the process of compiling a guide to county records concerning free blacks. This partial guide represented an amazing introduction to the documentary record. He generously gave me a copy of the draft-in-progress. Thanks to Vernon, I had a list of free black names as well as a set of basic directions for navigating often confusing collections—Vernon's guide provided the key for deciphering the story of free black life in Albemarle.

My time at UVA, around the Hopkins seminar table, and at academic conferences has been invaluable. I am lucky to know Jeff McClurken, George Baca, Andy Lewis, Dylan Penningroth, Natalie Ring, Josh Rothman, and Mark Thompson as good friends whose intellectual insights and humor continue to nourish me. I eagerly await my next fine dinner out at a conference with Jeff, Josh, and Natalie, as long as we never eat again at any place named Pancho Villa's. I am sure I owe each of them a drink.

My former colleagues in the Lynchburg College History Department—Nichole Sanders, Brian Crim, James Owens, and Scott Amos—provided critical commentary as well as companionship and support. I could not ask for better colleagues and friends. We also shared a few amazing students, whose own work on the antebellum South inspired me to persevere through the long publication process. Thanks to Charlotte Arbogast, John Marks, and Ashley Schmidt for their excellent research and writing. Jon Shipe spent the better part of a summer as a graduate assistant making manuscript-formatting corrections and chasing down whatever errand I sent him on.

I benefited greatly from my time as a Batten Fellow at the International Center for Jefferson Studies and from a year as a visiting scholar at the Carter G. Woodson Institute for Afro-American and African Affairs at the University of Virginia. There, Peter Onuf and Cinder Stanton did wonders for my understanding of Jefferson's writings on race and of the Hemings family. Lynchburg College also gave important support by providing both a summer faculty research grant and a travel grant for the project. The Virginia Foundation for Independent Colleges' Mednick Memorial Fellowship provided important financial support as well, allowing me to spend three comfortable weeks doing research at the Library of Virginia.

The knowledgeable archivists and librarians at the Library of Virginia, the Virginia Historical Society, the Virginia Baptist Historical Society, and the University of Virginia's Albert and Shirley Small Special Collections Library proved invaluable during my years of digging through all those musty county records. Any historian doing local historical research likely owes a huge thank you to at least one local lay historian, genealogist, or compiler. Bob Vernon graciously shared with me his draft-in-progress guide to African American records in Albemarle—it was my personal Rosetta stone that unlocked the mysteries of those county records.

At the University of Virginia Press, Dick Holway, Raennah Mitchell, and Morgan Myers patiently guided the book through acquisition and editing. All three happily answered my questions, solved my computing dilemmas, and caught mistakes. Melvyn P. Ely's guidance, first as a reviewer and then as a sensitive reader providing page-by-page editorial commentary, improved this book immeasurably. I cannot thank him enough for all the time he took to help me shape the book—the final product would not be what it is without his interventions. While I owe him for that effort, I remain solely responsible for any errors that appear within.

Since I began the long process of creating this book, my wife, Nicole Eramo, has been there at every moment, offering criticism of my writing, lending a copy-editing hand, providing critical analysis, listening to me fulminate at one thing or another, and always supporting me through the process. She did this while herself pursuing a doctorate, working full-time as a dean, and being a wonderful mother to our lovely son. She's the most beautiful, talented, and amazing person I have ever met, and this book could not have happened without her.

My parents, Fred and Nancy von Daacke, have always provided financial and emotional assistance and, far more important, moral and intellectual support. They have long been my role models in life and learning. I would not know where to begin in thanking them for all they have done. It was my father's own passion as a father, a mentor, a historian, and a teacher that pushed me toward this avocation. I dedicate this book to him.

FREEDOM HAS A FACE

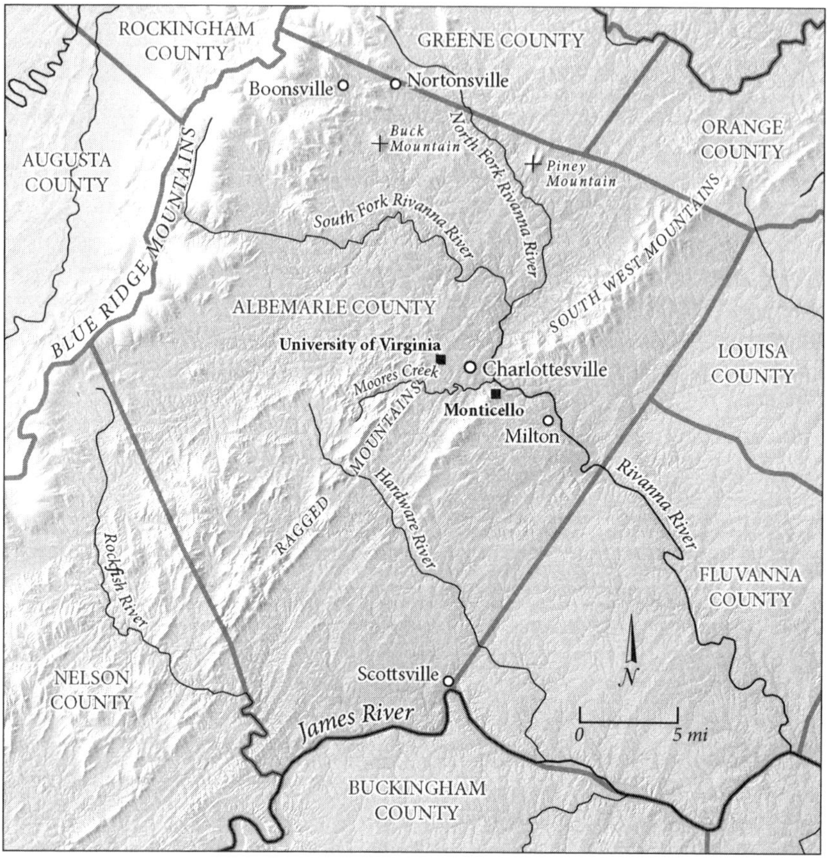

MAP OF ALBEMARLE COUNTY, VIRGINIA. (Map by Erin Greb)

Introduction

Ulrich Bonnell Phillips, in his systematic study *American Negro Slavery,* stated that "the main body of the free negroes were those who whether in person or through their mothers had been liberated purely from sentiment and possessed no particular qualifications for self-directed careers.... Wherever they dwelt, they lived somewhat precariously upon the sufferance of whites, and in a more or less palpable danger of losing their liberty." By liberty, Phillips meant simply not being slaves—self-ownership. Phillips's statement loudly declares his belief in black inferiority and condemns free people of color to a well-deserved status of slaves without masters. But Phillips's statement also contains within it the basic outlines of nearly a century of scholarship on free blacks.[1]

This view of free blacks as only nominally free and trapped in a precarious existence has had a long life. Scholars for decades after Phillips reiterated this basic view. Ira Berlin's seminal 1974 monograph, *Slaves without Masters,* confirmed the Phillips picture of free black life. Gone were Phillips's racism and his blaming of the victim. Instead, Berlin painted a picture of free blacks struggling mightily against virulent white racism, pervasive policing, and a legal system that both severely circumscribed their existence and was rigged against them. Such space as a few free blacks were occasionally afforded came about largely because of support by paternalistic white protectors. Berlin's powerful thesis remains perhaps the most influential statement on free blacks to this day. For Berlin and many other scholars, free blacks remain a historical anomaly in a society that equated whiteness with freedom and blackness with enslaved status. In Berlin's famous phrase, they were slaves without masters who spent their days avoiding a pervasive and racist white power structure.[2]

This paradigm remains attractive thanks to four main assumptions undergirding it. First, by the mid-eighteenth century, the legal system in every southern colony plainly announced white objections to free blacks. According to Ira Berlin, anti–free black laws grew out of white efforts to solidify and codify the slave system "by drawing a color line between free and slave." For Berlin and others, this effort virtually guaranteed that blacks who remained free would suffer despite their best efforts. In a slave society that equated darker skin color with enslaved status, little room seemed to exist for free blacks. They became anomalous, free but black, slaves by appearance but technically free, trapped in a liminal world between slaves and white citizens. A perusal of the legal code in any southern state would support this contention. This study, however, exposes a wide gap between state legal proscriptions on free blacks and actual local practice by examining free black interaction with the legal system in one rural Virginia county.

Second, the slaves-without-masters paradigm, which argues that free blacks wherever they existed were visible contradictions of an understood, racially coded socioeconomic system, sees rural areas as the most racist and inflexible of all locales.[3] There, the theory goes, the gaze of racist whites was all but impossible to avoid. Rural slaveholding white elites expressed the greatest concerns about the influence of free blacks upon their slaves. Most rural areas supposedly had tiny and dispersed free black populations. As a result, those free blacks, unlike those in southern cities, could not develop strong and protective communities. Nor could they achieve an anonymity that allowed them some comfortable room for living apart from the white community. Thus, free blacks who remained in rural areas lived in "palpable danger of losing their liberty" and often encountered a local legal and policing system that not only sought them out but also treated them as if they were slaves.[4]

According to this paradigm, the result was that free blacks moved continually from these rigidly racist rural areas to developing urban centers, seeking both better opportunity and a chance to live in relative anonymity. Thus, the existence of cohesive free black communities is considered a largely urban phenomenon. A gap between free black proscriptions and actual local practice is likewise seen as having existed mainly in urban areas. This book, however, suggests that rural areas may actually have been more permissive environments for the free blacks who lived there, because those free blacks were well-known and because many developed respectable reputations. A gap between state law and local practice thus developed as rural communities such as Albemarle County saw the people of color living in their midst not as dangerous free blacks but as people with names, faces, and personal histories that were tied to specific events, times, and places.

The third assumption supporting the slaves-without-masters paradigm involves a brief period of liberalization immediately after the American Revolution. According to this narrative, slave owners across America and particularly in the Upper South came to see their participation in the enslaving of people as a contradiction of the principles the colonies had fought for in seeking independence. Thus, Virginia's manumission law of 1782 becomes a patently liberalizing piece of legislation born out of the obvious contradiction of owning slaves while simultaneously accusing England of enslaving the colonies. The law of 1782 changed the rules for manumission. Prior to that year, the colonial assembly/state legislature remained the sole arbiter concerning the freeing of individual slaves. The law allowed for manumission only in cases of extremely meritorious service. But with the revised law in 1782, the power to manumit became the sole province of the owner. The result of the law was supposedly a spate of manumissions by slaveholders who explicitly mentioned revolutionary ideals as the reason for the emancipations.[5]

This body of scholarship correctly identifies a sizable aggregate surge in free black populations in the decade after the Revolution. The resulting free black population, now far larger and much more visible, supposedly became a problem for many white southerners. White racist fears about free African Americans in their midst grew with every passing year. According to these scholars, Gabriel Prosser's abortive rebellion in the Richmond area in 1800 brought the period of liberalization to an abrupt end. By 1806, Virginia amended the manumission law of 1782 by stating that any slave freed after passage of the law would have to leave Virginia within a year unless granted special permission by the legislature to remain. A brief and never fully realized moment, when a combination of egalitarian ideals growing out of the Revolution and out of evangelical Christianity coalesced to open the door to numerous manumissions, ended as racist whites and nervous slaveholders demanded the reassertion of a binary racial order. According to this interpretation, any chance of including in the broader community those people of color who were not slaves was lost by the early nineteenth century. This book argues that people of color remained integrally connected to the communities in which they lived at least until the 1840s and, in many cases, longer. Likewise, the evidence for Albemarle suggests that Revolutionary principles were rarely a motive for manumission. Instead, whites, free blacks, and slaves lived, worked, and played in close contact. They naturally developed close personal relationships. They came to know and trust one another. Manumissions, whether based on warm personal relationships or arising out of economic benefit, were predicated upon a high degree of intimacy between owner and slave.[6]

Finally, the slaves-without-masters model rests upon assumptions about the existence and maintenance of a strict color line. For white residents across most of the slaveholding states, the theory goes, black or brown skin color was equated with enslaved status. Whiteness indicated freedom and citizenship. We are told that most of the South adhered strictly to the color-coded hierarchy that allowed room for only two categories, white and black. No room existed for anyone with visible admixture. Mulattoes, no matter how light skinned, in most areas were coded as legally black. Thus, they too were anomalies: part white, but visibly possessing the debilitating stain of blackness. Their skin color linked them in the minds of whites with slaves. They occupied a status that was quasi-free at best. Places such as Charleston and New Orleans, in this view, were more permissive—urban areas influenced by Spanish and Caribbean societies, which had created de jure and de facto statuses between those of black slave and white citizen. These cities were the exceptions that proved the rule that black meant slave and white meant free. A newer body of scholarship has begun to complicate this portrait, examining interracial sex, free mulattoes, and class. This book continues that effort, arguing for a de facto free-mulatto status in Virginia. Free mulattoes in Albemarle County (who represented a significant majority of the free black population), by becoming well recognized and trusted, could enjoy a measure of comfort and success.[7]

Another smaller but growing body of scholarship seeks to complicate the slaves-without-masters model on nearly every level. Some scholars have highlighted the economic freedoms and opportunities available to free blacks and have found an at times startling degree of economic and financial success among individual African Americans. They shift the focus to free black agency in the face of racism and legal disability. Working especially with family papers, other historians have created in-depth biographies of free black families that bring to light lives that do not fit in the

Phillips-Berlin model. Still others have engaged in fine-grained community studies that have begun to resituate free blacks within the communities in which they lived. A few historians have done all these things. The combined weight of this body of scholarship suggests the need for a revision of the Berlin-Phillips paradigm. This book continues the efforts of those historians, examining the economic and social successes and failures of free blacks in one rural antebellum community.[8]

Chapter 1 charts the lives of a number of free blacks in Albemarle County. All were born free to free parents in the colonial period. All enlisted on the American side in the Revolutionary War effort. Their individual life experiences demonstrate, first, that Albemarle County had a stable and growing population of free people of color before the Revolution. Their stories also highlight the fact that these men were far more than "slaves without masters." They were active participants in the larger Albemarle County community that included whites, other free blacks, and even slaves. They may not have participated in that community as equals to the white male citizenry, but neither were they anomalous or marginalized. Their life experiences remain a testament to the power of personalism and the filling of useful roles in determining one's position in the social web. These men were commonly known by white and black alike. Their service in the Revolution would function throughout their lives as a calling card of sorts. Through that war service, they had established close relationships with local whites. They became known quantities. More important, they became trusted and respected people.

Chapter 2 continues that story, charting the experiences of the children of Revolutionary War veterans. This was the generation of Albemarle County free blacks born too late to participate in the war effort or even to appreciate fully that seemingly liberal postwar period when prospects appeared good for either a general emancipation or at least a less restrictive climate for free blacks. These people, lacking the valuable experience of Revolutionary War service, nonetheless successfully negotiated the social web in Albemarle County. They, too, learned the value of being known and respected within the community. These free blacks did not hide at the margins of Albemarle County society, ever fearful of white surveillance. Instead, they interacted in myriad positive ways with their white neighbors while remaining deeply connected to a web of free black families that stretched beyond the county's borders. As with the generation before them, this group did not experience a legal system that was unbearably repressive or rigged against them. They did not hide from local authorities, and they acted as if the local court system was a rational and responsive venue in which to settle personal disputes with white and black neighbors alike.

Chapter 3 examines the issue of free black residency and mobility in Albemarle County and in Virginia more generally. By focusing on how a rural county addressed the issue of free black residency, this chapter provides evidence countering the argument that the rural South was racially a rigidly defined space that spawned post-1800 anti–free black legislation. In this chapter, free blacks are shown to have demonstrated an impressive degree of mobility, moving easily back and forth from county to county and even from state to state. These same free blacks regularly managed to become known for their positive behavior, allowing them to live comfortable and unmolested lives in the area. And they did this without having a white benefactor or white relative in the county. The 1806 removal law, intended to give localities the opportunity to rid themselves of a presumably obnoxious free black presence, remained on the books but was ignored for decades in Albemarle County. Numerous slaves were freed in the county during that time, and most remained in the county in apparent violation of that law. Even in the 1840s, when local authorities, acting at the behest of a limited contingent of local whites, began to prosecute a small number of free blacks for remaining in the commonwealth, a much larger number of white residents came to the defense of people whom they were familiar with and considered respectable, trustworthy, and dependable. A rural culture of personalism was a key determinant of social status in Albemarle, even for free blacks.

Chapter 4 examines the members of the free black community in Albemarle County whose behavior should have marked them for the worst fate at the hands of the legal system. These people engaged in physical violence against white residents. Their face-to-face interactions with area whites often displayed the same fairly high level of familiarity and even intimacy that the earlier chapters highlight. But these men went further, asserting a rough sense of equality with whites through their actions. They all faced legal troubles stemming from violent attacks on whites, with the charges ranging from simple assault to premeditated murder. Yet they were treated in much the same way a white defendant accused of similar crimes would have been, rather than as particularly dangerous or frightening free blacks. As early as 1785, free blacks were legally forbidden by the state legislature to testify as witnesses in criminal or civil cases where whites were defendants or plaintiffs. In 1832, the state legislature denied free black defendants the right to trial by jury except in capital cases. Despite those legal disabilities, free people of color received what appear to have been fair trials, trials that evoke both the quotidian nature of interracial contact in Albemarle County and the immense importance of local knowledge of individuals' behavior and reputation to the functioning of the county's social structure. Some free blacks testified in cases that involved a white party. A guilty verdict was anything but a foregone conclusion for these people. Once again, these free blacks were active participants in local affairs, even if they were denied both full legal protection and access to the political arena.[9]

Chapter 5 tackles the issue of free black women and interracial sex in the rural context. This chapter exposes a sphere of interracial entertainments existing in Charlottesville, ranging from simple gaming and drinking to larger social gatherings and even houses of prostitution that catered to white and black alike. The activities that took place in those houses and fields seemed to violate both gendered notions of behavior and a sense of strict racial hierarchy. Yet policing of that sphere appears to have been minimal, with only occasional and mild enforcement. In fact, Albemarle County enforcement never involved the more comprehensive and concerted antivice campaigns that occurred in urban areas such as Richmond and Baltimore. Naturally, bawdy houses were sites of frequent and highly intimate interracial contact, and some white residents in Albemarle complained about their existence. They were sites often controlled by single women, both black and white. These women, despite becoming propertied and wealthy through prostitution, also managed to participate in Albemarle County's culture of personalism. Their stories highlight both the possibilities and the pitfalls awaiting unmarried women of color in the rural antebellum South.

The final chapter seeks to situate interracial sex within the context of one rural southern community. Here, miscegenation becomes a regular feature of society, one often not hidden at all from the larger white community. Free blacks, whites, and slaves interacted regularly and easily in Albemarle County. Such intimacy not surprisingly resulted in sex across a blurred color line. Miscegenation in Albemarle County was far more than white masters sleeping with their female slaves. It also included white men and free black women, as well as free black men and white women. Whatever the combination, interracial sex created a class of people who were neither black nor white and who did not fit neatly into the supposedly binary racial order.

In this chapter, color as society construed it is shown to be no longer simply a reflection of actual somatic condition or even parentage. The county's culture of personalism meant that proper behavior and reputation helped to determine how one's color was perceived. Local reputation derived from intimate, face-to-face meetings created a rough community consensus about individuals, social relationships, and color that carried far more weight than any law passed in Richmond. Once again, a pronounced gap between state law and local practice existed in Albemarle for free blacks at least until the 1850s. White Albemarle County residents felt no need to utilize anti–free black legislation against their black neighbors because they saw those laws as dealing with dangerous and unknown free blacks who lived someplace else.

This book argues for the existence and continuation of a relatively easygoing interracial social order in Albemarle County for more than two generations after the Revolution, stretching to the mid-nineteenth century and beyond. This culture continued despite the Gabriel conspiracy in 1800 and Nat Turner's Southampton revolt in 1831, but not because Albemarle was a highly unusual locale bent on creating an egalitarian interracial order. On the contrary, Albemarle County was a fairly typical rural Virginia Piedmont county socially, economically, and politically. No racial utopia existed there. It was a tight-knit county in which just about everyone knew almost everyone else. Face-to-face interactions determined social status and reputation. Free blacks, by participating openly and willingly in this culture of personalism, carved out lives for themselves that belie the slaves-without-masters model. White Albemarle residents did not look out upon the social landscape of their county and see simply black slaves and white citizens. Instead, they saw people who had names attached to faces and reputations attached to those names. As a result, the county recognized a de facto social position between the dangerous free black and the white citizen. This status did not have a formal name or any real legal backing, but it did have social power, which turned out to be far more important to those who possessed it.[10]

Again, this book does not argue for a blissful racial utopia in Albemarle County. The free blacks whose life stories are told here worked hard to carve out a comfortable space for existence, and they were denied full freedom. But they were not slaves without masters. Nor were they anomalies in a society that had room only for black slaves and free white citizens. Free blacks, Jews, Christians, mulattoes, masters, slaves, and mistresses: all could and

ALBEMARLE COUNTY POPULATION, 1790–1860

	1790	1800	1810	1820	1830	1840	1850	1860
Slaves	5,579	7,436	9,226	10,661	11,679	11,809	13,338	13,916
Whites	6,835	8,796	8,642	8,715	9,458	10,212	11,875	12,103
Free blacks								
Male	—	—	—	197	253	297	265	270
Female	—	—	—	176	231	306	322	336
Total	171	207	400	373	484	603	587	606

Source: Historical Census Browser, Geospatial and Statistical Data Center, University of Virginia.
Note: A breakdown by gender for free blacks is not available before 1820.

did engage in intimacies across a figurative color line that looks almost impenetrable when studied from the vantage point of law. But that figurative line in rural Albemarle County functioned more like a broad, elastic zone with porous, fluid boundaries between free people black and white. A de facto continuum of social status existed between those two poles, and not only in the Low Country and Louisiana. Albemarle County had a steep social hierarchy that allowed substantial inequalities to persist, and the vast majority of blacks there faced brutal exploitation as slaves, but it was nonetheless an intimately interracial society.

In arguing those points discussed above, I utilize a wide variety of source materials—court orders, minute books, law orders, surveys and deeds, marriages, wills, census reports, free black registrations, civil court lawsuits, criminal presentments, legislative petitions, personal memoirs, business records, and account books.

Taken individually, these sources often reveal little about life in Albemarle County for either whites or free blacks. Many source materials lack name indexes. Most records simply note the names of the participants without mentioning race—a practice that itself calls into question the idea that race was an indelible brand that governed an individual's fate absolutely. White and black families in the rural South often have similar or identical last names. Most poor, illiterate, or socially inferior residents, white as well as black, appear infrequently in the extant documents and rarely left behind personal records. Even when indexes exist, they often record only the primary names involved, such as the plaintiff and defendant, without mentioning the names of witnesses. The spelling of names frequently changes somewhat dramatically from document to document. This combination of factors makes it difficult to trace lives unless the researcher is willing painstakingly to sift through voluminous pages of materials. This book is the result of one such effort. I either wrote an abstract of or transcribed each and every entry in the will books, criminal presentments, legislative petitions, and other sources, taking care to capture the names of every individual involved in each entry.

Constructing a cross-referenced database containing individual records for nearly five thousand examined documents allowed that mountain of seemingly impersonal documents to reveal a picture of life in Albemarle County that a focus on the laws obscures. Individuals and families, and their lives, suddenly came into view. Documents that upon first inspection appeared to be unrelated revealed themselves to concern the same people. The completed database allowed me to create biographies of dozens of free blacks in Albemarle County. Who were their parents? Whom did they marry? Where did they live? What property did they possess? How many children did they have? Who were their neighbors? With whom did they have conflicts? Did they ever register their freedom? What did they look like? All these questions, and many more, could now be answered.

The database contains information on roughly one-fourth to one-third of the county's free men of color and a much smaller proportion of free women of color, for most years from 1780 to 1865. But many of those people do not appear in the documentary record with enough frequency to trace their lives in any significant way. Their lives remain largely invisible to historians. Thus, this book limits itself to those who left enough of an imprint on the historical record to be studied. Not only do these records provide details about individual lives, but they also allow the researcher to see how those people fit into the local community. It is this reinsertion of individual free blacks into the neighborhood, community, and county that exposes a different, more complicated picture of the life experiences of free people of color.

1

The Right Hand Men of the Revolution

Albemarle's Free Black War Veterans

Albemarle County, Virginia, situated in central Virginia just east of the Blue Ridge Mountains, was home to a few thousand whites, a few thousand slaves, and more than one hundred free blacks during the Revolutionary War.[1] It was a rural farming community producing tobacco, wheat, and corn as its cash crops. The county was home both to yeoman farmers working their own land and to plantation owners heavily dependent upon slave labor. Seventy miles west of the capital in Richmond, the county was neither part of the Virginia frontier nor central to the locus of political and economic power in the state. In many ways, it was a typically insular and tight-knit community of planters and farmers, the type of place that characterized Piedmont counties across the Upper South.

Rural counties in the Piedmont such as Albemarle that had substantial slave populations were characterized by residential integration. Small slaveholders dominated the landscape. Free blacks and nonslaveholding whites lived throughout the county, usually in areas with less productive land. Occasionally, this pattern was broken up by the appearance of a larger tobacco plantation; Jefferson's Monticello, where over one hundred slaves lived with a white family and white overseers, lay within a short distance of both Charlottesville and free black landowners. In such a world, family and neighbors formed the core of an individual's local and personal social networks. Local knowledge was maintained and disseminated by a social web built upon face-to-face interactions. Trust extended primarily to those who were known within these localized and highly personal social networks.

Free people of color, although part and parcel of these counties, neighborhoods, communities, and social networks, remained near the bottom of a steep social hierarchy. They were not slaves, but their often visible darker complexion, and more important, the local social coding of them as persons of color, left them in some ways trapped at the lower end of the southern social ladder. However, free blacks remained part of these communities, embedded in the web of social relations that existed in each locale, connections that crossed and confused apparent color lines. For free people of color to advance and prosper in such an environment, freedom had to have a face. They could be "known" personages, whose existence and productivity in the community had to be recognized and deemed worthy and respectable. They would need free black friends and family, as well as friendly relationships with whites whom they lived near or worked with, if they were to be successful and secure.[2]

At the beginning of the Revolutionary War in 1776, there were at most about 150 free people of color living in the county. The extant archival record indicates that at least six free black males between 1776 and 1780 enlisted in the war effort in Albemarle County. This chapter charts their lives and argues that their experience as soldiers helped them to cement highly personal and enduring bonds with white members of Albemarle's community. Decades later, these men continued to trade upon their service in that conflict as a credential showing their fitness for inclusion in the community. These men of color represent a small sample of the free black population, but they do not all appear to have been members of a free black social or economic elite. They are unusual or unique only in the sense that they appeared with enough frequency in public records that their lives can be pieced together by a modern researcher.

The county was a hotbed of Revolutionary activity and philosophy; Thomas Jefferson penned the Declaration of Independence and the Virginia Statute for Religious Freedom, and he served as governor of the fledgling independent state during the war. Many white men in the county served in the militia or the Continental Army. At least one hundred enlisted and fought.[3] Those white men were not alone in joining in the attempt to separate from England. A number of free men of color also enlisted, including a waterman named Johnson Smith. Born in 1763, Smith enlisted as a teenager sometime after 1776 and served at least one eighteen-month tour of duty.[4] Smith joined the navy and served as a seaman. After the war, he returned to Albemarle County along with other war veterans. In 1789, Smith was listed as living in St. Anne's Parish, which covered roughly the southern half of the county. Smith, described in that year as mulatto, lived with one other tithable (a person old enough to be counted for taxation purposes), a man aged between sixteen and twenty-one, likely a family member. At that time, he owned no taxable property. He seemed destined to remain a nearly propertyless free black whose imprint upon both Albemarle and the archival record would be faint indeed.[5]

By 1794, Johnson Smith's situation had changed only a little: he now owned one horse but still paid no tax. Two years later, Smith (now listed as "negro") no longer owned the horse. He remained a poor free black war veteran, apparently with little to show for his war service. Smith managed to purchase a horse sometime in 1798, however, and continued to own one through 1805. By the next year, 1806, he owned two horses, paying property tax for the first time. By then, he clearly had a family, with three free males listed as living in his household, including sons Wilson (age fourteen) and Pitman (age six). For the next five years, Johnson Smith's status barely changed. He continued to own one or two horses and to watch his family grow.[6]

County records sometimes call Johnson Smith "Johnson Scott," suggesting that Smith may not have become sufficiently well recognized. Regardless, Smith had fathered at least four children by 1810. County records provide little in the way of detail about the woman he started a family with, let alone much about Smith himself. The 1810 census has Smith listed as the head of a household of twelve "other free persons, except Indians, not taxed"—in other words, a household of black people.[7] By that time, some of Smith's children were old enough to be listed separately as free persons on personal property tax lists, but clearly still lived in their parents' household. Other extended family members also may have been living on the same property or even under the same roof as Johnson Smith. The family lived in the Scottsville area, the former county seat located at a bend in the James River on the southern border of the county. Perhaps Smith had put his experience in the navy to good use and was working as a waterman on the river.

The personal property tax list for 1812 suggests why the mother of Johnson Smith's children had not yet appeared by name in the records. In that year, Johnson Smith is listed as "Johnson Scott and son," free blacks with one horse and one female slave over the age of sixteen. For that one year, Smith owned an adult female slave. That slave, almost surely, was Smith's wife, Rachel. Though no deed of manumission exists to indicate how she achieved freedom, a Rachel Smith appears as a free woman starting with county records in 1813. Extant records do not indicate whether Rachel was that slave or whether she was actually the mother of all of Johnson Smith's children.

It was not uncommon in the Upper South, however, for slaves to be freed informally and recognized as such by locals. Since their children were considered free, Rachel Smith and her husband may have worked out a deal with Rachel's master that ended with Johnson Smith owning his wife for a time. Rachel, if she were indeed a term slave, may have been allowed by her master to go about as if free, all the while helping her husband, Johnson Smith, pay her master for the freedom of her children and eventually for her own. This, too, was not an unusual practice in rural Virginia. By the following year, Johnson Smith no longer owned an adult slave, and Rachel Smith is listed independently and by name for the first time on the personal property tax list for St. Anne's Parish. Court records that year clearly identified Rachel as Johnson Smith's wife. Prior to 1812, Rachel may technically have resided at least formally on a nearby plantation.[8]

On February 23, 1814, the free person of color Johnson Smith and his wife, Rachel Smith, ran afoul of the law. Any security they had managed to create for themselves was suddenly in jeopardy. She was arrested and charged with stealing three pigs from the white farmer John Patterson. The court, referring to her as Rachel Scott, a woman also known as Rachel Smith, stated that the pigs Rachel was accused of stealing were valued at nine dollars. Thus, although the original charge had been only petty larceny, the court now raised it to grand larceny. The court, apparently confused about her identity, remanded her to jail. Her husband was vigilant, and he had a number of white friends. Rachel was released only hours later when her husband, Johnson, and their white neighbor Chiles Brand appeared in court and filed three hundred dollars in recognizances guaranteeing her appearance in court. She was arraigned on March 7. The next day, Johnson Smith, along with four local whites, filed another set of recognizances totaling three hundred dollars on behalf of Rachel Smith, guaranteeing her appearance at the trial.[9]

Rachel Smith awaited trial for three months. While she waited for her case to come to trial, Smith busied herself rounding up material and character witnesses. On May 9, the white Albemarle slave owners Samuel Shelton, Joseph Eades, David Cobbs, and William Elsom, together with the free people of color Sally Lewis and David Martin, agreed to appear as witnesses on behalf of Rachel Smith. At the June court that same year, Rachel Smith's trial was held. Smith was found guilty of stealing pigs from her white neighbor John Patterson and sentenced to thirty lashes on her bare back at the public whipping post. Up to this point, the unfolding of events since the pig stealing back in March had largely followed a script typical of how historians describe the average free black experience in the antebellum South: economic and social marginalization, poverty, contact with a judicial system stacked against them, violent corporal punishment, and lengthy incarceration for minor infractions. For instance, Berlin's explanation is nuanced and recognizes the ability of a minority of free blacks to succeed, but sees that development as only possible for a few lighter-skinned mulattos who owned property and had white protectors. Berlin also privileges the role of law in his account and assumes that laws serve as a good indicator of actual practice. The large number of whites who gave security or testimony for Rachel Smith, however, undermines that interpretation.[10]

Rachel Smith immediately filed an appeal to arrest judgment, alleging that there were procedural errors committed both in her arrest and in the filing of the case against her. Two days later, the county court heard her appeal. The court sustained her appeal, agreeing that there were procedural errors in the arrest. The original verdict was thrown out, and Rachel was discharged from her recognizance and released. Rachel was once again a free woman. But problems stemming from the pig theft would continue to plague the Smith family. Rachel, along with her husband, Johnson, and their child Pitman, would be charged anew for the same specific theft in October 1814. On the seventh of October, a summons was issued ordering the sheriff to rearrest Johnson, Rachel, and Pitman Smith. Within the week, they were arrested and committed to the county jail. The family would spend the next three weeks there.[11]

But their story has further twists. For starters, at the second arraignment, three white slaveholders once again pledged security for Rachel Smith. Unfortunately, no record reveals the connections these men had to Johnson Smith and his wife. The repeated pledging of a substantial sum of money (three hundred dollars), as well as the agreement to testify on behalf of poor, politically powerless, and supposedly socially ostracized free people of color, however, belies the notion that for white antebellum southerners, free blacks were "slaves without masters" whose existence threatened a social fabric predicated upon the notion that dark skin color equaled enslaved status.

Johnson Smith and his wife were familiar with white men who at a minimum were their neighbors and likely had extensive contact with the free black Smiths. Perhaps the Smiths were regular hires as laborers or skilled workers on their white neighbors' farms.

After the Smiths spent three weeks in jail, the court acquitted Johnson Smith, his wife, Rachel, and their son Pitman and ordered their immediate release. Beyond evidence of following proper court procedure, the court records are silent about the reasons for the acquittal, but they hint at the possibility that free blacks could experience a judicial system at least locally that was not categorically prejudiced against them. The legal system was not necessarily a tool used to control a supposedly anomalous group—free people of color. The role of whites in this story suggests that interracial contact in the rural South entailed far more than solely violence and domination by whites in support of a brutally racist slave regime.[12]

Johnson Smith and his wife, Rachel, had a very busy year in 1814. After being freed from the county jail, they returned to life in Albemarle and continued to work to get the rest of their family out of slavery. Smith's 1814 personal property tax record, taken in December of that year, finds him again as the head of a household with two sons and two slaves aged twelve to sixteen. Perhaps those two slaves were the Smiths' children. Also listed separately as free black heads of household are Barnett, Bustard, and Wilson Smith, Johnson Smith's children who had reached adulthood. Whether Johnson Smith relied upon his service in the American Revolutionary effort remains unclear.[13] After 1814, however, the Smith family disappears from the public record. Perhaps they left the area for economic or familial reasons. Regardless, their experience in Albemarle demonstrates the positive potential for free people of color participating in a rural southern interracial community.

Other free black war veterans lived lives in Albemarle that differed vastly from those of the Smiths. Future Albemarle resident Shadrach Battles was a young man in the 1740s, living in Louisa County.[14] Though he was officially listed in public records throughout his life as a mulatto person of color, white Albemarle residents later described him as "half Indian and half mulatto." By 1752, he had moved from Louisa County and headed south and west to the eastern edge of the Blue Ridge Mountains, in what was then south-central Albemarle County. Battles crossed several counties on this journey to the rural tobacco lands in the James River basin, between Lynchburg and Charlottesville. Once he was there, his father, after whom Shadrach Battles was named, purchased 191 acres of land on the south branches of the Hardware River.[15]

For the next fourteen years, Shadrach Battles lived a quiet life on a farm in the heart of tobacco plantation country on the southern border of Albemarle, taking over his family's farm.[16] For reasons unknown, in 1775 the elder Shadrach Battles sold the family farm to the white farmer John Duncan for fifteen pounds and apparently moved south to the new Amherst County. Two years later, Shadrach Jr. was an itinerant laborer and carpenter with no fixed address, at the time working in Amherst. It was 1777, and the Revolutionary War had begun. Shadrach Battles Jr. enlisted that year and served two eighteen-month tours of duty. The Albemarle resident Clough Shelton was second in command when Battles joined the regiment and later became the leader of the outfit. Battles traveled far and wide in his military service, fighting at the battles of Brandywine, Monmouth, and Germantown and even at the siege of the fort at Savannah, Georgia. Decades later, white Staunton resident Archibald Stuart wrote to the Albemarle court, stating that Battles "was the right hand man of Clough Shelton at the storming of Stony Point" on the Hudson River in July 1779.[17]

In 1780, Shadrach Battles's second tour of duty came to an end. He was discharged in Augusta, Georgia. He made his way back to Virginia and first returned to his birth county of Louisa. There he quickly settled in, marrying Dolly Moss that same year. Within four years, the couple had relocated to Albemarle County. Upon settling down in the Charlottesville area, Battles quickly found himself in trouble. In November 1784, Robert Murray initiated a suit against Battles for trespass, assault, and battery. Shadrach Battles failed to appear before the magistrates and was thus ordered to pay Murray's court costs and to enter into a bond guaranteeing his good behavior for one year.[18]

Two years later, Shadrach Battles appeared at the courthouse in connection with the marriage of two free mulattos, Jonathan Tyree and Usly Goings. Battles granted surety to the court that there were no legal impediments to the marriage. From 1786 to 1792, Battles remained a landless laborer with a modest but not negligible amount of personal property—a few horses and a small herd of cattle. In 1793, Battles again ran into trouble in Albemarle. In August of that year, his fellow free person of color and relative Jane Battles charged Shadrach with trespass, assault, and battery. "Trespass, assault, and battery" functioned as a catchall for misdemeanors (or rarely felonies) ranging from simple violation of private property rights to actual physical assaults. Most cases in Albemarle that involved this charge appear to have involved physical confrontations. The extant records in this case do not state clearly what type of trespass, assault, and battery Shadrach was charged with. This time, the outcome was favorable for Shadrach. The court dismissed the case and ordered the plaintiff, Jane Battles, to pay his court costs.[19] Shadrach Battles thus had more trouble from fellow free blacks than he did from whites.

Battles's financial situation did not improve during the final years of the eighteenth century. The head of a household with a wife and at least one child, he did not better his situation by following his father's practice of purchasing land. He was becoming a known quantity in and around Charlottesville, viewed as a local resident and neighbor, but his color carried palpable disadvantages. In December 1800, he was ordered to work on a road being surveyed and repaired, something that only slaves and free people of color were compelled to do. This particular work order included Shadrach Battles and six other free black men.[20]

The following year, just a couple of months after he was ordered to repair the road, Shadrach Battles's financial world began to collapse. He fell deeply into debt. His creditors came seeking repayment in early 1801. At the beginning of February, both Joel Bennett and John Goodman took Battles to court. Bennett sought repayment of a ten-dollar debt. Goodman sought repayment of a nearly seven-dollar bill. After they filed suit and the cases came to trial, Battles again failed to appear at the courthouse. And just as it had back in 1784, the court had no choice but to rule in favor of the plaintiffs, Bennett and Goodman. A month later, the cycle repeated itself yet again. This time, a white man sought repayment of a debt. This case played out a bit differently, however, as Battles now had a white lawyer who appeared in court for him. William Waller Hening, a prominent Charlottesville lawyer and later the compiler of a multivolume Virginia legislative history, argued to the court that the debt had in fact been settled. After presentation of the evidence, the plaintiff agreed, and the suit was dismissed.[21] Thus, when Battles showed up in court—which he did about half the time—he fared well. His occasional failures to appear when sued fit with the general pattern evinced by whites and blacks at the time—both often failed to appear in court.

Shadrach Battles owned no land. He lived on the south edge of Charlottesville, in a low area adjacent to Moore's Creek, with a modest amount of property even in good years. But Shadrach did not live his life as an isolated and anomalous man of color. Several other free blacks owned land or lived in the same area, including Robert Battles and Daniel Farley. Just up the hill, within walking distance from Moore's Creek, was the southern end of the cluster of houses that made up downtown Charlottesville. Battles occasionally owned a few horses and cattle and likely lived on the farm of another free black (probably a relative). He lived in a community that included whites as well as people of color.

It is unlikely that he spent much of his time farming, however. He was a day laborer and carpenter for hire, performing odd jobs for people in the town of Charlottesville. One indication of this comes from the recollections of James Alexander, a newspaper editor in town during the antebellum years. Alexander recalled that during the first several years of the nineteenth century, town residents had a long row of locust trees planted. Alexander remembered that "these trees had been planted by a man by the name of Shadrach Battles. . . . His pay for the work was to be a quart of whisky for every tree that lived. He watched them carefully and watered them to aid in their growth, and when any of them gave evidence of life by putting forth leaves he would clap his hands and shout, 'Another quart saved.'"[22]

Living on the wild side of town, Shadrach Battles spent his time in the neighborhood containing a number of sellers of "ardent spirits"; some gaming houses; and the Sunday market where slaves, some of whom were allowed to work on their own time, sold the fruits of their labors. He may well have fallen victim to vices such as gambling and almost certainly had a problem with alcohol. He was friendly with Daniel Farley, a free black who ran an illegal gaming house, and also knew Joshua Grady, a local white man who lived openly with a free black woman and who was frequently in trouble for his gambling. But Shadrach's work seems to have been appreciated, as a number of white townspeople and merchants felt comfortable extending credit to him (several debt cases attest to that) and hiring him to perform work. William W. Hening, Battles's neighbor and sometime lawyer, likely had frequent contact with him. Defending Battles in court, whether the act of a solicitous neighbor, a protective patron, an attorney working for a paying client, or an occasional employer, did not reflect an unusual interracial worldview. Instead, the two men's interaction hints at how interracial contact could occur on the local level and be in many ways at odds with the proslavery and racist discourse prevalent at the time.[23]

Hening was not the only prominent white in Charlottesville to come to Shadrach Battles's aid. In May 1801, Battles was again in trouble for running up debts and failing to pay them—a situation that plagued many whites, too. This time, the white merchant Thomas Fretwell, who ran a store several miles to the northwest of Charlottesville, filed suit against Battles.[24] The court decided the case for the plaintiff. In the meantime, John Carr appeared at the courthouse and gave bond for Battles. Further details of John Carr's relationship with Shadrach Battles remain unknown; perhaps Carr had hired the black man in the past.[25]

As evidenced by the three free males living in Battles's household in 1802, his family continued to grow. By 1805, his son Shadrach III was in his teens. Apparently, Shadrach the elder had managed to keep his family out of court as defendants for several years. But in 1807, conflict of a different sort struck his family. In March of that year, Battles headed to the courthouse and filed suit against his fellow free black William Thacker, charging him with trespass, assault, and battery. The outcome of the cause is not known; the two men probably settled out of court. The lesson Shadrach Battles learned from his visits to the courthouse, however, was not that the courts were a dangerous place for free people of color, but that they offered a good way to settle disputes and air grievances.[26]

Shadrach Battles moved into old age still residing on the southern border of Charlottesville, still not owning any land, and remaining a day laborer. His son Shadrach III had become a head of a household in his own right and started his own family. Another son, Edward, also lived in the area. By 1820, Battles was well into his seventies. His health was in serious decline. On October 11, 1820, Battles was literally carried to the county courthouse on a stretcher. He appeared there to apply for a Revolutionary War pension, citing his three years of service between 1777 and 1780 (and thus repeating a pension application he had made in 1818). At the time, he owned "one broad axe, one oven, and one handsaw. His wife [was] aged about 60. He [was] a carpenter." He had returned to the courthouse because he had lost or mislaid his 1818 pension certificate. The elite white lawyer and jurist Archibald Stuart of Staunton (a town forty miles to the west) wrote a letter to the authorities affirming Battles's war service and terming him "the right hand man" of white officer Clough Shelton. The government granted him his pension, but he had little time to enjoy it. His infirmity relegated him to bed, so in March 1821 he gave his white neighbor Joshua Grady power of attorney to continue pursuing his pension claim and to handle his affairs. He died within the next two years. Grady was not the archetypal paternalistic protector, but rather a plain white man—a "frequent transgressor" in the same part of town that Shadrach lived in—and very likely an acquaintance or even a friend of Battles.[27]

Shadrach Battles himself, although never achieving landownership and remaining poor, managed to interact successfully with his neighbors and the community around him in Albemarle. He lived in technical violation of the 1793 registration law for seventeen years, yet he was in and out of court repeatedly as both defendant and plaintiff. He only registered once in his life, in March 1810, and he did so then because his son Shadrach III had reached his majority and was about to embark on a life as a head of his own household. Those instances where Battles failed to comply with the law, and the authorities ignored the lack of compliance, represented privileges granted social inferiors whom the authorities knew well and trusted. The ties of personalism created a space in which free people of color could live relatively comfortably amid whites and slaves. Battles's son was not yet fully connected and known, as his father was. Registration was a sensible choice for a father to make for his son, especially a son to whom he was giving property. The protections afforded free people of color who became known quantities in any community were a form of security, but registration could help formalize one's free status.[28]

Like most people white and black, Battles left no will, but other documents shed light on what choices his children made in life. Shadrach's children seem to have followed the examples of the other free blacks among whom they lived, including Robert Battles, a landowning farmer. The free black Stephen Coram was appointed to administer Shadrach's estate. In 1823, he filed a motion with the county court seeking to have Shadrach's daughter Dolly, William, and Edward Battles declared the only legal heirs at law to their father's estate. Shadrach's other children apparently had moved out of the state years before, whereabouts unknown. Perhaps they were following their father's example and spending their youngest years as itinerant laborers with no fixed address.[29]

Those children who remained continued to lead humble lives. In 1826, Shadrach III had his four-year-old son bound out to the white farmer Jennings Maupin. The apprenticeship system, intended to control poor whites and free blacks, was often utilized proactively by the poor as a way to acquire marketable skills. Thus, Shadrach III's decision highlights the poverty in which the Battles family remained, but the act also demonstrates how poor people, black or white, would attempt to free children from this burden. Battles's son would be taught farming and earn twelve dollars upon completion of the apprenticeship—the minimum pay for any apprenticed child. Another son of the late Shadrach, Edward Battles, remained in Albemarle even after the Civil War, always landless and with only a small amount of personal property, working as a day laborer and rough carpenter, much like his father before him. As with his father and other poor Virginians, he was no stranger to controversy with neighbors and likewise quick to sue those same neighbors. In 1823, he filed suit against David Markwood for trespass, assault, and battery.[30]

Shadrach Battles was not alone in either his war service or in finding that his veteran status helped to cement relationships with white neighbors. Charles Barnett, a free man of color born in Albemarle circa 1764, was a contemporary of both Johnson Smith and Shadrach Battles and, like them, chose to enlist in the Revolutionary War effort. In 1780, Barnett enlisted, serving for a year and a half under Captain John Marks of Albemarle before participating in the siege of Yorktown in tidewater Virginia, effectively the end of the war. From there, he marched to Powhatan Courthouse and then was sent north, driving baggage wagons on their way to Pennsylvania. Baron von Steuben oversaw Barnett's discharge in Philadelphia in late 1781. Like Smith and Battles, Charles Barnett chose to return to his home in Albemarle after the war. In September 1785, the twenty-one-year-old veteran married the free woman of color Lucy Bowles in a Baptist ceremony. Their fellow free man of color George Mann gave bond certifying the lack of legal impediments to the marriage.[31]

Over the next four years, Barnett made considerable progress as a free man of color living in a rural southern agricultural community. He appears in 1787 as a head of household owning one cow. Two years later, he no longer owned the cow, but he had become a landowner. In 1789 he purchased thirty-nine acres of land valued at over twelve pounds from William Johnson, a white man.[32]

In addition to becoming a landholding farmer, Charles Barnett was also becoming ever more enmeshed in a network of free families and friends of color in the county. George Mann, who had acted as surety for Barnett's marriage, lived with the Goings family. Charles, in January 1791, gave surety for the marriage of Richard Brock and Mary Goings. The white slave owner

William Michie witnessed the signing of the marriage bonds. The Barnett, Mann, Goings, Brock, Battles, and Bowles families were interconnected by marrying each other and by attending each other's weddings. Those same families found whites, including a member of the prominent Michie family, to witness the signing of marriage bonds.[33]

Although Charles Barnett did not spend any time in jail, his other experiences after 1793 echo those of Johnson Smith and his family. Without maintaining positive face-to-face relationships with local whites, and without cultivating a respectable reputation, free people of color would only have a relatively small free black community to turn to for help. Even a tight-knit rural subcommunity such as the free black familial network in Albemarle was not free from contention, conflict, and violence. In 1796, Charles Barnett and his wife Lucy went to Charlottesville to attend the May court. They filed suit against Robert Battles, the same free man of color who had married Lucy Barnett's sister two and one half years earlier, for assault and battery.[34]

Three months later, the county justices dismissed the case and ordered the plaintiffs to pay the defendant's court costs. On that same day, Barnett registered his freedom with the county clerk. Since the passing of Virginia legislation in 1793 mandating that free people of color were to be registered with the county or town clerk and obtain a new certificate once every three years, Barnett had not registered. Perhaps his appearance in court during his failed lawsuit may have impelled him to register.[35]

After this registration in 1796, Barnett would never register in Albemarle again. He continued to live in Albemarle County for another four years. In 1800, he disappeared from Virginia, wandering the South for the next several years. He first moved to Carter County, Tennessee, and from there went to Georgia. In 1807, he moved north to Granville County, North Carolina, where he remained for almost thirty years. He left behind in Albemarle his wife Lucy and their children and started another family in North Carolina. Despite a whole host of laws proscribing free black mobility—laws that existed in every southern state—Barnett moved freely and openly from locale to locale for eight years.[36]

During Charles Barnett's long absence from Albemarle, his abandoned wife, Lucy, struggled to raise their children. She relied on a network of friends and family in the county to do so. Lucy's mother, Amy Farrow, had died in 1798. Her will stipulated that her entire estate would go to her sons Zachariah Bowles and Thomas Farrow. Zachariah for several years held sole title to their deceased mother's 224-acre farm. In 1806, they evidently split the farm roughly in half after purchasing nine additional acres. In that year, Zachariah owned 121 acres and Thomas took possession of 112 acres. In 1810, ten years after her husband left her behind, Lucy Barnett was the head of a family with six free people of color in it. She almost certainly lived somewhere on her mother's sizable old farm north of Charlottesville, the one now owned by her brothers.

In April of that year, her brother Thomas Farrow died. He bequeathed his estate to both his brother Zachariah Bowles and to his sister Lucy and her children Judah (Judy) and Molly Barnett. The will also appointed Zachariah and Lucy as executors of the estate. Just weeks before her brother died, Lucy Barnett headed into Charlottesville to see the county court clerk. On March 9, 1810, described as forty-five years old and a mulatto, she received her first and only freedom certificate.[37]

Why did it take Barnett seventeen years since the passing of the registration law and ten years since her husband Charles ran away to register? Lucy surely decided to register in preparation for the death of her brother Thomas. She was to receive land from his estate and would find her "free papers" helpful in dealing with the court authorities who would prove the will. The family farm was located several miles north of Charlottesville, on the way to a crossroads called Earlysville and adjoining the property of the slaveholding white Samuel Carr, a nephew of Thomas Jefferson.

After Thomas Farrow's will and estate went through probate, the farm parcel was split up further. Zachariah Bowles continued to own and manage one piece and paid the taxes for the tract formerly owned by his deceased brother. He sold off a small plot to his white neighbor Samuel Carr. Meanwhile, Lucy Barnett had taken up residence on Thomas Farrow's place, and brother Zachariah lived next door and helped her. By 1816, Lucy Barnett was legally recognized as the owner of forty-four acres of land five miles north of town, joining the land of Samuel Carr, the land of her brother Zachariah Bowles, and a remnant of Thomas Farrow's estate.[38]

Battling illness and seeking to help her sister Martha, Lucy in 1818 leased a portion of her farm to Martha's husband, the free man of color Griffen Butler, who would pay her in rent a quantity of his income from the land. Butler, who had already been living on the tract, would further receive a discount on the rent for any lands he cleared for cultivation. For free families of color such as the Barnetts and the Bowleses, family extended well beyond a married couple with children.[39]

Unfortunately, Lucy Barnett had little time to enjoy her new status as both head of household and landowner. By the end of 1818, her health was failing. She was fifty-four years old and knew that writing a will would help to secure her estate for her family. In January 1819, Barnett dictated her will in the presence of the white witnesses Norborne Powers, Philip Phillips, and James Powers. She left all of her property to her daughter Judah Barnett and her niece Critty Bowles. Her daughter Judah was appointed sole executrix. In the years since her husband, Charles, had abandoned her in 1800, Lucy Barnett had managed to do quite well. With the help of an extended family, she had become a landowner and provided her immediate family with some economic security after she died.[40]

Charles Barnett, meanwhile, had settled into another life in Granville County, North Carolina. In 1832, after almost thirty years living in North Carolina, and fourteen years after his first, abandoned wife died, Charles Barnett left Granville County and his second family and headed north, back to Charlottesville. There, he sought out fellow war veteran Sabrit King. King was white, the town crier, and a man of modest means. On January 19, 1833, the two men appeared together at the county courthouse. King, himself already a Revolutionary War pensioner, declared to the court that Charles Barnett had served starting about 1780 in the Seventh Virginia Regiment, headed by Captain John Marks.

Charles Barnett was in fact a member of the same regiment as Sabrit King. For Barnett, freedom indeed had a face, a face recognized as familiar and worthy of assistance by at least one local white. Barnett had marshaled an additional witness: Sherod Goings, another free black war veteran from Albemarle. Goings stated that he "became acquainted" with Barnett at Chesterfield Court House and that they both fought in the siege of Yorktown before moving on to Powhatan Court House. Goings further stated that in Powhatan, they went their separate ways, with "Barnett sent to Philadelphia as a waggoner by General Steuben." Barnett's application for a war pension was in fact successful, and on November 25, 1833, he was issued a certificate guaranteeing him sixty dollars per year.[41]

For the next fifteen years, Charles Barnett may have lived a quiet life in Albemarle County as a pensioner. Upon his return to central Virginia in 1832–33, he was already in his late sixties. A poor, old man, Barnett does not appear in any county records over this period. He remained alive till at least September 4, 1848, the date of his last war pension payment. Almost a year later, on July 31, 1849, the white petitioner Thomas Peace of North Carolina wrote to the county government seeking information about Charles Barnett. Peace wanted to know whether he still drew a pension and mentioned that he had left Granville County "some time ago," leaving behind a wife and children who were now in a "very distressed condition." Peace sought to have Barnett's North Carolina wife receive the pension herself. Had Charles Barnett died? Had he once again migrated out of the area?[42]

Unfortunately, the complete story of Charles Barnett's peregrinations remains lost to history. The records are silent, except for one last appearance in the public record by a man named Charles Barnett. In 1850, the assistant marshal for the taking of the decennial federal census visited the free person of color Zachariah Brock's home. Brock was a farmer who owned over four hundred dollars in personal property. He was also the head of a household of seven free people of color. One of the members of Brock's household was a Charles Barnett, listed as a one-hundred-year-old mulatto who had been born in Virginia.[43]

The census taker's estimate of Barnett's age was a little high, as Barnett should have been approaching ninety, not one hundred. But this is very likely the same Charles Barnett, for Zachariah Brock was no stranger to him, and it was no accident that this was the house Barnett retired to. Brock was the son of Richard and Mary (nee Goings) Brock, who were married in 1791. Charles Barnett had certified that there were no legal impediments to the marriage. Zachariah Brock's neighbor Benjamin Goings Jr. was also Brock's uncle. Mary Brock and Benjamin Goings Jr. were both the children of Benjamin Goings Sr. Benjamin Sr. was the brother of Sherod Goings, the Revolutionary War veteran who had served for a time with Charles Barnett.[44] Barnett, through his frequent changes of address, had failed to develop deep connections to any community other than the one he was born into. Any respectability he had earned came as a young man fighting for the patriot cause. The rest of his life only served to attenuate the bonds of familiarity that he had established earlier. But he still had old friends in the free black community, and he turned to them.

Lucy Barnett's brother Zachariah Bowles had a life story with a similar starting point, but one that diverged drastically from that of Charles Barnett. Zachariah, born in 1754, about ten years before Charles, also served in the Revolutionary War. Like Charles, he moved about freely. He enlisted in January 1777 in Hanover County, over seventy miles and several counties east of Albemarle. His younger brother Stephen Bowles also served. Their family had been free at least since the beginning of the century.[45]

Like Charles Barnett, Zachariah Bowles returned to Albemarle after his term of service in the war ended. And, much like Barnett, Bowles took up farming with his extended family upon his return to the area. In addition, he had rough carpentry skills that he would use on his farm and as a part-time sideline occupation for much of his life. In October 1790, he signed the marriage bond for his sister Martha's wedding to Griffen Butler. For the rest of the decade, he lived with his half brother Thomas Farrow on their mother Amy Farrow's farm, several miles north of town. By 1797, he still lived with his mother and owned two horses.[46]

The following year, Zachariah's mother, Amy Farrow, died. In October 1798, very ill and near death, she had a will written out, and the local whites John T. Hawkins, John Newcum, and Usly Topence acted as witnesses. Topence was a plain white, no more literate than Farrow. Hawkins and Newcum had also fought as common soldiers in the Revolution. At that time, Hawkins was living in the same neighborhood, north of Charlottesville. These white witnesses were not lordly whites condescending to perform their duties as protectors of a free person of color. The will was officially recorded in the county court order book the very same day, Amy Farrow having already died. Her will bequeathed a 224-acre farm to her sons Zachariah Bowles and Thomas Farrow. She also divided her property equally between her two sons. She had accumulated some property, including a bed, household items, a horse, a "stock of hogs," and four head of cattle.[47] Amy Farrow, in her haste to have the will written, failed to appoint anyone to serve as executor. The white men Isaac Miller and Thomas W. Lewis, after giving bond and pledging security of one hundred dollars each, were granted letters of administration for Farrow's estate. Both Miller and Lewis lived in the same neighborhood as Farrow, also owning land several miles north of town. For Miller, Amy Farrow was not merely a "free black," but Amy, the elderly woman farmer who lived nearby.[48]

The county court, as it often did, ordered that an inventory and appraisal be conducted. For that job, the county appointed Robert Warner Lewis and the free man of color John Randol—an interracial appraisal team who lived in the same neighborhood, on the north side of the Rivanna River's North Fork. Amy Farrow's white neighbors Isaac Miller and Thomas W. Lewis handled administration of the estate. Zachariah Bowles, his half brother

Thomas Farrow, and their families continued to work Amy Farrow's old farm.[49]

There were difficulties for Zachariah, however. In November 1801, he was found guilty of assault by the county court. Unfortunately, the court's verdict is the only remaining evidence concerning the assault. No victim is listed. Bowles had appeared at an arraignment at an earlier date and filed a recognizance, along with "one or more securities," for his appearance at the trial. Until the trial, then, Bowles remained a free man, thanks both to his own pledging of money and to help from at least one white neighbor or benefactor. Having been found guilty, Bowles "received at the public whipping post on his bare back 15 lashes well laid on" and was required to give bond of fifty dollars to guarantee his good behavior for the following twelve months. Security for Bowles's bond came from the white Albemarle resident Francis Taliaferro and the free black John Randol. Bowles's experience in that assault case demonstrates the ways in which free people of color could connect with neighbors, including whites.[50]

Five years after Zachariah Bowles was punished for his misdemeanor, he and his brother Thomas Farrow finally divided their mother's farm. Zachariah took 121 acres, leaving 112 acres to his brother. That same fall of 1806, Zachariah decided he needed a gun and applied to the county court for permission to use firearms. On October 7, the court granted him permission to "make use of firearms during the pleasure of the said court." The network, both black and white, of friends, family, and neighbors that Zachariah lived in saw him not as a dangerous free black, but as a fellow landowning farmer. Despite his brush with the law and his violent public punishment at the whipping post years earlier, Bowles had no reservations about approaching white authorities for a weapons-use permit, nor did they hesitate to grant him one.[51]

For the next several years, Zachariah and his extended family continued to work the land on the two plots owned separately by him and by his brother Thomas Farrow. Thomas, however, fell ill in 1810. Like his sister Lucy Barnett before him, Farrow sought to protect his legacy fully by having a will drawn up. On May 25, 1810, Farrow dictated the terms of his will to two white neighbors, Norborne Powers and John Carr, who wrote it out and signed the document as legal witnesses. Carr was a close relative of Samuel Carr, whose plantation adjoined the Farrow property. Norborne Powers was also a neighbor, the same person who would dictate and witness Lucy Barnett's will in 1819.[52]

Farrow bequeathed the farm in equal proportions to his brother Zachariah and his sister Lucy Barnett (who was already living on the family farm). Realizing that Lucy had been abandoned by her husband a decade earlier and was the most in need of long-term security for herself and her children, Farrow gave her the right to choose which half she wanted. In addition, he gave Lucy his mare, his bedstead, his furniture, and a storage chest. Farrow also provided for Lucy Barnett's daughters Judah and Molly, who received his cow.[53]

Farrow was in fact deeply concerned with his sister Lucy's status. Not only did he give her land and property in an effort to secure a solid future for her, but he also worried about the whereabouts and actions of her absent husband, Charles Barnett. Understanding that the husband had control over any wife's property, Farrow went to great lengths to protect the property from any possible return of Charles Barnett. Thomas stipulated that:

> whereas my Sister Lucey Barnett was married to a certain Charles Barnett who has for many years absented himself from her, in case of his return it is my will and desire and I do hereby appoint my brother Zachariah Bowles as trustee for my said sister Lucey Barnett and do vest in him as trustee the interest in the said land and personal property hereby devised to my said sister Lucy, so that the said Charles Barnett is not to derive any advantage therefrom either present or future.[54]

Farrow considered his mother's old farm to be a family birthright, and Charles Barnett was distinctly excluded.

Zachariah Bowles continued to own his hundred-plus acres as well as half of Farrow's old parcel, and his sister Lucy Barnett and her family, already living at the farm, took over ownership of forty-four acres of Farrow's estate and remained there until she died in 1819. Together, the extended family working these plots of land owned a small herd of cattle and several horses. In addition to family, Bowles had help from at least one other person, the free black James Lott, who lived at the Bowles farm for a time between 1811 and 1819.[55]

On February 26, 1819, Zachariah Bowles successfully applied for and received his pension for Revolutionary War service. This annual stipend probably was not a significant source of income, but any money was surely welcome and useful in a stressful time. Zachariah's sister Lucy Barnett had died less than a month earlier. As discussed above, Lucy passed her forty-four-acre plot of land on to her daughter Judah Barnett.[56] Financially, the last several years had been good for Zachariah and the rest of his family. They continued to work a farm successfully. They did so on good land amid a number of neighboring plantations. Their white neighbors viewed them as well-behaved, respectable members of the Albemarle farming community. But on a personal level, these were trying times for the free family of color living on Amy Farrow's old estate. Thomas Farrow had died in 1810. Lucy Barnett passed away in 1819. Now, Lucy's daughter Judah Barnett fell ill. In early September 1822, Judah followed the same set of steps that she had seen her uncle and mother take. She asked her white neighbors John Hill and Carter Newcomb to come to her house to write down and witness her last will and testament.[57]

At this point, however, Judah's practices diverged from those of her uncle and mother. Thomas Farrow and Lucy Barnett left wills as a means to keep the familial estate intact and provide security for the next generation in the form of land, evincing an attachment to place. They could have called for the land to be sold with the proceeds divided among heirs, as many testators did. Judah, unlike her relatives, actually did order that "my land be sold and the money placed out at interest to be annually divided among my six youngest children for their support." Why the change in strategy? First, Judah Barnett was only thirty-seven years old at the time of her death. Her children were young, as she noted in her will: "It is my wish that my four youngest boys may be under the care of Robert Battles Jr., Elijah Battles, Stephen Coram and my sister Nancy Battles, and I do beg and implore them to treat them with tenderness in remembrance of me." All of her children were too young to live on their own without a parent or guardian, let alone possess a farmstead.[58]

Judah probably considered it too much of an imposition on her relatives to assume that they would gladly care for her children and incur all the expenses that would entail. The land would be of little use to the guardians of her children, or even an encumbrance for them. To provide for a division of the tract when the children grew up would result in breaking up the forty-four-acre farm into parcels too small to be of use. By selling the land and using the money derived from the sale, she could set up a trust for each child, ensuring that they would be provided for as they grew up.

Judah surely consulted Zachariah Bowles in her time of need. He was a favorite uncle who owned most of the farm that she had grown up on. She had spent most of her life with him as a father figure. Judah's will appointed both her uncle Zachariah and the free man of color Stephen Coram as executors. This action allowed her uncle to oversee the sale of part of the farm that he had worked for so long. He would have the opportunity to sell the parcel to himself if he so chose. He would execute the will with the assistance of extended family: Stephen Coram, who had married Judah's cousin Keziah Battles. Coram and the extended Battles family lived about seven miles south of the Bowles-Barnett farm, on a series of properties about one mile southwest of Charlottesville.[59]

Judah did not rely exclusively on her white neighbors or on her free black relatives to execute the will and settle the estate, however. In her will, she openly acknowledged both the all-important biracial web of highly personal relations that characterized her world and the social hierarchy upon which that web was built. After devising her property and naming executors, Judah "beg[ged] it as a last favor of Mr. Joel Terrell my excellent neighbor to lend his aid in seeing this my will faithfully executed." Barnett saw Terrell first as a neighbor whom she had dealt with before and who could be trusted to carry out neighborly duties honorably.[60]

One month later, the county court appointed John C. Wells, a white man, as curator of Judah Barnett's estate. Wells gave three hundred dollars bond to guarantee his performance in the role; Samuel Carr, the white planter whose plantation adjoined the Barnett-Bowles farm, gave bond in the same amount for Wells's performance. The court then appointed five white men to appraise Judah Barnett's estate. In January 1823, Samuel Carr filed a motion asking the court to order the sheriff of the county to take the estate into his possession and dispose of it in the manner that Judah's will directed. The same white men, Barnett's social superiors, but very familiar as neighbors, took charge of handling her estate.[61]

Not everything went happily for Judah Barnett's children. While her will was being executed and her estate administered, her children were caught in a legal limbo. They were too young to support themselves. The day after Judah's will was recorded at the courthouse in November 1822, the court ordered the Overseers of the Poor for the county to bind out James, Lucy, Jane, Mary, Thomas, and Zachariah Barnett, the orphan children of Judy Barnett. The family may have decided that apprenticeship represented the best situation for the children. This action would separate them from their family for years but could also provide them with the skills necessary to make it on their own as adults in Albemarle.[62]

For the better part of a decade after Judah's death, Zachariah continued to work his farm of over one hundred acres, as well as the forty-four-acre plot that Thomas Farrow had bequeathed to him. Bowles also continued to farm Judah Barnett's forty-four-acre parcel. Although no deed is extant, Zachariah clearly sold off about thirty acres of his estate sometime between 1819 and 1825, most likely to his white neighbor Samuel Carr, a man he had been doing business with on and off for years. His property was still valued at nearly eight hundred dollars, but listed as comprising only eighty-eight acres. Sometime in 1831, the administrator of Judah's estate sold eleven acres from her parcel to a white neighbor, once again the planter Samuel Carr.[63]

Did Zachariah Bowles have a family? Until the 1820s, the records are silent on this question. Zachariah is listed as a head of household and landowner with dependents, but the records do not tell who those dependents were. Were they his children? Were they the children of his siblings? We only catch a few glimpses of who these people might have been. The 1833 colonization census for Fredericksville Parish, however, makes at least one connection clear. In that year, two years after Nat Turner's slave revolt in Southampton County, the state legislature had ordered each county to conduct a special census of free blacks. The census detailed each individual's physical description, age, occupation, white neighbors, and interest in moving to Africa. Zachariah Bowles was listed as a sixty-four-year-old mulatto farmer residing near Samuel Carr and living with Critty Bowles, a sixty-four-year-old "negro" spinner. Also listed as living in Zachariah's household were Peter F. Bowles, a forty-five-year-old mulatto farmer, and his children Susan and John.[64]

Critty Bowles was in fact the wife of Zachariah Bowles. No record of the marriage exists because the pair married while Critty (sometimes spelled Critta) was still a slave, owned by Thomas Jefferson. Born in 1769, she was the daughter of Elizabeth "Betty" Hemings, a slave who came to Jefferson through his marriage to Martha Wayles. Martha's father, John Wayles, was the father of both Critty and her younger sister, Sally Hemings. At Thomas Jefferson's 1827 estate sale, his grandson Thomas Wayles Eppes purchased Critty for fifty dollars and freed her. The deed of emancipation states that "Critty, sometimes called Critty Bowles, [was] the wife of Zachariah Bowles, a free man of colour." Interestingly, although Critty was clearly living as if free after 1827 and residing with her husband Zachariah, the deed of emancipation was not entered into the record and acknowledged officially by

Thomas Jefferson Randolph, Jefferson's grandson and executor, until September 7, 1835.[65]

Why the eight-year delay in legally and officially recording the deed of manumission? Until 1835, Critty Bowles had little need for an official document. She had been a slave at Monticello, making it likely that many in the community were already familiar with her. She had been freed through the efforts of two of Thomas Jefferson's grandsons, so she had powerful allies among white elites in the area. Her husband, a free man of color, was already widely known, trusted and respected enough as a landowner and community member to carry and use firearms. She had a network of friends and family members among whom she could live comfortably and to whom she could turn for assistance if needed.

It was no accident that 1835 marked the year her deed of manumission was properly recorded at the county courthouse. In December 1834, her husband Zachariah Bowles's health was in serious decline. Early that month, he asked his wife, Critty, to call their white neighbors George Williams and George W. Saunders to their house so he could dictate his will to them. They came on the twelfth day of December, recording the will and signing the document as legal witnesses. Zachariah Bowles's will provides the most detailed account yet of just what his farm amounted to: he left all of his land, his growing grain crop, "dead victuals [freshly slaughtered animals and cured meats] on hand," all other grain and fodder, hogs, cows, and sheep, as well as all household and kitchen furniture, as a life estate to his "beloved wife Critty."[66]

He then appended a few exceptions to Critty's inheritance that reveal much about how Zachariah had gone about becoming a successful small farmer. He stipulated that Critty must "suffer my nephews Peter and Stephen Bowles, to remain in the houses now occupied by them, as heretofore, and cultivate the land aforesaid, by paying her a reasonable annual rent for the same." Leaving his entire growing crop of grain to Critty, Zachariah's will made one exception: "so much as my said nephew Stephen Bowles may require next Fall to seed the land cultivated by him." After giving all of his livestock as part of the life estate for his wife, he again made an exception: "one heifer and one bed and furniture, which I give and bequeath unto Martha Ann Colbert, a girl now living with me." Next, he provided his nephew Stephen with "my horse and cart and farming utensils" and ordered that his farmland, upon his wife's death, was to go to Stephen and Peter. Finally, he appointed Stephen Bowles the sole executor of his will.

In September 1835, Zachariah's widow, Critty Bowles, was granted letters of administration for his estate. To become the administrator for the estate, she gave three hundred dollars bond; like any such administrator, she also needed someone else to give bond guaranteeing her performance in the role. She chose Eston Hemings, who also entered a bond pledging against any malfeasance on Critty's part. These actions represented standard operating procedure in the administration of estates. Whites, too, had to put up security to perform these same duties. It was relatively unusual, however, for a free black to give security for another free black.[67]

Eston Hemings was a free man of color, but he had been freed only recently. He had been a slave at Monticello, the property of Thomas Jefferson. His mother was Sally Hemings, the younger sister of Critty Bowles. His mother, Sally, had almost surely been for some time the mistress of the widowed Thomas Jefferson. They produced at least one child together. That child was Eston. Madison Hemings and three other siblings were also very likely the children of Jefferson. Eston was one of only five slaves freed by Jefferson in his will. Jefferson liberated Eston and Madison by "giving their services" to their uncle John Hemings (also freed in the will) until the boys arrived at age twenty-one, at which time they were to gain their liberty. Madison, born in 1805, was already twenty-one; Eston, born in 1808, became free in 1829. In reality, from Jefferson's death until Eston Hemings's twenty-first birthday, Hemings lived as a virtually free man, working for his uncle as a carpenter's apprentice.[68]

Zachariah Bowles and his wife, Critty, clearly connect the free black world both with the white community and with the slave population in Albemarle. Critty in particular, as the slave child of a white planter who gained her freedom through the goodwill of wealthy white men, demonstrates one pattern of personal relationships that could bind Albemarle residents, black and white. Moreover, the social geography of Zachariah Bowles's farm vividly highlights the ways in which family functioned for free people of color living in the rural South. At the heart of a culture that privileged personalism lies the family, the most important social unit for the people who lived in that culture. The people to be protected and aided first, among whites as well as blacks, were family members. Occasionally, family loyalty even transcended the color line.

For Zachariah Bowles, all of this meant raising his siblings' children. Peter and Stephen Bowles were the sons of Zachariah's brother Stephen

Bowles Sr., who had fought alongside Zachariah during the Revolutionary War. Zachariah, now owning a portion of his mother Amy Farrow's farm, set up his own residence. His brother Thomas Farrow had a residence of his own. Lucy Barnett, who also came to own a portion of the original farm, had her own house as well. As the children living on this extended-family farm grew up, they were allowed to build their own houses and start families. At least partly on a collective basis, they worked the land, cultivating grains (probably corn and wheat) as a cash crop and raising livestock (pigs, cows, and sheep). Many free blacks lived on and cultivated land that another family member owned, land they might one day own.

The black girl "then living with" Zachariah was in fact an enslaved relative of his wife. Martha Ann Colbert was the daughter of Thomas Jefferson's trusted valet Burwell Colbert and Critty Colbert, the daughter of Critty Bowles's sister Nance Hemings.[69] Martha Ann, in 1809, after her mother had died, was given to Jefferson's granddaughter Ellen Wayles Randolph. At some point, Randolph allowed Martha Ann to be raised by Critty Bowles, who had become free in 1827. Ellen Randolph was moving west, and this was the event that likely precipitated the transfer of Martha Ann to the Bowles household. She was not freed, but she was not forced to move to Arkansas with Randolph, either. Critty and Zachariah Bowles raised Martha Ann Colbert as if she were one of their own children. And fifteen years after Zachariah died and bequeathed some property to Martha Ann, his widow, Critty Bowles, also passed away. In her will, she left all monies in the estate as a trust for Martha Ann. It was illegal at the time to leave property to a slave, and it is not known whether Colbert ever received the inheritance. Perhaps the law was ignored, and Martha Ann received payments from the trust. It is also possible that Colbert had indeed been sent to Arkansas in the late 1830s to live with her new master, Lewis Randolph, and never benefited from the gift.[70]

The public record remains conspicuously silent concerning any children Critty (Hemings) Bowles and Zachariah Bowles may have had. Those children born prior to her being freed in 1827 would have been slaves. Thomas Jefferson's records for Critty show only one child, James, born in 1787. No father is mentioned, and this very well could have been Zachariah's son. James, described as a nearly white slave, ran away from Monticello in 1804 after being severely mistreated by the white overseer. He became a boatman, working the James River from the fall line in Richmond all the way down to the mouth of the river, in the Norfolk area. He was captured as a runaway after six months, and Jefferson negotiated with him for his return, promising to let him work independently of the overseer if he came back. Just before leaving Richmond to return to Charlottesville, he fled, never to live in Albemarle as a slave again. If Zachariah was the father, he lived separated from his son for most of James's childhood.[71]

Zachariah Bowles's legacy in Albemarle was instead carried on by an extended family. After raising his nephews Stephen and Peter Bowles, he helped them become adults and start families of their own. Peter Bowles even named one of his sons after his uncle Zachariah. The two brothers and their children had lived for years in relative comfort thanks to the security provided to them by Zachariah Bowles and his farm. Zachariah had already ensured the continuance of this system after his death. As discussed above, the will guaranteed that the lands in Zachariah's estate were to be Critty's until she died. At that time, the land would pass to the ownership of Stephen and Peter Bowles.

In 1850, after Critty died, her money, "together with the debts . . . coming to me," all went into a trust for the benefit of Martha Colbert, and the lands that she owned as a life estate fell to the brothers, who quickly sought legal guidance in dividing the land. Peter Bowles by 1849 had also passed away, leaving Stephen Bowles to split the land with Peter's descendants. Peter did not leave a will, but his family chose to register for freedom papers on September 4 of that year. Peter's family now had business before the county court as legatees. Therefore, they were probably required, or decided it was wise, to register with that same court.

In February 1852, Stephen sued Peter's widow, Lucy Bowles, and three of her children—Zachariah, Peter S., and Susan Bowles. The dispute revolved around an argument over the proper division of the estate land. The court appointed the white county official Ira Garrett as the guardian of Zachariah and Peter S. Bowles, the juvenile defendants, for the purposes of this case. Next, the court appointed four white men as commissioners and ordered them to survey and divide Zachariah Bowles's land according to the provisions of his will. These were the same procedures that would have been followed if the deceased had been white.

Those white men were not randomly appointed. They were once again neighbors who likely were well acquainted with the Bowles family. Lilbourne Railey lived near Hydraulic Mills on the Rivanna, several miles north of town. The Carr family had kinfolk living immediately adjacent to the Bowles farm. The Goodman family resided across the Rivanna, on land sandwiched between the two forks of the river, and David Goodman had a sibling who married Joel Terrell's daughter. Terrell also lived in the neighborhood—back in 1822, Judah Barnett had enlisted his help in executing her will. The Bowles estate must have been settled quickly, because in March 1852, the court completed the division. Forty-five acres went to the heirs of Peter Bowles, twelve acres to Edward Bowles, and thirty-eight acres to Stephen Bowles. Later that same year, the property having been divided amicably, the Bowles heirs all came together on the same day into Charlottesville to register for their freedom certificates. The farm on the north side of the Rivanna River's North Fork remained in the family.[72]

The family stories of other free men of color who served in the Revolution echo the broad patterns that the lives of the Smiths, Battleses, and Bowleses demonstrate. Free blacks in eighteenth- and nineteenth-century Virginia faced a legal system that denied them citizenship and limited their freedom in a number of other ways. They could face severe punishments for relatively minor crimes. But the same legal system also allowed them to use the courts to parcel out legacies and allowed them to file civil suits—even against whites. Room likewise remained to forge personal relationships with whites as neighbors, business associates, and more.

For instance, the free woman of color Agnes Goings was born in Louisa County circa 1725. She was born into an extended family that had been free since the seventeenth century in places as far away as the Eastern Shore of Virginia. By the time that Agnes lived, the Goings surname had been spreading westward across Virginia for decades and was often attached to free people of color. By age eighteen, Agnes had run into some trouble with the county authorities. The county court sentenced her to receive twenty-five lashes on her bare back. The offense: giving birth to a bastard child. The bastard child was a lighter-skinned mulatto, the child of a poor laborer passing through the area (possibly a white man). What attracted the attention of the authorities was not a free black woman giving birth to a child out of wedlock, and not interracial sex, but rather that the father was a poor transient stranger. Although miscegenation was considered a social ill, particularly when practiced in a way that lacked discretion or when practiced by strangers, in this case the issue revolved around the father's transience—the county could not get child support from him.[73]

This was Agnes's first child, Moses. She had several additional children over nearly the next twenty years, and all were described as having "a yellowish complexion," suggesting that Agnes may have continued to have children by one or more white men. In 1762, she gave birth to Sherod Goings, her sixth son. In 1770, the churchwardens of Trinity Parish apprenticed all of Agnes's children under age twenty-one. Sherod served for six years, until his mother filed suit on February 12, 1776, in the Louisa court, complaining that her son was being abused by his master, William Phillips. The apprenticeship was voided, freeing Sherod. A poor free woman of color in Virginia, Agnes Goings, had sued a white man and won the suit. Sherod Goings, too, joined the military during the Revolution, for an eighteen-month tour in the Fourteenth Virginia Regiment. He served at the battles of Germantown and Monmouth. He reenlisted for a second eighteen-month tour. On the way to the siege of Yorktown, his company paused at Chesterfield Court House, where he became acquainted with another Albemarle free black, Charles Barnett.[74]

Sherod's mother, Agnes, had settled in Albemarle about the same time that her son was finishing his second tour of duty. In Albemarle by 1783, she became the owner of 250 acres of land, valued at over four hundred dollars. Sherod returned from the war and settled with her on her land and in fact may have had a hand in helping to purchase the property. Thanks to his three years of military service, he had received a Revolutionary war grant of 196 acres in Fredericksville Parish on Buck Mountain Creek that same year. Agnes and Sherod may have had further help from a white patron, perhaps Sherod's father. By 1787, Agnes was listed as owning the land. In that year, Sherod owned two horses and four head of cattle.[75]

Were Agnes and Sherod Goings living in a hostile world where anyone coded as nonwhite was perceived as threatening and dangerous? In 1789, the answer seems to be no. In that year, Sherod Goings and his older brothers, Joseph, David, and Joshua Goings, now landowning free heads of household in Albemarle County, signed a legislative petition that tobacco farmers in the county were preparing. The document sought the establishment of a tobacco inspection warehouse at the mouth of Ballenger's Creek on the James River, at a location that would soon become the hamlet of Warren. The Goings brothers had a common interest with their fellow farmers and were included in the effort along with a number of prominent white slaveholders. The right to ownership of real and personal property, among the most important prerogatives of white Virginians, applied to free blacks as well, and that helped to facilitate the neighborly link between free blacks and whites.[76]

By this time, Sherod Goings also had likely met his future wife. They may in fact have been cohabiting in a common-law marriage. In 1789, Sherod Goings already had a young male living in his house with him, probably Sherod Jr., who became a head of household in the 1790s. In June 1791, Sherod Sr. headed to Charlottesville, married Susannah Simmons, and had the marriage officially recorded at the courthouse. The white Albemarle resident William Simmons secured the marriage bond, assuring the court of the lack of legal impediments to the union. Though the records do not explicitly address Simmons's possible relationship to Susannah, he was most likely her father. Even in the Upper South, a de facto mixed-race class, the free mulatto, existed between white and free black. Free mulattos tended to marry among themselves and remained connected to whites through marriage, cohabitation, or parent-child relationships.[77]

Agnes Goings, now an elderly woman, used her son's marriage as an opportunity to transfer title for the farm to him. By the end of 1791, Sherod Goings had become the owner of 250 acres of land in Albemarle, with Agnes Goings now listed as a dependent living in his household. By then, the land had increased in value from forty dollars to about seventy dollars, probably because of improvements Sherod Sr. had made to the place. Throughout the 1790s, Goings continued to work his farm, situated on mountainous land with relatively poor soil. In 1798, Sherod received a Revolutionary War grant for 31 acres on the north side of Green Mountain in the county. By 1799, the now 281-acre pair of tracts was worth nearly eighty dollars. His white neighbor James Dunn purchased one hundred acres from Sherod and his wife, Susanna, in 1805 for two hundred dollars. The connection between Dunn and Goings ran deeper than simply sharing a property line. They had been privates together in the same company during the Revolution. For Dunn, Goings was a very well-known neighbor.[78]

Sherod saw his daughter Ann marry her cousin John Goings in January 1810. The Methodist minister James Gibson performed the ceremony, with Sherod himself consenting to the marriage and giving bond. By 1815, he still owned nearly two hundred acres of land, as well as several horses, and an eight-head herd of cattle. His property was seventeen miles north of town, near Buck Mountain. His sons William and Henderson Goings were still living with him but soon would become independent. In 1822, Goings approached his white neighbor Mace Pickett about possibly buying some land. Pickett at that time found himself "in [a] deplorable state" and was desperate to raise some cash to pay off creditors. He agreed to sell twenty acres of land adjoining Goings's farm for twenty dollars.[79]

Over the next few years, Sherod busied himself setting up his many children with property, real and personal, of their own. His sons William, Charles, and Henderson all appeared on tax rolls as heads of household during this time, and all lived on or near Sherod's farm on the north end of the county. Seeking his Revolutionary War pension in 1828, Sherod Goings enlisted the help of several white veterans. William Turner, Edward Hughes, and John Snow all came to the county courthouse to declare that they had served with Sherod Goings during the war. He received the pension and collected eight dollars per month for nearly a decade.[80]

His son Charles meanwhile had become a northern Albemarle landowner in his own right, purchasing ninety-five acres of land near his father's farm. His relative James Goings, possibly another son of Sherod's, also owned over one hundred acres of land in the vicinity, as well as one slave. Although the records do not reveal who this slave was, free blacks sometimes owned slaves, most often family members whom they had purchased but not yet freed. Since the Goings family had long been free, it seems unlikely that the slave was a family member. Perhaps James hired or even purchased a slave to labor on his farm.

In 1832, Sherod Goings gave bond for his daughter Virginia's marriage to Noah Tate, a free man of color from nearby Madison County. In 1833, as noted earlier, in response to the Nat Turner rebellion and the state's subsequent debate over the future of slavery, counties were ordered to take censuses of free people of color and poll them about their willingness to be colonized in Africa. At that time, seven children who had yet to reach adulthood still lived with Sherod and wife, Susannah. Noah Tate and his wife, Virginia, also resided on Sherod's farm. Twenty-four Goingses in total were described as living near James Dunn, and another eight were described as living in the vicinity at Buck Mountain.[81] Sherod Goings died in November 1837, surrounded by white neighbors whom he had known most of his life and by an extended family of children, siblings, nephews, and nieces in Albemarle. He had managed to provide well for his extended family both during his life and after. His wife, Susannah, applied in 1841 for a continuation of his war pension. Seven years later, she was granted eighty dollars per year.[82]

The Revolutionary War generation of free people of color in Charlottesville demonstrated a remarkable ability to interact with their white neighbors.

These same free blacks seemed to understand and accept the highly personal ways in which people in Albemarle conducted business. At the same time, they had to accept, at least outwardly, the social hierarchy. The legislation passed in Richmond concerning the rights, privileges, and duties of free people of color in Virginia by the middle of the 1780s was trending toward a steady diminution of free black liberties and a concomitant rise in explicit proscriptions, yet these laws bore little resemblance to the grassroots experience of many whites and people of color in rural localities such as Albemarle.

A degree of tolerance, combined with mores that determined a person's worth through personal interaction and shared experience, allowed a sphere of interracial activity that created a comfort zone for free people of color. Free black war veterans in Albemarle owned next to nothing at the commencement of the Republic. Within a half century, however, they had achieved some success in accumulating land and personal property. Even more important, their experiences participating in the war had prepared them for the vital work of connecting on a personal level with their white neighbors. Their efforts to carve out livelihoods in peacetime helped solidify those connections. Their efforts paved the way for the generations that would follow them.

2

Children of the Revolution

Post-War Free Black Families, Property, and Community

The Revolutionary generation of free blacks in Albemarle County forged solid and enduring connections with the white community. Their participation as soldiers in the war counted for something in their neighbors' eyes. In particular, the deeply personal connections that were created by serving together in combat would prove very useful to free black veterans well into the nineteenth century. Those same connections would also play a pivotal role at times for the families of free black veterans, who continued to receive military pensions even after the veterans themselves had died. The fact that the Revolution produced a period in which the racial hierarchy of the slave South temporarily weakened has been well documented by scholars.

These same scholars argue that this brief postwar period ended rather suddenly when enthusiasm for Revolutionary doctrine faded in the early nineteenth century. The abortive Gabriel's rebellion in the Richmond area, combined with reports of the excesses of the French Revolution and the successful slave rebellion in Haiti, supposedly put an end to a period of relative racial harmony. As the lives of these Albemarle free black Revolutionary veterans demonstrate, however, the door did not close so quickly on that period.[1]

And what about those free people of color who did not participate actively in the Revolution? What about those who were simply born too late even to consider getting involved? Did they merely experience a short post-Revolutionary time when the racial hierarchy weakened a bit? Were they denied participation in the local community as a result? The children of the Revolutionary generation and those born too late to participate in the war made slow but steady progress toward greater property ownership, wealth, and skills. It was a tough road to travel when their parents had had so few advantages.

Those who remained in Albemarle, however impoverished, continued to demonstrate sustained interaction with the white community. They became known people, whose behavior was respectable enough in the eyes of whites to allow them wider latitude in their actions. The man of color Robert Battles and his family represent an excellent starting point for such a comparison. Robert Battles Sr. was born in 1771 in Albemarle. He was too young to participate as a soldier in the Revolution. He was, however, acquainted with free black Revolutionary War veteran Charles Barnett. In December 1793, Barnett gave bond for Robert's marriage to Nancy Bowles. They were neighbors, living just south of Charlottesville.[2]

Until well into the nineteenth century, the documentary record of Robert Battles is sparse indeed. He appears yearly starting in 1794 on the county's personal property tax lists. These documents do not reveal anything dramatic about his life. Until at least 1820, he owned little personal property in any given year. Battles does not appear on land tax lists for that period. His marriage to Nancy Bowles in 1793, however, reveals some details about the neighborhood in which he lived. The ceremony involved three free black families: Battles, Barnett, and Bowles. All lived on the same side of town in a neighborhood that included free black property owners, white and black itinerant laborers, slaves, and free whites from a variety of economic backgrounds.[3]

Robert Battles's relationship with Barnett, clearly evincing a level of familiarity in 1793, quickly soured after that marriage ceremony. Less than three years later, Charles Barnett and his wife Lucy took Robert Battles to court. In May 1796, they charged him with assault and pleaded with the court for protection, fearing Battles's continuing intent to injure them. Robert Battles answered the summons for the charges, appearing at the Charlottesville courthouse, denying the charges and pleading not guilty. The case was continued until later that summer. At the August court, both the Barnetts and the Battleses returned to the courthouse. Barnett's case against Robert Battles was dismissed, and the Barnetts were ordered to pay all court costs.[4]

Both free men of color, contrary to the picture portrayed by much historical writing about free blacks, were ready, willing, and able to utilize the legal system in rural Virginia when it suited them. Neither had complied with state law by formally registering with the county as free black residents. That law had been in effect since 1793. Disregarding their apparent violation of the law, both men readily appeared in court: Barnett and his wife came first to file charges and again for the court's actual hearing of the case. Robert Battles, meanwhile, came forth to state his innocence and to give his side of the argument a proper hearing. While in town attending to the court proceedings, neither felt it necessary to take the time to register and comply with state law. Perhaps Barnett's willing appearance was the result of the local reputation he had earned as a veteran. But Robert Battles, only twenty-four years old at the time, a free man of color in the slave South just starting a family and with little property to his name, had no such obvious reason to feel safe. Yet he clearly did enjoy a relative level of comfort about his status within the community.[5]

Yes, the thinness of documentary evidence on his life prior to that 1796 court case could be read as confirming the prevailing theory that he lived as a free person of color in a virulently racist slave society that equated darker skin color with slavery and whiteness with freedom. In that world, free people of color failed to appear in public archival records because they kept a low profile, avoiding contact with whites or law-enforcement officers and constantly living in fear of being incarcerated or forcibly returned to slavery. Neither the actions of Barnett nor those of Battles, however, suggest that they were living in fear in 1796. Robert Battles eventually decided to comply with the 1793 law, but did so at a very leisurely pace. He first registered in July 1803, a full decade after the state legislature passed the registration law.[6]

In 1793, the unregistered Robert Battles owned two horses, was in his midtwenties, and was married. After the case brought by Charles Barnett was dismissed, Battles continued to own no real property and little personal property. That situation obtained until at least 1798, when he was taxed for owning one horse and one slave over sixteen years of age. Although the specifics of Robert Battles's economic life remain partially obscured, a picture begins to emerge. At first glance, Battles appears to have owned no real property until well into the nineteenth century. But then, on December 12, 1819, Robert and his wife, Nancy, sold one acre of land in Albemarle County to a Stephen Coram for $150. As part of the deed, Robert and Nancy Battles acknowledged that the sale was part of Coram's legacy. Essentially, they were giving this man an inheritance, but before anyone had died and well before their estate would go through the probate process.[7]

It seems likely that Robert Battles had in fact owned land in that same location since at least the 1790s. When he started his family, he may already have been in possession of some land. State governments in the late eighteenth century and first half of the nineteenth century lacked an efficient and ordered bureaucracy. Much of the modern work of government in that time fell upon the county governments, which were peopled largely by officials who fulfilled the obligations of public service on a part-time basis. These people were themselves residents and property owners. The courthouse, jail, and county court clerk's office were the sole physical manifestations of government with which a typical Virginian would be familiar. Robert Battles may have owned too little property for taxation. He may have been away the day the tax assessor came through Battles's neighborhood. The tax collector may also have conducted a less than exhaustive assessment of county residents.[8]

Regardless of the actual reason for Robert Battles's absence from the land tax records, he owned enough land in 1819 to part with some of it. But he did not simply post an advertisement for the land and sell it to the highest bidder. Instead, Battles looked among friends, family, and neighbors for a buyer. He chose Stephen Coram, another local free man of color. Stephen Coram, however, was not a business acquaintance within the free black community. Instead, Coram was family, a man who had actually married Robert and Nancy's daughter, Keziah, two years earlier. Coram most likely already lived on the Battleses' farm.[9]

In 1820, just shy of one year after Robert Battles sold a parcel of land to his son-in-law Stephen Coram, the real property tax assessor made it to Battles's neighborhood. The tax list for that year reveals that Battles owned seventeen and three-quarter acres of land lying one half mile to the southwest of the courthouse at the center of Charlottesville. The land was of middling quality, fetching a price of $25 per acre. This was a not insubstantial value per acre for the time. The tax collector assessed the parcel of land as being worth nearly $450. The tax lists that year also reveal that Battles had managed to do more than purchase land. He had worked to improve it, adding $150 in value to the property. Despite lacking the valuable connection to the local white community that veteran status provided, Robert Battles had nonetheless managed to do quite well for himself.[10]

Up to this point, Robert Battles's life reveals some detail about the lives of free people of color. They lived together, worked together, played together, and fought with one another. But Robert Battles was a member of a group that numbered only a few hundred people, all living in a county with thousands of white residents and thousands of slaves. None of these free people of color lived in isolation from the larger white and slave communities that they were immersed in. How, then, do we discover the ligaments of community that include Robert Battles and other free people of color? How were they connected to both the white and slave communities that shared the county with them? In that era of the incomplete state, what records can shed light on more everyday details of their lives?

First, the property tax lists highlight the ways in which free people of color such as Robert Battles might have connections with the slave community. Other family members might be enslaved, especially if the wife was a slave. Free blacks sometimes hired slaves as laborers at their businesses or actually purchased slaves for their labor. Most often, slave ownership by a free black was evidence of the purchasing of family members. In 1798, Robert Battles paid tax on one horse and one slave over sixteen years of age. This was the first year that he appeared on the tax rolls owning anything other than a horse or two. Suddenly, in 1798, he appears to have owned another person. His records never indicate that he owned any one slave for more than a short period of time. By 1799, that first slave was no longer in his possession, and he did not own a slave again until 1805. That second slave, too, was no longer owned by Battles the following year. These two periods of brief slave ownership were the only ones he ever had. The free person of color Robert Battles either occasionally hired a slave or had noneconomic connections to the larger slave community in Albemarle.[11]

Robert Battles had regular contact with white residents as well. He lived directly adjacent to the main east-west overland travel route between Richmond and Staunton, across the Blue Ridge Mountains, forty-odd miles to the West. His property and home were just outside the official limits of the town of Charlottesville. He had white neighbors with whom he had regular contact. His interactions with whites in the area, however, were far more than simply passive encounters that a free person of color such as Battles was allegedly at pains to avoid. No, Robert Battles maintained an active presence in the community, working with neighbors, conducting business with area residents, appearing in public areas, and utilizing the courts when necessary.

For instance, the free black Patrick Johnson, after a disagreement and public physical encounter with Robert Battles in 1804, hired a lawyer and sued Battles, claiming Battles had assaulted him. The court did little until March 1806. Both Battles and Johnson appeared at the courthouse on that day. The court referred to the plaintiff as "Patrick, a free negro, otherwise called Patrick Johnson," while also failing to indicate Battles's race. The court forwarded the case to trial, continuing the cause till the next term. In the spring of 1806, Robert Battles was summoned again to the courthouse to face the assault charges brought against him by Johnson. Battles appeared as required, heard the charges, and through his lawyer pleaded not guilty, stating that if there had been an assault, Patrick Johnson had started it by assaulting him first. The court ordered that the writ of inquiry be set aside and continued the cause till the next term. The case was continued once more in August and again in November, at Battles's request. Finally, on March 5, 1807, the court ruled in favor of the plaintiff, Patrick Johnson, and ordered Battles to pay court costs of $9.62.[12]

Typical for county records of the time, Robert Battles's race, physical description, and status were not recorded. The court documents, except in that one instance where Johnson is described as a "free negro," do not refer to either man by race—only by name. Both received due process of law, regardless of race. Both men were members of the community—known quantities; no further description was needed. Does such equal treatment before the law indicate that perhaps there was a great level of interracial social equality in Albemarle? No, the records give no sense of that at all. Battles was merely accorded the proper legal treatment that any respectable member of local society deserved. Respectability, while containing within it notions of at least a level of behavioral equality, did not preclude or supersede the local and steep social hierarchy that prevailed. Battles, as an active participant both in this social hierarchy and in attempting to live up to the norms of respectability, understood that the community knew him and that thus he had a reasonable expectation of receiving the privileges and rights that attached to such familiarity.

Robert Battles, an illiterate free black property owner in the antebellum rural South, remains largely inarticulate to the historical record. He left no stack of papers, no diary, no journals, no business account books. As a minor property owner and a small businessman, he simply did not engage in the complicated and larger-scale financial transactions that leave a clear footprint in the archives. The absence of such detailed sources, however, and Battles's fleeting presence in many other archival sources do not mean that Robert Battles was not an active participant in the community he lived in.

A year after Robert Battles faced assault charges brought by a white Albemarle resident, he was still living on the same property, still working, still leading a productive life. He was not hiding from white residents, from slave patrollers, from slave catchers, or from constables. He had not been incarcerated, intimidated, or driven from the area. Life went on in Albemarle County much as it always had. On June 17, 1807, Alexander Garrett, the executor for the estate of the white Albemarle resident Richard H. Allen, held an estate sale at Allen's farm. Local residents gathered that day for the auction. White and black residents stood in the crowd that spring day, all bidding on merchandise that interested them.

Battles attended, bidding on a grindstone. His freedom certificate, the only one he had registered for in nearly forty years of residence there, had expired the year before. Battles had failed to renew it but did not stop actively participating in the community. Battles saw no reason to hide and demonstrated no fear of attending public events where he would be seen by numerous local whites. Robert saw the auction as an opportunity to purchase some much-needed supplies.

He was the highest bidder on that grindstone. As the auction continued, Battles made arrangements with the estate executor, Alexander Garrett, setting up an account to pay for the grindstone over time. For the next fifteen years, Battles would maintain a running account with Garrett and the Allen estate, both for items purchased on credit and for services rendered by Battles for the estate. Battles was a carpenter by trade and constructed a school building for Allen's children on the Allen family farm property. Documents that at first glance appear only to reveal something about a white lawyer and a white landowner in Albemarle County actually reveal a fairly complicated series of transactions between white and black residents.[13]

The free man of color Robert Battles did not confine his contact with white Albemarle residents to one man. Alexander Garrett, a prominent local citizen who served for years as county clerk, owned property immediately adjacent to that of Robert Battles Sr. But Garrett was not Robert's sole connection to the white world. Remaining without a valid freedom certificate, Battles continued to conduct business in the area, both as a carpenter-for-hire and as a resident property owner. In December 1813, Robert Battles again made a purchase at an estate sale. The Jane Lewis estate was in the process of administration. Repeating what was surely a familiar process for Albemarle residents, Robert Battles heard of the estate auction, traveled to the Lewis property, and perused the sundry items for sale.

This time, Battles was less interested in what was for sale than in who would be in attendance. He came that day seeking payment for services rendered earlier. Whether the carpentry work was for Mrs. Lewis while she was still alive or was contracted for by the estate remains unclear. What is clear is that the free man of color Robert Battles Sr. showed up at Mrs. Lewis's estate auction on a winter day to make sure the account she had with him was paid. He was not afraid to be seen by whites or to encounter the sheriff or patrollers. He was not a dangerous free black; he was Robert Battles, local carpenter, respectable property owner.[14]

He continued to conduct business with area whites, marrying community custom and economic interest. In 1822, Robert and his wife, Nancy, sold a small lot that adjoined their seventeen-acre property. This parcel, about one-half acre, bordered both their larger property and the parcel they had sold years earlier to Stephen Coram. The lot, valued at twenty-five dollars per acre, sold for sixty dollars. William Burwell, a white resident in the vicinity of Charlottesville, purchased the plot. Robert and Nancy offered their land for sale to the highest bidder, white or black. A white man in the neighborhood was willing to do business with them and to pay a fair price for the land.[15]

Back on his nearly eighteen-acre farm just outside of Charlottesville, Robert Battles and his wife, Nancy, continued to raise a family. By 1817, Robert and Nancy had at least four children. The oldest was probably Keziah, the daughter who would marry Stephen Coram in March of that year. Personal property tax lists for 1816 and 1817 indicate that Stephen Coram was already living with the Battleses at least a full year prior to his marriage to Keziah. Next was the oldest son, Elijah, born in 1797. Robert Jr. was one year younger than Elijah. And the youngest was Wyatt, born circa 1804. In 1825, with his children grown and beginning to establish themselves as independent heads of household, Robert Battles Sr. decided to sell the nearly seventeen acres he owned just south of town. This sixteen-and-one-half-acre plot on the south side of Three Notched Road between Charlottesville and the University of Virginia was bounded by Alexander Garrett's land and the smaller plots now owned by Stephen Coram and William Burwell.[16]

In March, John Hartwell Cocke, a wealthy white man from neighboring Fluvanna County, purchased the entire plot. The Battles tract of land encompassed the two small plots that Battles had earlier sold to Coram and Burwell. The deed of bargain and sale that Battles and Cocke entered into explicitly excluded those two smaller parcels. Cocke agreed to pay Robert Battles Sr. two thousand dollars for the parcel of land. This was a considerable sum. In fact, the purchase price appears to have exceeded greatly the assessed value of the Battles land. The last time the parcel had been assessed, four years earlier, the land was worth twenty-five dollars per acre. The lot had about two hundred dollars in improvements upon it. The total assessed value in 1821 was about six hundred dollars. Battles jumped at the opportunity to sell the land.[17]

The great offer was certainly a factor driving Battles to sell the land. Other concerns, however, appear to have motivated him. In 1825, Robert Battles Sr. was a widower, but he had met a young woman who was soon to become his second wife—Martha A. R. Butler, the daughter of Griffen Butler, another free man of color living in Albemarle. The Butlers lived farther outside of town. Robert Battles sold his plot adjacent to town and then invested about half of the sale money in a new property located much closer to the Butler residence. At the end of April that same year, Robert Battles purchased forty acres of land on Moore's Creek from Dixon Dedman and Sarah Dedman for $925. The property was situated several miles southwest of Charlottesville. Dixon and Sarah Dedman were the last remaining members of the Dedman family still living in Albemarle. The rest of the family had already emigrated to southwest Virginia, Kentucky, and even points much further west. This sale was the beginning of the Dedmans' effort to sell off their substantial holdings and move west, a process that they completed in 1828.[18]

That series of transactions resulted in quite a life change for Robert Battles Sr. At the beginning of March 1825, he was a widower living on a small farm right outside of Charlottesville. First, in that month, he was taken to court by another free black. The free woman of color Rebecca Hughes filed a case against Battles, charging him with slander. Typical of both white and black residents, Hughes was concerned with her reputation and felt that Battles had publicly and verbally defamed her. The case would continue for over a year before being dismissed. Meanwhile, by the end of April, Robert had sold that first parcel of land for an excellent price, had remarried, and had purchased a much larger farm in the Ragged Mountains area southwest of town. His new neighbors included the free black Butler family, as well as Jesse Lewis, Claudius Mayo, and Michael Johnson, local white landowners. Topping it all off, he had made this transition while managing to profit nicely from the deal. After purchasing the bigger farm, he still had over one thousand dollars in his possession.[19]

There in the Ragged Mountains, the elderly farmer Robert Battles established a patrimony for his children and lived out the last several years of his life. His new farm became the support center for his extended family. According to the 1830 U.S. Census, it appears that some of his children or grandchildren had by then moved to the banks of Moore's Creek to work the property with him. Listed in adjacent dwellings are Bracken Battles, Betsy Battles, and Edward Battles. Robert continued to farm his land with the rest of his family, all the while managing to earn both their subsistence and extra income. Typical of small farmers in the South, the Battleses practiced a farming philosophy that privileged protection of family.

In August 1831, the administrator Richard Duke held an estate auction for the Charles Spencer estate. Spencer had been a well-to-do businessman who lived in Charlottesville along the main road running from Richmond to Staunton, the same road upon which Battles had lived until he purchased the Ragged Mountain farm.

The two men were quite familiar with one another. They had lived in the same general area for decades. Spencer lived in Random Row, which at the time was at the town boundary. He kept a carriage for hire, allowing one of his slaves to run the business for him. Charlottesville, although not much of a town center by any measure, remained a center of commerce and gathering for people in the area. This included slaves, free people of color, and whites.

A crowd appeared on that fourth day of August to peruse the items for sale from Charles Spencer's estate. Robert Battles Sr., now living a few miles away, purchased a number of articles. The estate records do not record specifically what he purchased, only listing them as "sundry items," for which Robert paid a little over four dollars. At the same time, Battles was involved in a lawsuit against the Spencer estate.

Several months earlier, the county court had awarded Battles a judgment of over three hundred dollars—money owed to Battles by the Spencer estate. The judgment covered outstanding debts dating back to 1828. On October 11, 1832, Robert Battles Sr. still had outstanding payments due from Spencer's estate. The administrator Richard Duke, willingly taking Battles's money at the estate sale, had refused to pay the debt Spencer owed Battles. Battles had been fighting Duke in the court since August 1830, when he first filed suit. On that date, the court had set aside temporarily a writ of inquiry to give Duke time to clean up the estate books.

But on that October day in 1832, things still had not resolved themselves. Eleven days later, Battles and the other plaintiffs filed a motion seeking an impartial accounting of the administration of the estate conducted by Richard

Duke. The court granted the motion and ordered the auditor to pay special attention to the debts and claims of the plaintiffs (including Battles) against the Spencer estate. Clearly, Spencer was more than a neighbor. Spencer and Battles had a business relationship, one that relied on a credit system. Spencer, a slave-owning white businessman, had evinced no concern about doing business with the free man of color Robert Battles Sr.[20]

Once again, a free person of color living in the rural slaveholding South felt comfortable enough to participate openly and directly in the economic affairs of the locality. Robert Battles saw the court system as a tool he should feel free to utilize in settling disputes he had with other area residents, black or white. A free black property-owning businessman such as Battles, regardless of actual net worth, belies the notion of free people of color in the rural South as poor, marginal, and living in fear of white reprisal. This lawsuit would drag on for another decade, not concluding until after Battles himself had died. In the short term, this business disagreement did not keep Battles from attending an estate sale on the Spencer property or from continuing to interact with white and black neighbors. In fact, the lawsuit brought Battles and some of his neighbors together.[21]

Robert Battles's forty-acre parcel remained a home for an extended family, one that did not just include some of his children and their families. A year after purchasing items from the Charles Spencer estate, Battles participated in a Presbyterian marriage service. The free people of color Staples Goings and Margaret Burrows married that August day. Robert Battles Sr. gave surety that the bride was of legal age and that there were no legal impediments to the marriage. The bride's mother, the free woman of color Elizabeth Randall, also attended and gave her consent. The connection between Battles and Burrows remains somewhat unclear, but a parish census of free blacks taken in 1833 indicates that Robert Battles headed a household that included one "Julian Burruss," a mulatto female seamstress. Apparently, another free black family, seemingly unconnected through kinship, resided with the Battles family at the Ragged Mountain farm.[22]

The day after the wedding, a fellow free person of color called upon Robert Battles for assistance, drawing on his long-standing neighborly connections to a number of whites in the area. Joseph Fossett, a former slave owned by Thomas Jefferson at Monticello, had been freed in 1827 by the provisions of Jefferson's will. Fossett, however, had a wife and children, all of whom were slaves owned by Jefferson. Jefferson freed only five slaves in his will, and none of the others were Fossett's family members. Fossett needed the help of a number of people in Albemarle if he were to reunite his family. He would turn both to local whites and to free people of color.

Robert Battles was one of the people whom Fossett contacted. Battles until 1825 had lived just outside Charlottesville, practically at the base of the mountain on which Monticello was located. One of the adjacent property owners was a man named James Dinsmore, who until 1809 had been a master carpenter working for Jefferson on the mountaintop. Dinsmore continued working as a carpenter from his shop and farm on the outskirts of town. Interestingly, all of Robert Battles Sr.'s male children became carpenters while growing up next door to Dinsmore. In addition, Dinsmore likely knew many of the Monticello slaves, including those who would become free after Jefferson's death. White, free black, and slave intermingled with ease there on the south side of Three Notched Road.

By 1831, James Dinsmore had died, and his brother John came to town to execute distribution of his estate. Included in the estate holdings were a few slaves. The records remain silent as to the names of these slaves. But the records clearly state that Joseph Fossett and Robert Battles together made purchases of a slave or slaves from the estate. Joseph Fossett, recently freed, made a payment of nearly twenty-five dollars on July 15, 1831. The newly freed man of color Joseph Fossett made his purchase only a few weeks before Nat Turner's Rebellion exploded in Southampton County. Robert Battles paid his bill in full on May 2, 1832, paying an additional fifty-two dollars. No one in Charlottesville appears to have raised any kind of commotion that May day, less than ten months after a number of white Virginians had died at the hands of the Turner rebellion. A free black purchasing slaves for another free black who probably intended to free them did not strike fear in the hearts of locals because both men—Joseph Fossett and Robert Battles—were known personages with long-standing connections to the community.[23] They still conducted business, moved about in public in relatively free fashion, and interacted with slaves, other free people of color, and white neighbors on a regular basis. Almost all of this occurred well after that fabled brief post-Revolutionary period. Much of it took place after Gabriel's Rebellion in 1800. And the pattern continued even after Nat Turner's bloody slave revolt of 1831 in Southampton County.

In November 1835, Joseph Bishop, a white businessman who ran a tanyard in Charlottesville and had frequent contact with local free people of color, filed with the court the accounts he had kept while executing the estate of William C. Burton, a fellow tanner and businessman in town.[24] Bishop and Burton lived in the same neighborhood that Robert Battles Sr. had lived in until 1825. Burton, in fact, had hired Battles to do work for him, probably rough carpentry. The two men maintained a running account, with Battles performing occasional work and Burton making payments to Battles as he could. Joseph Bishop, functioning as executor after Burton's death, continued this arrangement, using Battles when work was needed and paying him later.[25]

Those payments in 1835 were the last Robert Battles Sr. would ever receive. Approximately sixty-five years old, Battles died sometime that year. His estate was inventoried and appraised in November 1835. On March 7, 1836, the court recorded the dower allotment for Robert's widow, Martha Battles. She received possession for life of nine and one-quarter acres of his Ragged Mountain farm. Her acreage included Moore's Creek frontage. The division of Battles's estate was now under way, and problems would predictably arise. He appears to have left no will, and he had an extended family sharing his forty-acre plot with him. Only his widow, Martha, quickly received a portion of the estate. The rest of his property would be fought for or divided up amicably by his surviving heirs.[26]

Robert Battles Sr. was the best-known, most respectable, most independent, and best-connected of the Battles family members. With his estate in the process of administration, surviving family members continued to live on the farm. Meanwhile, a group of nearby property owners, including whites and their neighbors, the free black Battles family, completed a petitioning of the county court, seeking the establishment of a public road through the neighborhood.[27] This road, as proposed, would cut through the Battles tract and the property of neighboring white Jesse Lewis. In May 1837, county officers Opie Norris and John R. Jones ordered the county sheriff to call a panel of twelve white property owners. This panel would meet at the farm of Robert Battles, deceased, now the "lands of Elijah Battles, Robert Battles [Jr.] and others as well as the widow of Robert Battles Sr. and Jesse Lewis on June 3, 1837." This jury was to consider the lands, the proposed path of the road, and the locations of fencing and gates necessary for the installation of the road and then assess damages that the property owners (Battles and Lewis) would suffer.[28]

The panel met as directed in early June. They surveyed the proposed route of the road and considered damage to both the Battles and the Lewis properties. The panel asserted that the property then owned by Robert Battles Jr., Elijah Battles, and others would sustain thirty dollars in damage if the road were put in as proposed and if they were permitted to erect one or more gates. The panel further asserted that white neighbor Jesse Lewis would sustain damage of sixty dollars if permitted to construct one or more gates, but six hundred dollars if not permitted to do so. The road inquiry dragged on for at least another year. In December 1838, the court ordered William Garth and the rest of that panel to report formally to the court concerning the establishment of the proposed road. The road would go through the lands of Robert Battles Sr. and four white men, three of whom were on the panel reporting on the road. The road would connect the Lynchburg Road, which ran south from Charlottesville, to the Rivanna and Rockfish Gap Turnpike, which continued west over the Blue Ridge Mountains.[29]

Robert Battles Sr. and his children may not have shared equal citizenship with the white neighbors affected by the proposed road. They may not have considered them intimate friends. But they had had extensive face-to-face relations with them, had done business with them, had discussed matters of interest to the neighborhood with them. To those white men, Robert Battles Sr. was a respectable independent farmer and family man. He had been free as long as they had known him. In turn, Robert Battles Sr. respected them and probably trusted them to make the road cut through their combined properties in such a way as would best advantage all of them.

Interpersonal relations in the rural antebellum South were structured around all-important face-to-face interactions, and these interactions by necessity occurred between whites, free people of color, slaves, and people from all points across the economic spectrum. In this instance, the new road would make the Battleses' travels to and from town easier and would likely better connect them with other neighborhoods in the county, perhaps even increase business opportunities for them. Laws passed by the legislature in Richmond had little direct bearing on the lives of people who were well-known in their home localities.

Road construction issues aside, the Battles family now had an estate to execute. The oldest surviving male heirs, Robert Jr. and Elijah Battles, became the executors. As prescribed by law, they first had to pledge bond and security of two hundred dollars each. In addition, the law required a security, a bond filed by someone else on their behalf attesting to their respectability and trustworthiness. Elijah and Robert Jr. turned to the white local resident John Pollock, a neighbor living in the vicinity of their father's Ragged Mountain farm. Pollock pledged security for them, but Elijah and Robert Jr. did not give bond as administrators. Pollock, after pledging security for both Battleses, would return to the courthouse in November 1838 to file a motion against the administrators (Robert Jr. and Elijah) "to show cause why they should not be compelled to give further security."[30]

Assigned as administrators of the estate, Robert Jr. and Elijah were in a bind: they could not yet demonstrate that they possessed sufficient assets to give bond. This was understandable and to a degree foreseeable. They were cash poor, and what assets the family actually possessed were currently tied up in the administration of their father's estate. Luckily, although their father had left them without a will to speed the process of administering and executing the estate, he had begun to provide for his children before he died.

Robert Jr. and Elijah Battles turned to the old family homestead on the south side of Three Notched Road, just south of Charlottesville. Originally, their father had owned nearly eighteen acres of land. He had sold off one acre to son-in-law Stephen Coram and then sold another sixteen shortly before he moved to the Ragged Mountain farm. But he had kept one acre of land for his family. He had purchased this acre of land from neighbor Jacob Waltman. Elijah and Robert Jr. mortgaged the land, selling it to the local lawyer Egbert R. Watson for one dollar. In return, the Battleses received securities from the local white Fontaine Wells and the free man of color Jesse Scott. Through this deed of trust, Watson would hold title to the land as long as the Battles brothers were administering the estate and as long as Scott and Wells did not call in their securities. As soon as Elijah and Robert Jr. had successfully completed administration of their father's estate, the mortgage agreement would be voided, and the land would return to the possession of the Battles family.[31]

The entire plan was designed to protect the bond given by Wells and Scott. Elijah and Robert Jr. further gave bond for $1,600 payable to Pollock and another white area resident, John D. Craven. Jesse Scott and Fontaine Wells, those two benefactors, would not endure considerable financial loss if the Battles brothers failed to administer the estate properly. This complicated legal arrangement required extensive personal connections with other area residents. Whether they relied on their father's reputation among town residents or utilized their own connections, the Battles brothers fulfilled the security obligation for estate administration.[32]

Once all the legal wrangling involved in securing proper administration of the estate had been completed, the Battles brothers set to the task. Again, there was no will, but it seems clear that the family had worked out an arrangement as to how the property would be divided. Robert Jr. and Elijah received legal authority to administer the estate only in December 1838; yet early in the following year, much of the work had already been completed. On February 4, 1839, Elijah Battles submitted to the county court his administration accounts for his father's estate. The court approved the documents and submitted them to the record, and a portion of the estate was settled. Elijah had completed his duties as administrator, and it took less than two months.

Elijah's brother Robert Jr. would need another three months to finish his portion of the administration. First, on March 4, Robert submitted partial accounts for the estate. These accounts detailed his father's economic life and gave a sense of the distribution of his estate to heirs. The estate made payments to the white residents Nathaniel Wolfe, John R. Jones, and Walter Perry, settling transactions that the father had been involved in. The accounts showed payments to a list of free people of color as well, including Martha Battles (his widow); Elijah, Robert Jr., and Wyatt Battles (his sons); and Eliza Foster.[33] On May 3, 1839, Robert submitted his finalized administrator accounts. The court then released him from his duties as administrator. The Robert Battles Sr. estate was now finally fully administered. That same day, Fontaine Wells and Jesse Scott returned the property mortgage to Robert Jr. The mortgage with Egbert Watson was thus satisfied. Robert Jr. bought back the acre of land, paying Egbert R. Watson one dollar.[34]

With the legal formalities of dealing with the estate finished, the family could now turn their attention to the intrafamily details of distributing estate assets. Over the several months after Robert Jr.'s May completion of estate administration, the Battleses continued parceling out land and property. On July 18, 1839, Robert and his wife, Mary, sold off their interest in the father's estate. Their interest consisted of one-fifth of the Ragged Mountain parcel. They sold it to their deceased father's second wife, Martha Battles, for sixty-four dollars. This sale was not completed until February 17, 1840, when William A. Bibb and John R. Jones, white county officials that year, examined Mary Battles (the wife of Robert Jr.). Once they had confirmed that Mary had not been coerced into selling the land she owned jointly with her husband—standard procedure in such cases—and that she actually approved of the sale, the transaction was confirmed. The widow Martha Battles now possessed nearly twenty acres of the original Ragged Mountain farm.[35]

The sons of Robert Battles Sr. had already demonstrated that they had enduring connections to the community. Their actions and interactions with white and black neighbors strongly suggest that they most likely did not rely solely upon their father's respectability. Through face-to-face interaction, they had developed a reasonably secure reputation for proper behavior in the community. But what would happen to Robert Battles Sr.'s widow? Though her race and her status as a married woman had long imposed civil disabilities, there is some evidence that she, too, had managed to maintain those all-important face-to-face interactions with neighbors that established a person's reputation in rural and small-town southern communities and applied to white and black residents alike.

At around the same time that Martha was becoming an independent property owner in her own right, both securing a dower portion from her deceased husband's estate and purchasing several more acres of the old family farm from other heirs, a white neighbor was dying. William Goodwin, the white man who had been the prime mover behind that earlier effort to establish a road that would have cut across the Battleses' land, died sometime between 1838 and 1840. Another white neighbor from the Ragged Mountain neighborhood, Michael Johnson, was appointed as administrator for the Goodwin estate. His estate accounts for 1839 and 1840 include payments to Robert Battles Sr.'s widow, Martha. No records exist that detail just what Martha Battles did for Johnson or Goodwin. But the 1833 colonization census contains a hint. In that year, Martha was the thirty-four-year-old wife of Robert Battles Sr. She has no occupation listed, but a young female living with them at the time is described as a seamstress. In all likelihood, Martha Battles ran her own sewing and garment-making business out of the home, dealing directly with other locals, black and white.[36]

Three full decades into the nineteenth century, Robert Battles Sr. and his wife Martha demonstrated an enduring connection to the community in which they lived. They almost never complied with the 1793 free black registration law. But this lapse did not arise out of concern for the visibility that going to the courthouse or interacting with white county officials demanded. They were not in hiding, nor were they avoiding attention. They conducted business with white and black people in and around Charlottesville, in their old neighborhood just south of town, and in the neighborhood of the larger family farm several miles southwest of town. They used the courthouse and the local legal system when it suited their needs and even as they did not feel compelled to register their freedom or even renew expired papers. They did not need to do these things: they had established relatively secure reputations through face-to-face interactions. Their children to this point had demonstrated similar behavior. But with Robert Sr. deceased, what would happen to those children? Would they be able to replicate their father's accomplishments?

Robert Battles Sr. by the early 1820s had at least three sons. Robert Jr., Elijah, and Wyatt Battles were all young men in their early to mid-twenties, and they all sought to achieve independent manhood through marriage and real property ownership. Well before their father's death in 1835, they all were seeking to establish themselves as respectable and trustworthy members of the local community. The oldest son, Elijah, would be the first child to demonstrate the desire to protect his own interests. Albemarle, though no longer a rough-and-tumble frontier, retained some of that flavor. The town in the rural South was a trading center, a location for court sessions once a month, and a gathering place for young men. And young men, both black and white, often participated in a boisterous masculine culture. Sellers of spirits, gamblers, horse racers, itinerant preachers, traveling salesman, braggarts, laborers, skilled craftsmen: all convened in various public spaces in and around town. Fighting occurred with some frequency; it sometimes resulted in lawsuits and often in the filing of criminal charges. Whites and free people of color alike vigorously defended their persons and reputations through the court system.

In June 1820, Elijah Battles filed a complaint with the county court, charging the white resident John T. Bishop with assault and seeking one thousand dollars in damages. Bishop was about the same age as Elijah and, like Elijah, was following in his father's footsteps. Bishop's father owned property just west of Charlottesville, along Three Notched Road, and ran a tanyard on Main Street in town. The two young men lived and worked in the same general area. The records remain silent about what their affray was about. That same month, the court ordered the white defendant to appear.[37]

Two months later, the suit against Bishop still pending, Elijah Battles walked the half-mile or so from his father's farm into Charlottesville. In town, he headed to the courthouse to meet with the county clerk and register for his freedom certificate. Elijah was twenty-three years old, born only four years after the registration law went into effect and then five years delinquent in registering his freedom with the court, yet this was his first trip to the courthouse to register. The county clerk filled out his certificate, noting that he was a "bright mulatto." In November, the county court set aside Elijah's suit against Bishop.[38]

Five months later, Elijah returned to the courthouse, this time to have his marriage legally recognized. On April 25, 1821, Elijah Battles married Nancy Farrar, a free woman of color, daughter of James Farrar, in a Baptist ceremony. He had not registered as a free man of color simply in an effort to comply with state law concerning free blacks, nor does he appear to have been motivated by his suit against a white man; instead he saw the registration as a useful step in providing proper and full legal documentation for his impending marriage.[39]

Elijah Battles followed in his father's footsteps, learning the trade of carpentry, possibly by working as an apprentice for his white neighbor James Dinsmore. Elijah, too, was an active and willing participant in the county's economic life and in the affairs of the free black families in his neighborhood. A little over a year after marrying, perhaps unsatisfied with the court's initial ruling or responding to a second altercation, Elijah Battles again charged the white county resident John T. Bishop with assault and battery. This time, the case was continued repeatedly through the summer of 1823. At the August court, Battles appeared before the court as directed. The court made a finding of "nonsuit" and then charged Battles five dollars for court costs. Although the suit did not end favorably for Battles, the fact that a free man of color would feel comfortable enough to file an assault case against a white man says quite a bit about how the web of social relations functioned at a local and personal level.[40]

In 1821, Robert Battles Jr. turned twenty-two. He had reached manhood, and like his brother he sought to maintain the same respectable reputation his father had. But he lacked the independence that came with owning real property and thus lacked some of the credentials for independent manhood.[41] Like his brother Elijah months earlier, he went to the courthouse at the beginning of the year to register. The court clerk described him as "age twenty-two, a bright mulatto." Again like his brother before him, he needed proof of freedom to have his marriage legally recognized.

Three days after obtaining his first freedom certificate, Robert Battles Jr. married the free woman of color Mary Farrar in a Baptist ceremony. Both families attended, with Robert Sr. serving as a witness. Mary's father, Reuben Farrar, gave his consent to the marriage, and James Farrar, an uncle of the bride, gave bond for the union. The marriage cemented bonds between the two families, bonds already well established both by living in proximity and by previous intermarriage. The Farrars resided near the old Battles homestead on the outskirts of town. Free people of color and whites in rural Albemarle turned first to friends and neighbors, whether seeking spouses or contracting for business.[42]

The next month, September 1822, the Battles family was shaken by news of the death of Elijah's aunt Judah Barnett. Judah Barnett's sister was Nancy Battles, the deceased first wife of Robert Battles Sr. and the mother of Elijah. Judah Barnett, although most likely unable to read or write, made sure that her legacy would be protected. Before dying, she had had a proper will drawn up. Her will highlights the interconnectedness of the various neighborhoods and residences across the county. Barnett lived several miles north of town. In her will, she left her four youngest children in the combined care of her sister Nancy Battles; her two nephews Elijah and Robert Battles Jr.; and Stephen Coram, the husband of her niece Keziah. She then appointed Stephen Coram as one of the executors for the will. Last, she asked her white neighbor Joel Terrell "to lend his aid in seeing [her] will properly and faithfully administered."[43]

Thus, these documents reveal a free black community dispersed throughout the county and yet intimately connected to each other through marriage. They also highlight how Albemarle's free people of color demonstrated a fair degree of residential integration with whites and routine interaction with white neighbors. The Battleses, living just south of town, had white and black neighbors on adjacent plots. Judah Barnett, connected to the Battles family by marriage despite living several miles away in a different neighborhood, also had white neighbors with whom she had regular contact that included far more than a one-way relationship with a hegemonic white patron.

Now Elijah, just starting a family of his own, had taken on the extra burden of caring for his aunt's children. He did not avoid white scrutiny, nor did he steer clear of the legal system. Instead, he continued to participate in the daily life of the county, working around town as a carpenter. He conducted business with whites and other free people of color. He relied upon face-to-face interaction with other people in the community to secure his reputation, place, and status, among both whites and other free blacks.

All of the Battles boys were part of this culture. Their interaction in public likely included primarily other free people of color, some slaves, and laboring whites. Unfortunately, these gatherings sometimes ended in violence. At the beginning of July 1823, some young men gathered at the edge of town, and tempers flared. The Battles brothers engaged in an affray with another local free man of color, William Spinner. The court records do not give details of exactly what went on that July day, but they do make it clear that William Spinner thought he had been assaulted unfairly by all three Battles brothers. Thus, he brought suit against Elijah, Robert Jr., and Wyatt Battles, charging them with a breach of the peace and pleading with the court for protection from them.[44]

The court ordered all three Battles brothers to file recognizances ensuring their good behavior and promising to keep the peace. All three complied, filing fifty-dollar bonds for their good behavior. Their brother-in-law Stephen Coram appeared with them, filing an additional bond promising that they would keep the peace. The court then adjourned, continuing the cause till the next court, which would meet at the beginning of August. On successive days in August, the court convened. William Spinner, along with Elijah, Wyatt, and Robert Battles Jr., appeared at the courthouse. The court heard the details of the case, eventually deciding to dismiss it due to insufficient evidence in support of either side. With the dismissal, the court also released the Battles brothers and Stephen Coram from the peace recognizances they had filed in July.[45]

These men appeared before the county court time and again, but not a single one of them registered more than once from the time they turned eighteen until at least 1850. Their technical noncompliance with the 1793 free black registration law never posed a problem for any of them.[46] This public appearance at the county courthouse for rowdy, unseemly behavior apparently had little effect on the status of the brothers in the community. Proper behavior in this context primarily meant recognizing and visibly legitimating the hierarchy Albemarle social networks were built upon. Rowdiness, for white and black men of any social station, did not damage their reputations.

Free black reputation was secured in two major ways. First, it helped greatly to achieve independent property-owning status and demonstrate upstanding economic behavior. This often required routine contact with whites in the community. Those experiences ensured that free people of color became known within the broader white community, even if they had to defer to their social superiors when it was required. That court experience with William Spinner probably also failed to change the Battleses' perception of the court, and of the white power structure of which it was a part, as the final arbiter in disputes.

For Elijah and Robert Jr., the conflict with a fellow free person of color apparently had little effect on their activities in the area. They were not arrested. They did not leave the area. Instead, both lived and acted as they had for most of their lives. Both men continued to work as carpenters, maintaining connections with both black and white families. In August 1825, Robert attended an Episcopalian wedding officiated by the prominent white minister F. W. Hatch. Robert gave bond for the marriage of the free people of color James Farrar and Critty Hawkins. Robert affirmed that Critty was indeed of legal age. Farrar was an acquaintance who lived not too far from the old Battles homestead on Three Notched Road. The Hawkins family were neighbors at the new Battles farm at Ragged Mountain. Robert's participation in the wedding hints at how social networks could cross neighborhood boundaries and link families and friends over more considerable distances.

The following year, Robert Jr. had earned and saved enough money to purchase his own land. He bought a plot on the southern edge of Charlottesville from Jacob and Martha H. Waltman for one hundred dollars. The Waltmans had earlier purchased the plot from their neighbor Alexander Garrett. This one-acre lot facing Ridge Street bordered Garrett's property, as well as the property of the Waltmans and William W. Hening. This lot was in fact only a short distance toward town from where Robert had grown up. At the time of the purchase in early February, Battles could only afford to pay the Waltmans fifty dollars. They agreed to a deal by which Battles could pay them the remainder over a six-month period. Battles mortgaged the property to Ira Garrett (the brother of his new neighbor Alexander Garrett), who took possession of the deed until Battles either successfully paid off or defaulted on the debt, which was due at the beginning of September.[47]

Battles did indeed manage to pay the Waltmans the remaining fifty dollars of the purchase price on time, and his mortgage to Ira Garrett was paid off. He took possession of the land, worth ten dollars per acre, a parcel that was as close to his old home as he could get. By engaging in honest and faithful business, he had once again demonstrated to the community his trustworthiness and respectability. Battles continued to extend his personal networks, completing work for a number of area residents.

Meanwhile, starting in 1826, Elijah Battles began doing both rough carpentry and more skilled construction work for the John C. Ragland estate. Ragland had been a wealthy and well-connected white doctor in Charlottesville. Opie Norris, a prominent local white businessman related to Ragland by marriage, was the executor. He hired Battles to do carpenter's work at the Ragland farm. This business arrangement would continue for at least a decade, bringing Elijah Battles into contact with locally powerful whites and with a number of other free black laborers and artisans.[48]

In 1830, Norris used Ragland estate monies to pay Elijah, who had done work fencing a number of lots. Two years later, both Elijah and his brother Robert were paid for more fencing and additional skilled work. The Battles brothers hewed all the timbers for a stable at the Ragland farm and then constructed the stable.[49]

That same year, Elijah Battles went to court and filed a case against the white area resident George Spreigle. Through his attorney, Elijah sought to use the court as a collection agency, recovering money Spreigle owed him for services rendered. Spreigle must have been a particularly recalcitrant client, who had dodged every attempt by Elijah to receive payment for his work. Elijah was not alone—Spreigle had developed a reputation as someone who did not repay debts. Battles's lawyer that August also filed a motion seeking to join the suit to another that had been filed by Spreigle's creditors. The court granted the motion, and an attachment was awarded against another white Albemarle resident, John D. Craven, who was listed as a garnishee in the case, because Craven at that time likely held Spreigle's assets, which the creditors wished to seize.

Craven then failed to appear at the courthouse. He again failed to show up two days later, and another judgment was awarded against him. The records do not mention whether Elijah and the other creditors ever successfully collected the debt from Spreigle or from Craven. But this case remains important for a number of reasons. First, a free man of color cavalierly violated the 1793 registration law yet eagerly used the court system to resolve an economic dispute. Second, this free man of color felt at ease filing a suit against a white person. Last, the existence of the case suggests just how prevalent white-black economic interaction was.[50]

In 1831, Robert Jr., continuing to appear regularly at public events in Albemarle, attended an estate auction at the home of Benajah Gentry. He mingled in the crowd that day with white and black alike, purchasing one cotton wheel for seventy-five cents. Also at the sale that November day was the free man of color Edward Battles, the son of the Revolutionary War veteran Shadrach Battles. Edward purchased a skein of yarn for three dollars and change. For most white Albemarle residents, seeing free black neighbors mingling with whites and bidding on items at an estate sale for a wealthy planter remained an unremarkable occurrence.[51]

Two years later, in 1833, the county commissioner George M. Woods interviewed the Battles families as part of an effort by the state legislature to conduct a detailed census of free African Americans living in the state. The census order was part of a flurry of anti-black legislative activity in the aftermath of the Nat Turner Rebellion in 1831. If ever there was a time when stricter compliance from free blacks would be demanded, this was surely it. Fascinatingly, the General Assembly, in ordering the free black census, required county commissioners to ask free blacks whether or not they might want to leave the state. Even state legislators in the wake of Nat Turner demonstrated that they implicitly understood that free people of color were in some significant way Virginians entitled to exercise their free will.

This colonization census provides a snapshot of an extended Battles family continuing to dwell in the area, living on lands often originally purchased by Robert Battles Sr. He, too, was listed on the survey, at age sixty-two, a farmer residing near Charlottesville. His first wife, Nancy, had died sometime between 1822 and 1824. At that time, Robert Sr. was in his early fifties. He had promptly married Martha A. R. Butler, a twenty-four-year-old free woman of color. In 1834, a year after the colonization census, they were still together, living on Ragged Mountain, several miles southwest of Charlottesville. Living with them was Julian Burruss, a nineteen-year-old seamstress.[52] Robert Battles Jr., age thirty-five, a carpenter, lived in a separate household but in the same vicinity. Elijah, a carpenter residing near Charlottesville, was a thirty-seven-year-old head of household. Both men were successful carpenters continuing to do business with a number of local clients.[53]

Most of the growing Battles family continued to reside in a tight-knit cluster on the edge of town. They were not wealthy, but they owned property, had skills, and could feed every member of the family. The statewide anti-black backlash in the wake of the Nat Turner Rebellion looks far less powerful when viewed from Albemarle—the Battles family remained active participants in the neighborhood and in the larger community in the area.[54]

For example, Robert Battles Jr. continued to ignore free black registration requirements and moved about town in relatively free fashion. Despite failing to register, he did not hesitate to use the legal and economic structures that local government and economy provided. Later in 1833, he found himself indebted to the white hatter Andrew McKee for more than thirty dollars. Once again, Robert Jr. gambled his economic independence, mortgaging his one acre of property just south of town to Twyman Wayt, and in return secured payment of his debt to McKee. As with his previous mortgage, the plan involved Battles paying off the debt in a timely fashion. If this were done, the mortgage would be voided, and he would retain legal possession of his land. The financial agreement was signed by McKee, Wayt, and Robert Battles Jr. Like the other male members of his immediate family, Battles had picked up at least a basic literacy somewhere along the way. He could sign his name to documents, instead of simply leaving his mark.[55] Five years later, in 1838, Battles completed paying off the debt, with interest. Two white men trusted a free black carpenter enough to underwrite a debt-relief package for him. Upon completing payments to McKee, Battles handed Wayt one dollar and in return received full title to his one acre of land.[56]

Elijah also continued to do work for Opie Norris and the John Ragland estate, as well as for John Dinsmore, the brother of James Dinsmore, the white carpenter and former neighbor of the family. In working for the Dinsmore estate, Elijah Battles had contact with Eston Hemings, the carpenter and musician, formerly the property—and also the son—of Thomas Jefferson. The business dealings with the Dinsmores would continue well into the 1840s.[57]

The Battles family continued to maintain their reputation as hardworking and trustworthy neighbors. The personal connection Elijah and his brother had forged with Opie Norris had already proved to be lucrative, and it would continue to deliver excellent business opportunities to them. In 1835, Norris again hired Elijah, this time to build a kitchen on one of the Ragland estate lots. While working on this project, Elijah had to work with other craftsmen. The free men of color Frank Hatter and Tucker Isaacs were also hired to work on portions of the kitchen project. Hatter helped with final construction of the kitchen; Isaacs painted the house and the new kitchen building. Norris continued to hire Elijah Battles time and again for carpentry work at least through 1838.[58]

For Elijah and other free people of color in Albemarle, a job well done was good for business, as it strengthened an individual's reputation within the community. And for Elijah, his respectable and trustworthy business dealings with Opie Norris indeed created other opportunities. In the fall of 1835, having finished the kitchen for the Ragland estate only a few months earlier, Elijah Battles signed on to perform labor on another property, this time for the administrator of the William C. Burton estate.[59] In a pattern already familiar from Battles's work for Norris and the Ragland estate, Elijah would do carpentry and work alongside a number of other free black workers, as well as the occasional white worker. Administrating the Burton estate was the local white businessman Joseph Bishop, the man who ran a tanyard on Main Street and lived a short distance west of the Battles family on Three Notched Road. Bishop was the father of John T. Bishop, the white man Elijah had charged with assault thirteen years earlier.[60] Elijah Battles, by virtue of his hard work and respectable behavior, had become commonly known in the area. This recognition guaranteed Battles a measure of security in the county. Even families with whom he had had physical conflict and legal wrangles saw him as worthy of being hired.

Working for Joseph Bishop on the Burton estate, Elijah Battles interacted with a familiar cast of characters: free black artisans and laborers whom he knew well. On this project, Elijah worked with his brother Robert, his cousin by marriage James Farrar Sr., the skilled artisan Robert Scott, and Thomas Jefferson's former slave Joseph Fossett. The Burton estate was a center linking wealthy whites, skilled free black artisans, white workers, and slaves.[61] James Farrar Sr.'s niece Mary was married to Elijah's brother Robert Battles Jr. Elijah Battles, through hard work, had managed to make himself known to a fairly large group of local residents. In so many ways, Albemarle County remained a tight-knit rural community in which regular interracial contact occurred. This contact seems to have been viewed as unremarkable by most residents.

In Albemarle, life for the free black Battles family continued much as it always had. Gabriel Prosser and Nat Turner were distant names that evoked fears of slave rebellion or perhaps raised vague concerns about dangerous free blacks. But those names did not direct negative attentions toward those members of the Albemarle community who happened to be free people of color and had established themselves. On February 4, 1839, Elijah attended an estate sale on the property of the deceased white Albemarle resident Caleb Stone. On that winter day, Elijah purchased a mahogany bureau and a coffee mill, spending over ten dollars, a sizable amount in those days. The white and black people gathered there that day did not eye him suspiciously. For his white clients and neighbors, he remained Elijah Battles, neighbor and trustworthy carpenter, not a dangerous and rebellious free black who lacked freedom papers and whose presence threatened the community.

Elijah's relationship with the local white businessman Joseph Bishop would pay off again. In 1843, Joseph Bishop was assigned to administer the estate of Henry Pace. As Bishop worked to settle the estate, he realized that the Pace homestead was falling into disrepair. He hired an old business associate, Elijah Battles, to fix the roof on the house and make repairs to the well and the garden house. The connections developed through face-to-face interactions allowed Elijah to coexist comfortably with other free people of color, hired slaves, and whites. Elijah busied himself as a carpenter and as a free man of color trying and succeeding to comport to respectable behavioral expectations in rural Albemarle.[62]

All of the Battles males living in Albemarle managed to carve out a comfortable niche in which their families could live. Each of these men utilized the localized web of social relations to the best of his abilities, and each benefited from the reputation and respectability of parents or siblings to facilitate face-to-face dealings with other residents, white and black. In December 1843, the wealthy local white George Carr was once again serving as an estate administrator. This time, he was settling the estate of Thomas Grady. Grady had been the "bar-keeper and chief manager at the Central Hotel" in Charlottesville. In the last years of his life, he had run a grocery on Main Street in town. James Alexander, a newspaper editor in Charlottesville, described Grady in reminiscences: "Mr. G. was of a tall, lank and ungainly appearance, his clothes fitting loosely about his person; he was full of jokes, very free spoken and often using, like many of the older residents, profane language; he was, however, friendly, sociable and kindly disposed."[63]

Carr's estate account books hint at the easy interracial interaction and commingling that likely took place regularly across lines of class in and around Charlottesville. The estate administrator George Carr was a wealthy white planter and lawyer who lived six miles north of town. The Carr family represented the upper class in Albemarle. George was active in county politics; he taught for a time at a boys' academy in town. While Thomas Grady was clearly not a member of the highest social or economic classes in Albemarle, he was well respected in town and the surrounding area.[64]

Carr's records from administering Thomas Grady's accounts repeatedly include income from or payments to a number of free blacks. These included Jane West, a seamstress and milliner who ran a thriving business in town. Robert Battles Jr. was also a regular in those account books. Unfortunately, the records are silent as to the exact nature of those transactions. Any way the story is explained, one thing remains clear. Whites and free blacks interacted regularly on the streets of Charlottesville and in the neighborhoods of Albemarle County.[65]

Robert Jr.'s family continued to grow. In 1844, his daughter Ellen, then twenty-three years old, married into the Harris family, many of whom were watermen, working bateaux on the navigable waterways in the area. The Harrises resided in the southwestern portion of the county, over fifteen miles away. They lived on Hogg Creek, just west of Green Mountain. The Baptist minister James Fife, who lived near Robert Jr., close to Ridge Street in Charlottesville, officiated the ceremony. Ira Garrett, a white man who knew Robert Battles Jr. very well, served as a witness.[66]

Three years later, Robert Jr. continued to have regular interactions with free people of color and whites in the community. Susan Pace, administering her deceased husband Henry's estate in 1847, made a payment of $9.78 to Battles for work he had done repairing estate property. Even a white widowed woman had no problem dealing directly with a respectable local free man of color. For Pace, Robert Battles was simply that hardworking carpenter who could be trusted to do the work for a fair price. In October, Robert Jr. called another white Baptist minister, William P. Farish, to his Ridge Street property to officiate at the wedding of Robert's youngest daughter, Susan, to John Kenney, another local free man of color.[67]

Robert Battles Jr.'s acre of land just south of Charlottesville along Ridge Street had served him and his family well. A number of his family members continued to dwell with him there. Two of his children were married at the family homestead. Robert, however, had bigger plans. Like just about any other small landowner of the time, he wanted to increase his holdings. In April 1849, his neighbors Alexander and Evelina Garrett agreed to sell a couple of acres to Battles for $246. The parcel was located on the north side of Ridge Street, and adjacent lots were owned by whites. Now the Battles family had tripled their acreage. All this took place in 1849, on the eve of open, heated, and seemingly continuous sectional conflict and antislavery agitation. This free black family was not properly registered, displayed relative prosperity, and lived comfortably and openly at the edge of town and with the approval of their white neighbors. The family's reputation as respectable and hardworking people maintained for them a social space in which to operate.[68]

For Elijah Battles, too, that general trend continued. In October 1848, he attended the marriage of his twenty-one-year-old daughter Sophia to the free man of color John Shelton. At the Baptist wedding ceremony officiated by James Fife, Elijah gave his consent and stated that no legal impediments to the marriage existed. The court recorder filed all of this information in the marriage register, misidentifying Elijah Battles as Elijah Farrar. But the original certificate makes it clear just who was the father of the bride and bondsman at the ceremony: Elijah Battles. Elijah actually signed the document, as his brother Robert also was accustomed to do.[69]

Elijah Battles had managed to outperform his father, building upon the nest egg and training Robert Battles Sr. had provided him. Elijah was the head of a household, a landowner, and a successful businessman. His success as a free man of color in a slave society, in this accounting, is not measured by political power or actual dollar amounts. Instead, success is defined by the basic economic power and personal security he had managed to carve out for himself, as well as the respectability that he had achieved in the eyes of whites. In 1850, Elijah Battles ran a homestead carved out of his father's Ragged Mountain farm. He was fifty-five years old and lived there with his wife, Nancy, and three children, aged ten to twenty. His immediate neighbors were all free people of color: Joseph Hawkins and family, Dolly Cousins and her children, brother Robert Battles Jr. and family, William Kinney and family, and Thomas Farrar and family. All lived on or immediately adjacent to the old Battles farm.[70]

One year later, life in Albemarle continued in much the same way it always had. Elijah continued to work as a carpenter, at that time for George Carr and the Andrew McKee estate. McKee's executor accounts also include an intriguing note. On March 1, 1852, George Carr, McKee's executor, recorded that the estate had received income from the local white Thomas R. Bailey. He also noted that the payment was part of a court judgment in a case Bailey had filed against Elijah Battles. Apparently, Bailey had lost the case and had been forced to make payments to Elijah Battles. Upon a request from Elijah, Bailey simply paid an outstanding debt Elijah owed to the Andrew McKee estate. Long after the Gabriel Prosser and Nat Turner rebellions, and after slavery had become an extremely divisive issue on the national agenda, Elijah Battles continued to conduct the same face-to-face interactions that had served him and his father so well for so long. He had not registered since a few days before he was married, some thirty years before, yet he continued to be active in local affairs and to assert his rights.[71]

In 1856, just five years from the outbreak of civil war in America, Elijah Battles found himself a contented man. He still maintained his homestead. His children were rapidly growing up. He had lived his whole life in Albemarle and had managed to become a literate and skilled craftsman and independent landowner. On January 4 of that year, Elijah Battles opened his homestead to friends and family, who gathered for the wedding of his daughter Joanna. Joanna was twenty-one and no longer lived at home, but rather in Charlottesville. She was marrying William F. Farrow, a twenty-six-year-old Charlottesville native who was working as a carpenter. He was related to Thomas Farrow, who lived next door to the Battleses. The white Baptist minister A. E. Dickinson traveled out to the Battles farm to conduct the service.[72]

The social space for free people of color in a rural community that depended on face-to-face interaction and reputation, on knowing and being known, was about to contract momentarily. Trouble had been brewing for free blacks since early 1850, when antislavery agitation nationwide had created new efforts to control all nonwhite residents in Virginia, whether slave or free. In 1850, over one hundred free people of color in Albemarle were suddenly brought up on charges of violating the 1806 residency requirement. That law stated that any slave freed after 1806 had to leave the state within one year of manumission, or they could be arrested and returned to slavery. Former slaves wishing to remain in Virginia had to apply for permission. For over forty years, the law had rarely been enforced in any way in Albemarle. The Battleses were not among those who had to answer charges about residency that December, but the message was clear: the social space for black-white interaction and the maneuvering room for free people of color in the rural South had narrowed for some. The local court in most cases simply continued these cases repeatedly without resolution. Ultimately, court records indicate that in seven instances local justices listed the accused as "not found," "not known," or "no inhabitant." Perhaps those seven people responded to the charges by moving away. Three free people of color were found not guilty or had their cases dismissed before a verdict. Two free blacks were granted permission to remain, and only two were found guilty.[73]

The ultimate result of these efforts was not to drive out the free black population, but instead to force the majority of free people of color who continued to live in Albemarle to keep their free papers up to date. In this respect, the crackdown was successful. Robert Battles Jr. and his family were not cited for violating the laws regarding either registration or residency, but they did feel the pressure.[74] For the first time in nearly forty years, Battles went to the courthouse to register properly and receive a current freedom certificate. He took his family with him. Robert; his wife, Mary; and their children John, Reuben, Robert III, and even Susan Kenney (nee Battles) appeared together at the courthouse on the third of the month and formally registered. The Albemarle County Minute Books for 1848–50 and 1851–54 are filled with entries from 1850 for free people of color pouring into the courthouse to establish their freedom and to request permission to reside in the county.[75]

Attending events at the courthouse that winter must have suggested to all present that the old racial system that privileged local context over state law was then in danger of withering away. Comfortable coexistence might no longer be possible. The Battleses may have felt the pressure. By 1852, they had picked up everything they owned and moved to the Cincinnati area in southern Ohio, just across the river from Kentucky.[76] On February 6, 1852, Robert and his wife, Mary, completed the sale of two of their three acres of land in Albemarle to their white neighbor John H. Bibb for three hundred dollars.[77]

Thus, by 1852, though they were living in Ohio, they still possessed one acre of land on the outskirts of Charlottesville. This was the first acre of land Robert Battles Jr. had purchased from Jacob Waltman, back in 1826. By early 1853, the Battleses knew they were never returning to Charlottesville or Albemarle. They had moved from Cincinnati to Franklin County, Ohio, near Columbus. Franklin County, Ohio, would be their new home. They hired William Scruggs to serve as an intermediary and real estate agent in Virginia. Scruggs sold the one-acre parcel to John C. Patterson and Julius Mundy of Charlottesville for $350. When the notarized document from Franklin County confirming sale and dower relinquishment by Mary Battles arrived in Charlottesville in early May 1853, most of the Battles family closed the door on Charlottesville, Albemarle, and even Virginia. In the end, the Battleses' choice to leave Virginia represented an atypical decision for Albemarle free people of color. Most appear to have chosen to continue living in Virginia.[78]

For the rest of the decade, free people of color in Albemarle continued to register far more often than they had prior to 1850. For instance, in October 1857, Elijah Battles, for the first time since he married nearly forty years earlier, went to the courthouse to renew his freedom certificate. Several of his immediate family members and neighbors went that same day, and all had their freedom certificates recorded. On these certificates, the court clerk made a point of mentioning that they had been born free to free parents or to parents free prior to May 1806.[79]

Again, renewed white vigilance was in some measure counteracted by local officials, who took care to spare the Battles family any serious trouble. Within a year, Elijah Battles would be dead. Yes, strictures on free people of color in Albemarle had tightened in the 1850s. But Elijah's freedom and that of his family rested relatively securely. In January 1859, not long after Elijah's death, his son Noah Battles was married at the family farm. Another white Baptist minister, John A. Broadus, officiated the ceremony. Noah followed his father's career path and worked as a carpenter. On that winter day in 1859, the young free man of color married Martha J. Farrar.[80]

Another son, Elijah Battles Jr., also continued the family tradition of relative success and inclusion in Albemarle society. According to the 1860 census for the county, Elijah Battles Jr. was a forty-year-old carpenter owning two hundred dollars in real estate, fifteen dollars in personal property, and a proper dwelling house. He lived there with James Battles, a twenty-year-old carpenter (a cousin). They lived next door to Nancy Kenny, a free black female head of household, and Joseph Watson, a seventy-year-old white farmer who had moved to the area from Indiana. If the social space for free people of color had contracted considerably in the last decade, if white-black residential integration were also on the way out, the experience of the Battles family did not demonstrate it on the eve of the Civil War.[81]

Clearly, regular interaction between white and black, slave and free, remained central to the lives of the Battles family in Albemarle, as it had since the eighteenth century. Reputation, respectability, and property-owning independence formed the backbone of this system. And the Battleses had managed to sustain interactions and even social relationships with their white and black neighbors for at least sixty years. Relative racial harmony, at least for those who maintained respectable reputations, and especially for those who owned property, existed in Charlottesville and Albemarle well into the nineteenth century. Gabriel Prosser and Nat Turner, though creating two spates of anti–free black legislation, had done little to change the nature of interracial interaction at the local level in Albemarle County. As late as June 1850, Robert Battles and his family were still living comfortably on Ridge Street. They continued to work and play in and around town, and these activities often involved interaction between whites and blacks. On June 3, the white resident James Watson returned guardian accounts to the courthouse. He had been assigned guardianship duties for the now-deceased young girl Mary June Railey. His accounts included payments to Robert Battles Jr. over a three-year period, running from 1847 to 1849. White residents continued to see Battles as a respectable and trustworthy part of the Albemarle community. He was safe, good to do business with. Although he chose to move, most of his fellow free people of color decided to stay.[82]

Home to thousands of slaves and thousands of whites, this Virginia piedmont county remained largely rural throughout the period. A rough residential integration predominated. Free people of color, slaves, and whites of all classes mingled easily in neighborhoods throughout the county and even more so in and around town. It was the highly personal nature of social relations in this place that allowed such interracial activity to take place. This interracial commingling, however, was structured around great inequality, under a social hierarchy running from slave to wealthy land-owning white planter. In between were free people of color, laboring and itinerant whites, small business owners, and yeoman farmers both black and white.

All worked in a world where contact between the races was a regular feature of local life. People of all races met in the fields and on the streets not as members of groups or classes, but as individuals. It was these individual-to-individual encounters that structured the tenor of race and social relations in the area. Face-to-face meetings were literally the foundation of social commerce in the area. Relationships were built upon those meetings, which established reputations, created trust, and strengthened connections that subsequently went well beyond initial one-on-one meetings. Laws passed in Richmond, while surely reflecting more general white concerns, most often had little impact on local life in Albemarle, where local and personal relationships formed a tight-knit web, superseding legislation. This privileging of local knowledge and local context remained intact at least until 1850, when slavery exploded onto the national scene as an issue of great political divisiveness. The free black population of Albemarle in 1850 stood at 587, down from 602 in 1840. But even after 1850, most free people of color in Albemarle remained, and life continued much as it had for the past eighty years. By 1860, there were 606 free blacks living in the county.

3

Good Blacks and Useful Men

Reputation and Free Black Mobility

Many scholars have argued that the immediate post-Revolutionary years in the South represented a unique moment when the egalitarian principles promulgated during the Revolution challenged the slave system and the way of life that it supported for masters. Slavery at the time faced another assault from Quakers and from evangelical Christian thought propagated in particular by Baptists and Methodists. For a short time, many historians have written, this combination of secular and religious egalitarian ideals appeared to be on their way to ending slavery. Master after master, spurred by the apparent contradiction between those lofty ideals and the act of slaveholding, manumitted their slaves. The free black class ballooned across the Upper South.

But racism soon reared its ugly head, and many white southerners saw this new class of free blacks as physically menacing as well as threatening to the slave system. Some in Hanover and Henrico counties petitioned the legislature as early as 1784, complaining of the "many evils [that] have arisen from a partial emancipation of slaves." A petition from King and Queen County in 1800 argued that "a general emancipation . . . is impossible with our safety beside a commixture to our minds is abhorrent."[1]

Thus by the early nineteenth century, according to those same scholars, that small window of opportunity for slavery's demise at the hands of Revolutionary ideals had closed. Racist views hardened everywhere in the midst of the visible reality of a burgeoning and often newly manumitted free black class and in the wake of slave rebellion. First a slave revolt started in August 1791 in Haiti, making southern slave owners nervous. Then, the arrival of exiled Haitian planters and their slaves on the U.S. mainland worried many

Americans that the bloody Haitian revolution might be imported as well. The Haitian revolt against slavery and French domination would continue until 1803, when France gave up its effort to reclaim the island, and Haiti was declared an independent republic. For Virginians, however, the pivotal event that supposedly brought the period of liberalization to a close occurred in 1800. Gabriel's abortive rebellion in the Richmond area seemed to embody fears of a Haitian-style revolt in Virginia. Suddenly, white Virginians focused on the growing free black population in their midst as a real problem, one that had to be dealt with because those people of color might become the fuse that, when lighted, would explode the slave system and white supremacy along with it.

A survey of legislation concerning slavery and free blacks in Virginia from roughly 1780 to 1810 appears to confirm that interpretation—post-Revolutionary egalitarianism followed by a rising tide of white racism. In 1782, the Virginia legislature loosened a nearly sixty-year-old manumission rule. Until that year, the individual slaveholder had to seek approval of the colonial and later state assembly for any act of manumission, and only unusually meritorious or heroic service by the slave warranted freedom. The 1782 law allowed individual masters or mistresses to manumit slaves by will or by deed. Now, the individual slave owner became the final arbiter of a slave's fitness for freedom. This loosening of manumission restrictions allowed slaveholders troubled by the contradiction between their religious or revolutionary ideals and the holding of people in bondage to divest themselves of slaves.

Some scholars argue that as early as 1793, Virginia's experiment with a less restrictive racial hierarchy was drawing white opposition, especially in urban areas such as Richmond, Petersburg, and Norfolk, where newly freed blacks congregated. The rising urban fears of a burgeoning and unruly free black class that intermingled all too freely with slaves and working-class whites prompted the Virginia state legislature in 1793 to pass a law demanding that "free negroes or mulattoes shall be registered and numbered in a book to be kept by the town clerk, which shall specify age, name, color, status and by whom, and in what court emancipated. Annually the Negro shall be delivered a copy for twenty-five cents. . . . Every free Negro shall once in every three years obtain a new certificate."[2]

In actuality, that 1793 registration law did little to alter Virginia's social landscape. White masters continued to free individual slaves as they saw fit.

The state's free black population not only did not disappear but continued to grow. From 1790 to 1820, the free colored population witnessed a nearly threefold increase, from just under thirteen thousand free blacks in 1790 to almost thirty-seven thousand in 1820. The state legislature, meanwhile, did not address the fears of those who worried about free blacks until 1806. In that year, the legislature passed a statute specifically addressing the growing free black class.

The 1806 law stipulated that any slave "hereafter emancipated who shall remain within the Commonwealth more than twelve months shall forfeit such right, and may be apprehended and sold by the overseers of any county . . . in which he shall be found for the benefit of the poor." Suddenly, according to that new state law, any person of color who found himself manumitted had to prepare immediately to leave the state. The new law partly placated urban whites concerned about free blacks. Scholars typically portray the Virginia legislature's passage of the removal law in 1806 as the ending point for a relatively brief moment of more relaxed race relations. According to those scholars, however, more relaxed conditions only occurred for a brief time and mainly in urban areas, but even there, white racism arose quickly and by 1806 had resulted in strict repression of free people of color. The rural South during that same time period, however, supposedly remained a rigidly defined place in which black meant slave and white meant free citizen. But how did the 1806 law function in rural areas? Was it actually used to control even more tightly the modest free black population in the countryside?[3]

The 1806 law actually represented a compromise measure that sought to satisfy both hardliners and more liberal laissez-faire whites. That neither group monopolized public opinion at the time helps explain why this law, often portrayed as a response to Gabriel's attempted revolt, was passed fully half a dozen years after that event. Thus, the law fell short of banning manumissions yet nevertheless discouraged private emancipations. After the state legislature passed the 1806 removal law, it began receiving petitions from free people of color seeking permission to remain in the state.

Virginians of color, both slave and free, considered the state home and had no desire to leave. Scholars have argued that this free black class was also unwilling to leave the small known world in which they lived because of fears of violent white racist repression elsewhere. They often had neither the means nor the desire to move this argument goes, and the world beyond appeared fraught with danger. The law frequently went without any enforcement, however. One scholar estimates that up to a third of the free people of color living in Virginia in 1860 were in technical violation of the 1806 law.[4]

Since the law was in theory designed to reduce the free black population in the state, it appears to have been a failure. If the legislature was deeply concerned by the free black presence, it could have simply denied any and all residency requests. It instead approved many of the requests, spurring more and more free people of color to apply. Believing it had more important governmental matters to consider, the legislature in 1815 gave local courts power to decide whether free people of color should be permitted to remain in the state in cases of "extraordinary merit." By 1837, the legislature had authorized the individual county courts to make residency determinations for free people of color in all cases. If the commonwealth was so concerned about dangerous free blacks threatening the racial order and spurring slaves to revolt, why did they fail to capitalize on the 1806 removal law? Why were so many residency requests granted? What happened in localities when they gained the power to make their own local residency decisions?

The experiences of some of Albemarle County's free people do not conform to the older story of a curtain falling down on white open-mindedness by 1800 or so. For instance, Charles Barnett spent years traveling across the South, settling in several states and putting down roots in both Virginia and North Carolina before returning. In Albemarle County, the supposed flood of residency applications never occurred. Free blacks between 1806 and 1815 simply failed to petition the state legislature. After 1815, they again failed to petition the county court for residency permission. In 1815, the free black population of the county stood at nearly four hundred persons. Since the removal law went into effect in 1806, six different masters in Albemarle County had freed by deed or will sixty-one slaves.[5] None ever applied to the state legislature seeking permission to remain in the commonwealth. Neither, apparently, did they depart the area. After 1815, when control over residency devolved to the county courts in cases of "extraordinary merit" only, eighteen more slaves were manumitted over the next decade. Out of all of those manumissions since 1806, only two ever applied for residency.[6]

On September 2, 1816, Lodwick Quarles received residency permission from the Albemarle County Court. Quarles had been freed by the will of John Bourne. His notice of application for residency was nailed to the courthouse door for two weeks. No one came forward to rail against the free black presence in Albemarle or to denounce Lodwick Quarles. Instead, the white resident William Woods came to the court to testify on Quarles's behalf. The court recognized that Bourne had freed Quarles "on account of his extraordinary merit." Woods provided yet more verbal evidence, stating that he knew Quarles to be a man of "extraordinary merit and of generally good conduct." Quarles was first and foremost a respectable neighbor whose behavior mattered more than his free black status. Even though Albemarle's free black population had swelled after 1782 in much the same way that it had in Richmond and Norfolk, at the first opportunity to expel a free black, the court instead chose to approve Quarles's residency application.[7]

Three years later, the Albemarle County Court again had an opportunity to send a message to the county's nearly four hundred free people of color. After all, this was a largely rural slaveholding community, one that later historians would say was deeply troubled by the free black presence and seeking rigid maintenance of the racial hierarchy. On March 1, 1819, the free woman of color Rachel came to hear the court's decision concerning her residency request. As with Lodwick Quarles before her, Rachel had to wait two weeks as the notice of her residency request was posted on the courthouse door, as required by law. Again, no one came forward to denounce Rachel or to raise concerns about a troublesome free black presence. The white planter Jesse Garth had emancipated Rachel in November 1818 on account of her "extraordinary merit and conduct." The court agreed with Garth's assessment of his former slave: "her former good and exempliary [*sic*] Conduct and her long and faithful services" meant she deserved "full license and permission" to reside within Albemarle County. Once again, a person of color's behavior carried more weight than actual skin color or status. Local context trumped state-level concerns.[8]

For nearly forty years after the passage of the 1806 removal law, Albemarle County authorities and citizens alike did not demonstrate any great concern about enforcing the removal law. In that period, nearly one hundred slaves received their freedom through manumissions granted by deed and by will. Not only did most fail to leave Albemarle County and Virginia, but they often failed to register and did not file residency applications with the county court. Even after the bloody Nat Turner Rebellion in Southampton County in 1831, Albemarle did not dramatically change its maintenance of the racial hierarchy. Free people of color were not rounded up and charged with violating the removal law. After an initial scare that swept the county, a panic that evinced far more concern over the slave population than over free blacks, life in Albemarle returned to the way it had been before. The highly personal web of social relationships in the county continued to determine individual status for most area residents. Once again, local context framed white officials' understanding.

Free people of color, by becoming known persons with positive behavioral attributes, managed to live unmolested and at times in relative comfort in Albemarle. For instance, the highly personal relationships that led to masters manumitting slaves and to white residents valuing the presence of individual and known free people of color were all on display in 1835. In January of that year, the Albemarle resident Fontaine Wells filed a petition with the General Assembly asking the body to permit his former slave Yarico to remain in the county. His petition portrays a close and lifelong relationship with Yarico. Yarico had been a slave owned by Wells's father, Thomas. Thomas Wells had died "totally insolvent" and had been forced to sell property, including his "faithful" slave Yarico. Fontaine Wells described himself as "attached" to Yarico. Thus, he "became the purchaser of her and since that time, influenced by the same considerations in her behalf, he has permitted her to receive, principally, if not entirely, the earning of her own labor." Fontaine Wells allowed the trusted slave he had grown up with and since purchased to live and conduct herself as if free.[9]

Fontaine Wells was not satisfied with this arrangement, however. He wanted to reward Yarico for her life of dedicated service to his family by giving her legal freedom. He described her "character . . . as that of an honest and harmless and unoffending creature." Wells knew Yarico to be a respectable person and feared that emancipating her might force her to leave the commonwealth. As a result, he emancipated her and at the same time filed a petition seeking permission from the state legislature for her to remain in Virginia. Forty-eight white male residents joined Wells in signing the petition. One signer, John R. Jones, would sign a similar petition four years later, but then sign an anti–free black petition in 1850. His behavior over that fifteen-year period illustrates perfectly the dichotomy in many whites' minds between free blacks as an impersonal mass and a problem and free blacks as individuals one knew personally and could respect.[10]

The assembly rejected the petition on February 14, but not on its merits. The assembly instead chose to refer the final decision back to the county court in Albemarle, where many whites knew Yarico. Unfortunately, Yarico's fate remains lost to history. Although no county court decision is extant, it seems likely that the General Assembly assumed local authorities would rule in her favor or table the request permanently, preferring to privilege local knowledge and informal practice over state-mandated legal procedure. For Yarico, a respectable reputation and close personal relationships with a number of area whites overcame in some ways her disadvantaged status. To Fontaine Wells and the other signers of the petition, Yarico was not a dangerous anomaly, but a familiar and trusted person.[11]

Not until the 1840s would any free black in the county be charged with remaining in the commonwealth contrary to the removal law. Jesse Jones manumitted Randolph Jones in October 1841, but not for meritorious service. Instead, Randolph had much earlier worked out an agreement with his master whereby he would be freed once he had paid his master eight hundred dollars. Randolph would live in the county as if a free person and hire himself out, paying a percentage of his earnings directly to his master, but pocketing the remainder. The deed does not explain how long the agreement had been in effect, but the price suggests that Randolph Jones had been working for years to earn his own freedom. This was term slavery, a process in which masters agreed to a future manumission date as an incentive for more efficient labor from the slave. Such an agreement was predicated upon a personal relationship between master and slave. These arrangements were mutually beneficial, with the slave earning freedom and the owner eliminating the financial loss associated with manumission. The owner, in this case Jesse Jones, likewise benefited from his ultimate right of refusal or denial of the agreement, because slaves could not legally make contracts. Thus, a slaveholder had little to lose from term slavery. Jones had agreed that Randolph could purchase himself after paying his master the purchase price.[12]

Master and slave, in this case, had about as formal an agreement as master and slave could have. Willis H. Woodley, "an agent mutually chosen by me [Jones] and a certain coloured man Randal, commonly called Randal Jones, my former slave," acted as an agent facilitating the completion of the manumission agreement. Woodley acted as a "freedom broker," either because of a personal relationship he had with the master or the slave or because of money he stood to make in brokering the deal. Either way, this arrangement required a series of face-to-face relationships among three people, relationships that lasted years.[13] Again, a forging of personal connections was often necessary to create the conditions under which term slavery or even a slave hiring his own time could come about, since the master had to cede some effective control to the slave himself.[14]

Randolph Jones managed by October 1841 to pay Jesse Jones in full. Jones honored their agreement and came to the courthouse to file a deed of manumission with the county clerk. Two weeks later, Randolph Jones returned to the courthouse to file for his first freedom certification. Jones did not leave the county, much less the state. He did not petition the same court for permission to remain in Albemarle. He simply stayed. His years of hard work and close contact with a number of whites demonstrated to the white community that Randolph was an industrious and trustworthy individual.[15]

Randolph Jones returned to what he had always done well: working constantly to earn more money. For the next two years, he remained in Albemarle, a free but propertyless man. At this point, in late 1843, one might conclude from the documentary record that Jones was unsuccessful in freedom: he still owned no taxable property. But Randolph was actually quite busy and successfully earning money; he was working to purchase his sister Rosanna. In late November 1843, he sought the help of another Albemarle County free man of color, Nelson Roberts, Rosanna's husband. Once again, this was no spur-of-the-moment sale by Lewis. Randolph Jones and Nelson Roberts had earlier worked out a purchase agreement with Lewis that included a purchase price and payment schedule. On November 27, 1843, Nelson Roberts purchased and freed his wife, Rosanna. He had been very successful both in his last years of enslavement and in his first years of freedom.[16]

Almost four years after purchasing his own freedom, Randolph Jones continued to live in violation of Virginia's 1806 removal law. But he did not live as a shrinking violet, spending his days avoiding contact with whites hell-bent on policing free blacks and rigidly enforcing the racial hierarchy. Instead, he continued to maintain and expand the face-to-face relationships that had proved so important to him. Now free, he industriously applied himself to earning yet more money. To do this, he had to have regular contact with a number of area whites. As the summer of 1844 dragged on, Randolph Jones must have been encouraged about his prospects. The last few years had been busy but fruitful for Randolph, his sister, and her husband, Nelson Roberts. But on August 27, Randolph Jones had an encounter with two white men, Willis Woodley and Jesse Heiskell. Jones knew Woodley well, for Woodley had acted as the middleman between Jones and his former master as Randolph worked to purchase his own freedom. No record remains of the conversation these men had, but the meeting would have serious consequences for Jones.[17]

Several months later, the county court brought charges against the free man of color Randolph Jones for "unlawfully remaining in the Commonwealth more than twelve months." He was the first free person of color in Albemarle County formally charged with violating the 1806 removal law. The commonwealth's attorney, citing that meeting on August 27, 1844, among Jones, Woodley, and Heiskell, summoned Woodley and Heiskell as witnesses for the prosecution. The two men had filed a complaint with court officers. On May 21, 1845, the court convened to hear testimony in the case against Jones. He had reason to worry. He was, after all, living in Albemarle in clear violation of the 1806 removal law. He had been freed over thirty years after 1806, had not left the state as the law required, and had not sought permission from the local court to remain. Yet the court did not take the opportunity to make an example of Randolph Jones. He was not exiled from the state. He was not sold back into slavery. Instead, the court dismissed the case. Again, local knowledge and context appear to have been more important to the county court than state-level law.[18]

Perhaps the court decided that the public presenting of the residency charges against Randolph Jones would be enough to send a warning to all free people of color in the county. Maybe the court thought that Jones had learned his lesson and would immediately seek to leave the area or at least properly file for permission to remain in Albemarle County. Or maybe the court had to consider the case because Woodley and Heiskell had filed a formal complaint. At that time, however, the court remained unconcerned about Jones's apparent violation of the 1806 removal law. The court may have seen in Randolph Jones a sober and hardworking free black community member, who, though occupying an inferior station, was not a threat to the county's racial order. Whatever the court's motives, Randolph Jones after May 21, 1845, remained a free person of color living in Albemarle County. If the court intended to send an implicit message to Jones, it was not immediately received or acknowledged. Jones did not take the opportunity that day in May to file a request for residency. He simply returned to his life as a laborer in the county.

By 1848, however, Randolph Jones had changed his mind. He had since become acquainted with another free man of color in Charlottesville, James Munroe. The two men shared a similar life story. Both had purchased their own freedom. Both had worked successfully to purchase and liberate family members. Both continued to live in the county. But something had changed. Munroe had only very recently earned his freedom, and his deed of manumission suggested that his master thought Munroe would be departing Virginia for Ohio after receiving his freedom. Together, James Munroe and Randolph Jones came to the courthouse on June 5, 1848, and filed for permission to remain in the commonwealth. No records exist detailing the court's response to their joint request, but the request may have been rejected. Less than a year later, the commonwealth's attorney for a second time charged Randolph Jones with violating the 1806 removal law. Amazingly, in May 1849, this second case against Jones was also dismissed. Randolph Jones remained a free man of color living in Albemarle County in clear violation of the 1806 removal law. He had survived not one but two cases brought against him for remaining in the commonwealth.[19]

Both James Munroe and Randolph Jones managed to continue living in Albemarle County. For three decades after the passage of the removal law in 1806, no one in the county appeared concerned about the numerous free blacks living in the area, in clear violation of the law. By 1850, however, some white residents in the county had begun to notice; they began to police the racial hierarchy more carefully. In November 1850, Randolph Jones came to the courthouse to renew his papers, originally filed back in 1841 and technically in need of renewal every three years. Jones should have renewed his certificate back in 1844 and again in 1847, but did not become concerned about his status until late 1850.[20]

In early March 1851, a grand jury that had been convened with the express purpose of bringing charges against free blacks for violating the 1806 removal law brought criminal presentments against eleven free people of color. Both Randolph Jones and James Munroe were included in the indictments. For Jones, the message seemed to be that the white community had become concerned about the growing free black presence in the county. If Jones had failed to hear that basic message in the first two cases brought against him, he acted as if he heard it the third time. In the first two cases, Jones did not hide. He came to the court to answer the charges against him. He eventually filed a residency petition. He continued to live and work in and around Charlottesville. But in 1851, he did not appear. Two months after the initial indictment, he had still not come to the courthouse to answer the charges. On May 1, the court issued summonses for Randolph and his relative Charles Jones.[21]

Apparently, the county sheriffs either had trouble finding Randolph Jones or were not trying very hard to find him. Over a month after the first summons had been issued, the county court issued a second summons for Randolph. The sheriffs still had no luck hunting him down. One sheriff scrawled "not known" on the back of the second summons—he was saying he had never heard of Jones and could not find anyone who had, which almost surely was not true. In late January 1852, the county court for a third time issued a summons for Randolph Jones so he could be brought before the court to answer charges of violating the 1806 removal law. Finally, in February, the sheriffs found him. He was arrested and jailed sometime that month. Now Jones found himself the victim of the new climate in Albemarle. The racial hierarchy was for the moment being rigidly policed. Some free blacks suspected of violating that hierarchy were charged and, in a few cases, arrested and incarcerated. Jones likely spent well over a year sitting in the county jail. Finally, in October 1853, the court found time to hear his case. The court found him guilty of violating state residency laws concerning free blacks and "ordered that the said defendant forfeit his freedom and be sold as a slave."[22] Despite the harsh sentence, there is no evidence anywhere in county records that he was actually sold. Perhaps the court tacitly allowed him to leave Virginia. Randolph Jones's years of cultivating close personal relationships with his master and white employers had brought him and his sister to freedom and initially held out the promise of a comfortable and secure existence in Albemarle. Unfortunately, Randolph Jones entered freedom in troubled times.

Others, such as James Munroe, experienced similarly drawn-out trial processes and eventually chose to move out of Virginia. In June 1842, a white woman named Mary Rose died. Her will bequeathed her slave man "Monroe" to her daughter-in-law, Maria Rose. This Monroe was in fact James Munroe, who would soon become a free black in Albemarle County. James Munroe was born a slave at the household of Captain John Rose of Amherst, a town about forty miles southwest of Charlottesville. Munroe's parents were also slaves owned by Rose. Munroe, in the year he was passed as property from one master to another, had been laboring as a dining room servant for the keepers of the University of Virginia's hotels and for the professors at the university. Munroe lived as if free, but was really a hired slave working beyond the day-to-day control of his master.[23]

James Munroe followed and even exceeded the example set by Randolph Jones. He worked very hard and behaved in a respectable fashion, even as a slave. His job put him in very close contact with numerous white elites in the area. Five years after he was bequeathed to Maria Rose, Munroe still found himself a hired slave working in the same dining rooms he had labored in for the last fifteen years. His owners, Erasmus and Maria Rose, had moved to Memphis, Tennessee. They had left James Munroe behind after negotiating a term-slavery agreement with him. Munroe would remain in Albemarle, because he was married to a woman named Evelina, the property of the Charlottesville merchant Opie Norris.[24] The arrangement Munroe had negotiated with his owners sent most of his wages from the university to the Roses. He pocketed the remainder and was free to work for himself in his free time. He moonlighted in that free time at taverns around the university and in town so that he could earn extra money to pay his way to freedom.[25]

Finally, in 1847, James Munroe achieved what he had worked so long and hard for. His absentee masters received the final payment from Munroe and complied with the agreement. On September 28, 1847, the transaction was finalized, with the recording of the deed of manumission at the Albemarle County courthouse. Munroe's wife, Evelina, was still enslaved in town; by 1847 they had had a number of children. Adhering to the 1806 removal law would be painful and difficult for Munroe. He instead decided to stay in the commonwealth. On December 15, 1847, just a few months after earning his freedom, Munroe petitioned the General Assembly seeking permission to remain in the commonwealth. This decision, until then an unusual one for Albemarle people of color, may indicate a changed local climate at that moment. Munroe told the court that he "had demeaned himself as a person of good character." He closed by further reminding the assembly that "he has a wife and four children residing in Charlottesville and that were he compelled to leave the state he would be separated from them forever."[26]

Fortunately, Munroe's occupation as a servant in the university dining room and in taverns in town had allowed him to forge powerful and intimate relationships with many local white people. He would need their help if he were to petition successfully for permission to remain. He was able to call on the help of the planter George W. Carr, as well as the professors William McGuffey, St. George Tucker, John B. Minor, and Addison Maupin. Other university staff and Charlottesville residents, including Cynthia Norris, the widow of merchant Opie Norris and owner of James Munroe's family, also agreed to help. Yes, as a recently freed person of color seeking to remain in the county, he had to ask whites to come forward as character witnesses. But many people were ready to do so, willingly signing a petition in praise of James Munroe's respectable behavior, based upon the long-standing personal relationships they had with Munroe, the hardworking dining room servant who had served them for years.[27]

More than fifty individuals came forward and signed James Munroe's residency petition. The petition attested to Munroe's personal merits, describing him as "a free man of color [whom we know] to be a person of good character, peaceable, orderly, and industrious, and not addicted to drunkenness, gambling or any other vice." The petition continued, outlining in plain language the long-term attachment to the community James Munroe had already demonstrated: "[He] is now residing at the University of Virginia in the capacity of dining room servant and attendant upon the students, and . . . he demeans himself so far as we know with uniform propriety, and by his attention to his duties in both of these capacities gives entire satisfaction." The petitioners concluded, stating clearly to the court their feelings about Munroe's request: "We unhesitatingly recommend him to the General Assembly of Virginia as a suitable person to whom permission should be granted to remain in the Commonwealth."[28]

Working zealously to secure permission to remain in the commonwealth, James Munroe did not stop with that first petition. He circulated a second petition that garnered nearly 150 additional signatures. This second petition included fewer university faculty and staff, but a far greater number of important local whites, who may have known Munroe from his work as a servant in the taverns in town. Surely the signatures of two hundred respected whites would be enough to sway even the most rigid of legislators—but Munroe took no chances. He also approached individually those people who knew him best and asked them to write and sign affidavits attesting to his respectability and worthiness for residency in Albemarle County. The university professor and slaveholder John B. Minor said that Munroe had worked for him as a house servant for several years and "has given me entire satisfaction. He has been attentive, quick, willing and capable, and has demeaned himself in every particular with uniform propriety." Again, Minor stressed that he "knew" Munroe and knew him to be a respectable and trustworthy person.[29]

Others reiterated Minor's strong support for Munroe as a respectable person. The planter George Watson Carr in 1845 had hired Munroe as a servant. By 1847, Munroe had worked part-time for Carr for over two years. Carr "believed him [James Munroe] to be an honest and respectable man, [and I] respectfully recommend him to the honourable court of Albemarle County, as such." Carr finished his affidavit by stating that "he is a free man of colour, desirous of obtaining permission to remain in this state, and in the opinion of the undersigned, in every way worthy of it." Cynthia T. Norris, the widow of merchant Opie Norris and the current owner of James Munroe's wife, Evelina, also filed an affidavit in support of Munroe's residency request. The widow stated that "James Munroe has had a wife at my house for eleven years and has always behaved with the utmost propriety. I should be very sorry for him to be separated from his family."[30]

John Carr, the owner of a Charlottesville hotel, wrote enthusiastically to endorse James Munroe as an excellent and trustworthy employee:

> Munroe . . . has been living with me for 18 months and I can say with pleasure that he is a servant worthy the confidence of any one who may wish to employ him either in a Hotel or any home business. He is perfectly honest and industrious; as I have entrusted to his care and management about 17 rooms with all their appurtenances; and never heard of anything being taken out of his department; I recommend him to any one who wishes to employ him as a bedroom servant and dining room also.

A patron of Charlottesville's Eagle Hotel also weighed in. P. Francis Auguste said, "I take pleasure in stating that James Monroe, having had the care of my room in the Eagle Hotel for 10 months, has been faithful, strictly so in discharging his duties. I have abundant reason to believe him entirely honest."[31]

James Munroe's stellar reputation was not confined to a small geographic space stretching merely from the university to the hotels in downtown Charlottesville. That space certainly represented the epicenter of his reputation, but he was a known figure over a far greater distance. His former masters now lived in Memphis, Tennessee, but they had originally lived in a county neighboring Albemarle to the south. Munroe had grown up with them in Amherst County. Even after fifteen years residing and working in Charlottesville, at least one Amherst County resident was willing to speak favorably of Munroe. John Thompson Jr. came to Charlottesville in October 1847 and filed an affidavit with the county court supporting Munroe's residency request. Thompson remembered Munroe from his childhood days in Amherst: "I know Monroe a coloured man who was raised by Capt. John Rose and believe him to be an honest peceable and good man. His father and mother both the slaves of Capt. Rose were well disposed and faithful servants." For Thompson, Munroe's reputation came first from his parents, who had been hardworking and trustworthy. Munroe's actions during his life served merely to strengthen Thompson's opinion of Munroe.[32]

Numerous other Albemarle residents appear to have agreed completely with Thompson. James Munroe had done an excellent job of establishing intimate personal relationships with many white residents. On June 3, 1850, another petition on his behalf arrived at the General Assembly. This time the petitioners stated, "James Munroe is desirous to remain in the state in consequence of having a wife and five children, slaves, the property of Opie Norris' estate, whom he cannot purchase so as to remove with him; and maintains a good character with his employers." Once again, the petitioners described James Munroe as a respectable, hardworking family man. Thomas Jefferson Randolph, Alexander Garland, Nimrod Branham, and six other justices of the peace for the county were signatories to this petition of June 1850. The signers of this petition represented every administrative district of the county. James Munroe's world stretched well beyond a few blocks in the town of Charlottesville. In filing the petition, they were "expressing [their] willingness that leave should be granted him to remain in the Commonwealth."[33]

Perhaps as little as ten years earlier, in the 1830s, James Munroe would have relied on his reputation and local connections to remain in the state informally and quietly. He would not have needed to rally his white supporters so publicly. He likely would not have felt it necessary to apply formally for residency, and if he had chosen to do so, his request would have been granted with ease.

For some Albemarle residents, however, James Munroe's residency application in 1847 was a bigger issue than simply that of one free black worker. For these proslavery ideologues, the application raised the specter of northern abolitionists invading Albemarle, a violent end of slavery, and subsequent racial chaos. They saw in James Munroe's application and the white petitioners in support of his residency a line in the sand, and they chose to take a stand. In publicly voicing their opposition to Munroe's petition on December 12, 1850, they denigrated James Munroe personally, questioning both his reputation and his free status: "We, the undersigned, citizens of Albemarle County, having learned that a petition has been presented to your honorable body praying that a certain free man of color, by name of James Monroe, may be permitted to remain . . . respectfully ask that the prayer of the said petitioner may be rejected. . . . The petitioner has, as far as the undersigned are informed, no individual merit in his claim, being a slave who says he purchased his freedom." For these Albemarle residents, whiteness meant freedom and citizenship, and blackness indeed connoted enslaved status and nothing else. This petition denied James Munroe legitimate freedom, figuring him instead as basically still a slave.[34]

How did this angry group of proslavery citizens come into existence? This petition against James Munroe's residency request was not the spontaneous reflexive gesture of a virulently racist society that could only envision people of color as slaves and was threatened by any other possibility. But it did come from one vociferous defender of slavery and of a strict racial hierarchy. At the time of Munroe's residency request, Charlottesville was home to two competing newspapers, the *Jeffersonian Republican* and the *Review*. The *Review*, edited by Green Peyton and James C. Southall, was the more moderate newspaper when it came to sectional issues and would only belatedly come to support secession in 1861, when Virginia's secession had already become a reality. Nevertheless, this paper was still proslavery. The *Jeffersonian Republican* was edited by James Alexander, northern born but by the 1840s Albemarle's leading proponent of slavery and defender of the southern culture predicated upon it. He used his paper as a bully pulpit from which to denounce anyone and anything that he believed might weaken or question the slave system in any way.

By 1850, slavery had become "a burning political and moral issue" across the nation and even in Albemarle County.[35] James Alexander and his mouthpiece, the *Jeffersonian Republican*, throughout the decade carried on a heated and running argument with the *Review*. Slaveholders in the county were engaged in discussions about the treatment of slaves. The Albemarle resident William W. Gilmer, writing in the *Review* in 1852, felt that slaves should be trained at an early age in proper respectful behavior: "Talk to them, take notice of them; it gives them confidence and adds greatly to their value." The *Review* published commentary critical of slave owners who mistreated their slaves. This was no abolitionist editorializing. The *Review* was proslavery but espoused the use of positive reinforcement in slave management and sought to ameliorate harsh treatment of slaves. For the *Review,* slavery's vigor was predicated upon open and honest discussion of its ills: "when slavery becomes a hypocrisy, when slavery is to be carried on in the dark, when it cannot stand *in the light;* when it sulks and cries Oh, there comes a Northern man . . . then we are against slavery!" William W. Gilmer agreed and further counseled masters to avoid whipping slaves: "Kindness when sick, and at all times when they deserve, or will *permit* it, is a great thing. . . . Never scold or threaten."[36]

James Alexander, an acolyte of the positive-good school of slavery defenders, fumed in the *Jeffersonian Republican* that the *Review* and Gilmer aided and abetted northern abolitionists by "parading before the public the blemishes of our social system and the incidental evils of our peculiar institution." For Alexander, any discussion of problems in the slave system was tantamount to being an abolitionist. Proslavery ideologues such as Alexander saw the *Review*'s position as a heresy. Clearly, by 1850, the rising tide of antislavery agitation nationally had begun to affect some locals' views of slavery and slaveholding. Men such as Alexander figuratively circled the wagons, preparing to defend slavery at all costs. In this climate, free blacks would become for some a much more visible threat to the racial order and to the white southern way of life, rooted in slave owning.[37]

It was James Alexander who circulated the petition attacking James Munroe. For Alexander, James Munroe was not significant as a person. He had no face-to-face relationship with Munroe. All he could see was a free black whose residency in the county visibly questioned the entire slave system. Alexander preferred that all people of color be slaves. Thus, for Alexander and the other signers of the anti-residency petition, James Munroe as an individual was a secondary issue. The petition said as much: "We have no doubt that there are several other free persons of color in this county awaiting a favorable result of the said Monroe's petition, who will also solicit similar favors from the Legislature; we are now endeavouring to get rid of the free colored population of our county." These people were challenging the more fluid system of race relations privileging local knowledge and context that had predominated in Albemarle County since the Revolution. A small group of anti–free black people, who had probably been present in Albemarle all along, was challenging the longstanding dominance of laissez-faire whites. James Alexander was leading the charge to turn the "black is slave, white is free" concept into a lived reality in Albemarle County. Narrowing the gap between state law and localized social practice by rigidly enforcing anti–free black legislation was for Alexander the starting point.[38]

The threat of abolition and the continuing national debate over the morality of slavery, the issue of the institution's geographic expansion, and the fitness of African Americans for freedom and citizenship had become cause for visceral concern for some residents in Albemarle. Some felt so strongly about maintaining the status quo that they signed Alexander's petition demanding the eventual removal of all free blacks from the county. Among the signers was the white merchant John R. Jones. Fifteen years earlier he had signed two different petitions supporting free people of color in residency requests. Either the times had changed, or Mr. Jones was not acquainted with James Munroe. Regardless, the number supporting Alexander's position was relatively small. Only forty white residents signed Alexander's petition, while about two hundred signed James Munroe's petition seeking permission to remain in the county. And six of those two hundred offered detailed testimonials about James Munroe's respectable, sober, hardworking character and his dedication to his family. The General Assembly declined to make a decision, withdrawing the petition from consideration and forwarding the request to the attorney Egbert R. Watson in Charlottesville.[39]

James Munroe found himself trapped. His petition, although drawing impressive support from the white community, had also drawn the ire of a smaller contingent of proslavery ideologues. In June 1851, Munroe had not left Albemarle. The county court issued a warrant for his arrest, but the sheriffs did not find him that summer. On August 3, 1851, a grand jury convened by the county court made presentments for ten free blacks who were in violation of the 1806 removal law. James Munroe was one of those free people of color. He had remained in the county, hopeful that the significant white support he had managed to muster would overcome the indictment and the opposition to his residency. The court went ahead and issued a verdict, finding Munroe guilty. By January 1852, James Munroe was still in the county. Finally, in early February 1852, the warrant was successfully executed.[40]

Strangely, James Munroe had been found guilty of remaining in the commonwealth contrary to the 1806 law, but he was not sold into slavery; he was not even exiled. He remained in the county after February. The close personal connections he had with so many whites provided him with some cover while he worked to free his family. As long as he remained peaceable, respectable, quiet, and hardworking, he would likely be allowed to remain in Albemarle. Unfortunately, just five months after the court found him guilty, Munroe had a confrontation with a slave. That slave, James, the property of S. D. Williamson, appealed to the county court seeking "protection from James Munroe, who threatened to assault slave James." Munroe still had personal connections. He called on the white attorney Egbert R. Watson, who came to the courthouse and filed a matching twenty-five-dollar recognizance guaranteeing the good behavior of Munroe toward the slave James. Court officials did not take the opportunity to arrest or apprehend this already convicted free man of color. Rather, they handled the breach-of-peace case in the customary fashion.[41]

A month later, in July 1852, James Munroe was still in Albemarle; he came to the courthouse with the white resident James Norris. Norris was the son of Opie Norris and one of the executors of his deceased father's estate. Opie Norris owned James Munroe's wife, Evelina, and their children, including Mary Ann, Thomas Jefferson, and James Jr. James Norris came to the courthouse that day to file a deed of sale. James Munroe had paid $650 to the Norris estate, purchasing Evelina along with Mary Ann and Thomas Jefferson Munroe, two of his children. James Munroe was not finished purchasing his family. He still had two children held in slavery. But his altercation with a slave the previous month had narrowed considerably the comfort zone in which he could maneuver. At some point between that July 7 purchase and 1860, Munroe took what family he had freed and moved to Ohio.[42]

In Ohio, Munroe continued to work to earn money to purchase the remainder of his family. In January 1860, he made the trip back to Charlottesville from Ohio to purchase one of his two children who were still slaves—son James Jr. In Albemarle, James Sr. met a man who had been acquainted with him back in the days when Munroe lived in the county: the attorney Egbert R. Watson, one of the executors of the Opie Norris estate. Munroe paid Watson twelve hundred dollars for the freedom of his own son. That meeting with Egbert Watson was Munroe's last act in Albemarle County. The records do not reveal what might have happened to Munroe's other child.[43]

When the deed of manumission was signed, the Munroes left Albemarle for the last time, returning to Ohio. James Munroe's life in Albemarle demonstrates the possibilities free people of color had there. Through a highly personal culture based upon reputations established through face-to-face meetings, James Munroe and other free blacks managed to carve out comfortable spheres of existence, both as slaves living with great autonomy and as free people of color. But Munroe's experience, in which his well-maintained personal connections explain how much latitude the authorities gave him, also shows how the gap between law and social practice in Albemarle (and Virginia) had narrowed to the point where being known was not necessarily enough. The population statistics for the county bear out this image. In 1840, the free black population reached 602, up 50 percent from its 1830 numbers and a high point in a fifty-year climb. But by 1850, the free black population in Albemarle had dropped slightly, to 587.[44]

Some free blacks, including James Munroe, responded to increasing anti–free black rhetoric by moving to free territory. But the highly personal culture allowing a number of free people of color the space to live comfortably and even flourish did not disappear. Yes, the free black population declined slightly from 1840 to 1850, but the numbers vividly illustrate that a massive exodus of free people of color did not occur. James Alexander and other proslavery ideologues in the county, who by 1850 posed a serious but essentially unsuccessful challenge to the white majority favoring a "live and let live" approach to local free people of color, did not win the debate. Free blacks were not driven from the county. Most free blacks who lived in Albemarle County as 1850 approached did not find it necessary to depart the area. And most free people of color who had been freed since 1806 did not find themselves facing criminal charges. In fact, of the fourteen free blacks in the county who were actually charged with violating the 1806 removal law, some were granted permission to remain in the county.

For example, the free man of color William Swingler was born free in 1810 in Augusta County, which lies adjacent to Albemarle County to the west, on the other slope of the Blue Ridge Mountains. Swingler at age thirty-one decided to head east, crossing the mountains and finding his way some sixty miles to Scottsville on the James River, at the southern end of Albemarle County. In 1840, Swingler does not appear to have been concerned that his movement over significant distances as a free man of color might pose a problem. For the next decade, Swingler lived a quiet life in Scottsville, Albemarle's only port on the James River. Scottsville's population when Swingler arrived was about three hundred. The town consisted of a little over one hundred houses. Scottsville was located at the eastern terminus of the Staunton and James River Turnpike.[45]

As a result, Scottsville became a center of far more activity than might be expected for a town of its size. It was the main point of departure for river traffic bound east from other points in Albemarle and even from the Shenandoah Valley. The Charlottesville resident Dr. William S. White explained the importance of the turnpike to the town: "A turnpike had recently been constructed, extending to Rockfish Gap, and inviting the trade of the Valley of Virginia in that direction. The result was that so small a village rarely ever commanded so active a trade. A hundred large Valley wagons have been seen unloading their rich freight of flour, bacon, venison hams, butter, cheese, beeswax, etc., in one day." Scottsville had developed a thriving mercantile trade, with fourteen stores and retail craft production of clothing, leather, shoes, and furniture. As a center of both overland and river shipping, the town developed a bustling service industry supporting wagon making and repair, bateau repair, and stabling for horses.[46]

William Swingler moved to Scottsville at a very opportune time. A mere twenty years earlier, Scottsville had been little more than a few buildings erected at the location of a ferry crossing across the James. In addition to the ferry, it was home to two stores, a warehouse, and several modest houses. By the Civil War, Scottsville's boom would have passed forever. Thus, William Swingler's move to the small but booming entrepôt in southeastern Albemarle was likely a move based in optimism. For the next ten years, Swingler worked in Scottsville. By 1850, he headed a household of eight people. His wife, Mary, kept their home, raising their seven children, ranging in age from one year to fifteen years old. After a decade working in the busy little town, William Swingler had established himself as a reliable blacksmith. He lived in an extremely modest dwelling with his family.[47]

Most of 1850 passed quietly for Swingler and his family. He continued to work as a blacksmith, living next door to his white neighbor William Wright, a thirty-seven-year-old contractor, and his fellow free person of color Madison Hubbard. Neither Swingler nor his neighbor Hubbard was swept up in the anti–free black spurt in late 1850. Unlike James Munroe and Randolph Jones, they did not find themselves charged with violating any law. But Swingler was living in technical violation of the 1806 removal law. Yes, he had been born free in Augusta County and had not left the state. But he was born after 1806 to parents freed after the removal law went into effect. As a result, the authorities could have argued that he lived in technical violation of the removal law. No one in Scottsville, however, seemed concerned. Swingler's work as a blacksmith made him a valuable, if relatively minor, contributor to Scottsville's success. The community on the north bank of the James River did not see him as dangerous.

Swingler, however, inadvertently caught the attention of certain public authorities. As a native of Augusta County who resided in southern Albemarle, Swingler surely had family connections back on the other side of the Blue Ridge. He clearly moved back and forth between the two locales with some regularity. Although Swingler and his family are listed as residents of Scottsville in census reports and tax lists from 1840 to 1850, William also showed up as a resident of Augusta County. On January 27, 1851, Swingler went to the Augusta County courthouse and registered his freedom. Despite possessing free papers in 1854, he was charged with violating the 1806 removal law. On March 6, the Albemarle court summoned Alexander Johnson and eight other white men of Scottsville as witnesses for William Swingler. Johnson, a thirty-two-year-old white merchant with a four-thousand-dollar estate, lived on a lot in 1854 that was located adjacent to Swingler's humble dwelling.[48]

The list of William Swingler's supporters continued to grow as the year wore on. The Augusta County court clerk's office forwarded an affidavit on June 3, 1854, attesting to Swingler's proper registration and to his free birth in Augusta County. By February 1855, a number of Scottsville men had testified on behalf of William Swingler. But Swingler wanted to avoid a negative outcome such as that experienced by Randolph Jones or James Munroe. So he wisely followed Munroe's example and garnered additional support. He was a widely recognized person in the village of Scottsville and had little trouble finding supporters. Two petitions were filed in Albemarle in favor of Swingler's residency.

The first, signed in 1855 by Peter Field Jefferson, Thomas Shelton, James Pace, Benjamin Eubank, Thomas Wash, and several members of Scottsville's Johnson family, stated that he "is a good black and a usefull man in the neighborhood as regards his trade; and his attention to business." These petitioners dealt with Swingler first and foremost in a business capacity, hiring him to do blacksmith's work. They knew and trusted him as an honest and hardworking resident of Scottsville. The petition continues in this vein: "we certify that said free man of color has resided in this county for nearly fifteen years. . . . We consider him a peaceable, orderly and well disposed man." They finished their petition by "asking the court to grant him the liberty of remaining in said county."[49]

The second petition, signed by a dozen other Albemarle whites, reiterated many of the same points about William Swingler. These white Scottsville residents could attach a name, face, and reputation to Swingler and therefore found it easy to include him in their community: "The undersigned have known William Swindler [*sic*] for some time and know him to be an industrious hard working man." As with the first petition, these white residents saw more than labor when they looked at William Swingler. There was a social aspect to his respectability: "he has a large family and has been supporting them by his industry. He is as far as we know & believe an honest & sober negro."[50]

William Swingler's application for official residency, like James Munroe's, generated some resistance, however. On March 9, 1857, fourteen white men were called as witnesses for the commonwealth in the case against Swingler. Even a slave was summoned to provide information against Swingler. At this point, the case against Swingler had dragged on for years, and he still remained in Scottsville. Swingler, moreover, encountered far less vociferous opposition than that faced by James Munroe. First, far fewer people were summoned by the prosecution to testify. Second, no one filed a petition demanding that the court reject his residency request. Last, of the fourteen people summoned as witnesses for the commonwealth against Swingler, at least four failed to appear.[51]

On April 6, 1857, after over three years of delay, the court ruled in favor of Swingler. The court granted him permission to remain in the commonwealth and approved his request to register his freedom with the county where he then resided. Three years later, Swingler remained a resident of Scottsville. In that year, he continued to work as a blacksmith and was the head of a household of eight people. These included his wife, Mary and three sons and three daughters ranging in age from eleven to twenty-one. By the eve of the Civil War, Swingler had managed to purchase some taxable personal property, owning a personal estate worth twenty dollars. His house in Scottsville was adjacent to a much fancier home owned by the white merchant A. Johnson and the home of Rebecca Hamlet, a white widow who had an estate worth over five thousand dollars and continued to run the family farm on the outskirts of Scottsville. The town's boom years had passed, but the highly personal culture that helped to determine the network of social relationships still allowed for interracial residential patterns and amicable face-to-face interactions across the color line. William Swingler may not have been on an equal footing with his white neighbors, but neither was he seen as anomalous or marginal.[52]

The experiences of the free man of color Stephen Byars also demonstrate vividly just how the highly personal social culture that characterized Albemarle County crossed both racial divides and class lines. Byars was born a slave in Albemarle County. By the time he was in his thirties, Byars was a skilled slave whose master agreed to allow him to go about as if free and hire himself out. This practice was technically illegal in Virginia, but it remained widespread throughout the first half of the nineteenth century. Letting slaves handle their own hiring out was an informal arrangement that afforded benefit to both parties. The master could free himself from the burden of paying for the upkeep of an individual slave and from the effort of finding people to hire his skilled slaves. Additionally, the master received cash payments from the slave. The slave gained a measure of freedom, living and conducting himself as if free. The slave also had the opportunity to make some money for himself.[53]

This practice was predicated upon a personal relationship between master and slave. The master, in agreeing to allow a slave to live as if free and hire himself, had to believe that he could trust the slave implicitly. That trust was created through years of working together in close face-to-face interactions. A slave had to achieve a reputation as a trustworthy, hardworking, and sober person before a master would allow self-hiring. Slaveholding communities tended to be of two minds about the practice. Some saw the practice as potentially dangerous, because slaves who hired themselves out lived free from direct white oversight and control. These slaves, by virtue of their liminal position between freedom and slavery, posed a visible problem for some white slaveholders. At the same time, many masters found the relationship economically satisfying. Nonslaveholding whites benefited from the system, too, because they gained access to affordable labor without having to earn enough money to buy a slave. Slaveholders tended to see the practice as problematic in the abstract, but they routinely tended to act as if their personal slaves would not cause any difficulty. As long as those slaves behaved in a respectable fashion, people usually felt no need to complain.[54]

No one in Albemarle County seems to have raised an eyebrow about Stephen Byars living as if free. For years, Byars lived and worked in and around Charlottesville, hiring himself out, sending payments to his master, Joel W. Brown, and saving what he could for himself. The deal worked so well for Brown that he eventually agreed to let Byars purchase himself. In agreeing to let Byars purchase himself, Brown did not betray any interest in divesting himself of connections to the peculiar institution. Brown's motives likely were purely financial—he had already benefited monetarily from the arrangement. For Brown, Byars had proved that he was, whether slave or free, trustworthy and unlikely to present any problems for the Charlottesville community. Brown knew that he would continue to receive payments from Byars in addition to any money that Byars would pay toward his freedom.

By 1835, Byars was nearing completion of the purchase agreement. Technically still a slave, but having spent quite a few years living in the Charlottesville area as if a free man, Byars decided it was time to prepare himself for the transition to documented legal freedom. He understood that if he received his manumission and remained in Virginia, he would be in violation of the 1806 removal law. But he had family in the area whom he was working to free. He needed to stay in the county at all costs. So, while still a slave, he petitioned the state legislature requesting permission to remain in the state.

In his petition, Byars told the assembly about the agreement he had with his master, stating that "he was born in the County of Albemarle and raised in the town of Charlottesville where he now resides, that by the indulgence of a kind master he has been enabled to accumulate a sufficient sum of money to purchase his freedom, which he has done." Byars continued, "he [Stephen] is liable to be reduced to a state of slavery if he remains within the limits of the Commonwealth without leave obtained from your honorable body. . . . He is now an old man, he has a wife and children who are slaves and it is on their account chiefly, that he desires to be permitted to spend the short remainder of his days in the land of his birth." Byars was in his fifties at the time he filed the petition, but he did not beg simply for mercy. He made it clear to the assembly that he was in fact a respectable and trustworthy citizen: "Your memorialist is proud to recollect that never during his protracted life has his honesty been impeached, and that his demeanour has been such as to secure him the good will of many who know him." Stephen Byars demonstrated that he clearly understood the importance of maintaining a positive reputation in the highly personal and reputation-based social culture of Albemarle.[55]

Thirty-seven white Albemarle residents concurred with Stephen Byars's assessment. They agreed that he was an honest and trustworthy member of their community. They knew him to be a hardworking and dedicated family man. One signer, William Wertenbaker, not only signed the petition but left a very personal inscription: "for twenty years my friend." Wertenbaker at the time was a middle-aged man who had served as a private in the War of 1812 and attended the University of Virginia. At the time he signed the petition, he was the proprietor of the University Book Store and postmaster for the university community. Wertenbaker evinced no abolitionist sympathies during his life. Back in 1830, he had captained the county slave patrol for a time. But he did act as if certain free blacks, including Stephen Byars, were worthy of trust and even what he termed "friend[ship]." Face-to-face relationships facilitated these interracial bonds. The General Assembly read the petition and simply referred it back to the county court. The county court, on February 19, 1836, deemed Byars's request "reasonable." But the petition appears to have stalled there. The court never completed the process by granting residency permission. Neither, however, did they reject the petition outright.[56]

Almost two years later, on November 2, 1837, Stephen Byars's long-absent master, Joel W. Brown, came to the county courthouse in Charlottesville. There, he entered a deed of manumission into the record. Brown had signed that deed on October 25, when Byars delivered the last payment of the agreed-upon $300 purchase price. Stephen Byars was legally a free man. That same day, Byars was involved in filing yet another deed. He came before the county clerk a second time, this time with the white resident Anderson Wingfield. Wingfield entered a deed of manumission for Jane, a slave woman owned by John Winn. Wingfield was acting as a middleman for the purchase agreement. Byars had paid John Winn $150 through Wingfield so he could purchase his wife. Byars, in addition to working for years to purchase his own freedom, had been busy earning extra income to purchase his family, including his wife, Jane (also known as Ginney). Now they were both legally free. They returned to the courthouse on November 7 to apply formally for their freedom certificates. The county clerk described Byars as fifty-five years old and his wife, Ginney, as thirty-six years old.[57]

With Stephen's residency request stalled, however, they decided to emigrate out of the state. They moved to free territory, heading to Ohio. Their Albemarle County story, however, does not end there. They experienced a form of culture shock in Ohio. As Stephen Byars would describe it, "much to his surprise and regret . . . he found after a trial of about six months residence there, that so marked was the difference in the manners and habits of the people of Ohio when contrasted with those amongst whom he had been raised that he would not remain amongst them with the least happiness or contentment." Byars and Ginney chose instead to return to Albemarle, knowing full well that they could face legal difficulties as a result of their actions. A few months after returning to Charlottesville, Stephen Byars once again filed a petition with the General Assembly of Virginia seeking permission to remain in the commonwealth. He explained that he was a native of the county, that he had purchased his freedom and that of his wife, emigrated to Ohio, found it hard to live there because the culture was so foreign, and returned to Albemarle. Last, he again reminded the assembly of his "general good character for honesty, industry and sobriety."[58]

As with his 1835 petition, Stephen Byars rounded up the signatures of nearly forty white residents, including seven justices of the peace. They reiterated their feelings that Byars was a "person of good character, peaceable, orderly, and industrious, and not addicted to drunkenness, gaming, or any other vice." They reminded the General Assembly that they were "well acquainted with Stephen Biars now a free man of color for many years and have no hesitation in recommending him." The petitioners added one last flourish, telling the "Honourable Body" that they "cheerfully unite with him in his prayer to remain in the Commonwealth." This time, however, Stephen Byars made it clear just how intent he was on spending the remainder of his life in the county where he was born. He reminded the assembly that he "was now about sixty-two years of age" and further "declared to your Honourable body that he would prefer being sold into Slavery in Virginia to being compelled to emigrate to and reside in the State of Ohio."[59]

For any free person of color, making such a suggestion would appear to have been a risky proposition. Any locale that found itself deeply concerned about a free black presence could use residency requests as opportunities to deport free blacks or to return them to slavery for violating the removal law. If the local magistrates were zealous ideologues intent on rigidly enforcing the racial hierarchy, any petition such as that filed by Byars would present a perfect opportunity. Since Byars had himself suggested a willingness to return to slavery if he could remain, the court could easily have accommodated him by bringing charges against him, convicting him, and selling him back into slavery. But the court did not jump at that opportunity. The residency request sat for several months. In June 1839, the court still had not reached a decision.

Byars returned to the courthouse on the fourth of June with his wife, Ginney. That same day, one Eliza and her children, also free people of color, appeared. She and her children had recently been freed by the will of John Rogers Sr. They all applied to the clerk of the county court seeking permission to stay under the 1837 rules that put full decision-making power in the hands of the localities.[60] Both residency requests, the petition filed with the General Assembly, and the request made to the local court remained undecided for months afterward. Byars and his family were not granted permission to remain in the commonwealth, but neither were they prosecuted for violating the removal law. Although the residency request remained as unfinished business, they were allowed to stay and to keep their free status.[61]

Byars did not sit idly and wait meekly for the court to render a decision. He returned to work as a hostler at the taverns and hotels adjacent to the university. Byars also made money and personal connections with white residents by running a service for horses. Many students, professors, and county residents left their horses with Byars when they came to the university area. He housed them in a stable, fed them, watered them, and otherwise prepared them to be ridden again. But Byars was not content simply working as an employee for someone else. He had done that for decades. He started saving money in 1839 so he could purchase his own place. By June 1840, he had found a suitable tract of land on which he could establish his own stable and home. It was a two-and-one-quarter-acre plot of land near the university, located advantageously along the Three Notched Road, the main east-west artery in the county. The white resident Andrew McKee, a hatter by trade, at the time owned the lot and agreed to sell it to Byars. The purchase price was seven hundred dollars, a significant sum by any standard.[62]

Stephen Byars had already demonstrated to his neighbors in Albemarle County that he was extremely hardworking, trustworthy, and respectable. But this purchase price was far more than he possessed at the time. Byars, however, still had his reputation. Andrew McKee had known him for decades. Byars completed the purchase by taking out a seven-year deed of trust with McKee, a white man, acting as trustee. Under this agreement, Byars was to repay McKee one hundred dollars each year. The final payment would be due October 1, 1846. Until the last payment was made in meeting the obligation, a third party, the Charlottesville resident and county clerk Ira Garrett, would retain possession of the actual title to the land. Such an arrangement represented a rather routine agreement for both whites and blacks at that time.[63]

That same year, the county conducted the federally mandated decennial census. Byars was listed as a free colored male, age fifty-five or older, living as the head of a household containing one free colored female age thirty-six to fifty-five (Ginney) and one free colored female under the age of ten. His family owned their own two-acre plot of land, enough to run a hostling business. It must have been fairly lucrative for Byars, because by 1841 he owned one slave over the age of sixteen, two horses, and one carriage worth forty dollars. Extant county records do not indicate whether this slave was a family member he had purchased and liberated de facto or simply a slave he had bought or hired because he needed help with the business. Either way, he was successful enough to have income to buy or hire a slave. Stephen Byars and his family had so far comfortably resettled into the Charlottesville area, basically picking up where they had left off back in 1836, when they departed for Ohio.[64]

The county court in 1842 reopened the court case concerning Byars's petition for permission to remain in the county. The county clerk ordered the justices of the peace once again to assemble and consider the petition. Yet again, nothing happened. For Stephen's family, daily life continued much as it always had. But that residency request still hung over them as unfinished business. Much of 1843 progressed in the same fashion. The residency request had stalled again, but Stephen and his family busied themselves in the neighborhood of the university. Finally, on October 17, the court initiated activity concerning Stephen. Charges were filed against him regarding his illegal residency in the county. He had been freed well after 1806, had not been granted residency permission, and thus was in violation of the twelve-month residency limit after manumission. To make matters worse, he had emigrated to Ohio. Now an additional law might also be used against him by terming him a free black who had gone north to get an education. According to an 1838 law, any free person of color who moved beyond the limits of the commonwealth "to be educated" was not allowed to return.[65]

After over six years of patient waiting, Byars and his family received their days in court. On October 12, 1843, the county court finally responded to Ginney's application for permission to remain in the county. The court examined a number of witnesses and found Ginney not guilty of violating the 1838 residency law. The court also granted her permission to stay in the commonwealth. Less than two weeks later, the court convened to consider Stephen's petition and the testimonials of Byars's white supporters and then examined a number of witnesses. As with his wife nine days earlier, the court found Stephen not guilty and granted him permission to remain in Albemarle. That same year, Albemarle County handled a total of six criminal presentments for violating the residency law. Three cases were dismissed, one was found guilty, and two were acquitted. By being known and respected in their neighborhood, Stephen and Ginney Byars, along with three other free people of color in 1843, had developed such a reputation that they were seen first as neighbors and only second as people of color.[66]

For the Byars family, 1843 represented a watershed year. Their decades-long struggle to become free and remain as residents in Albemarle County had culminated in two court victories that October. They were free and at liberty to remain in the area. But that was not the only happy event for Stephen Byars that year. Two months after the successful conclusion of his residency request, Byars met with the county clerk and his creditor, neighbor Andrew McKee. According to the terms of the deed of sale for his land purchase, he was not due to make the last payment to McKee until 1846. But Stephen had worked hard since returning to Albemarle. On December 22, he made the last payment to Andrew McKee, the last of the seven hundred dollars that the two had agreed upon as the purchase price for the two and one quarter acres of land. Byars did this in less than half the time available to him under the mortgage agreement. McKee honored the agreement and on the same day filed the final deed of sale for the land. Stephen now owned his land outright. The county clerk recorded the completed deed of sale on January 1, 1844.[67]

The experiences of a handful of free people of color seeking residency and unmolested existence in Albemarle in the 1840s suggest that a few may have faced increasing difficulties, especially as the decade came to a close. As 1850 approached, a few free blacks found their room to maneuver in Albemarle in some ways diminishing. Personal relationships with whites still allowed free people of color to move toward security and perhaps even something approaching an informal social whiteness through establishment of respectable reputations, but the class of whites truly opposed to a free black presence was growing. These virulent racists and proslavery ideologues would make life difficult for several free blacks, including Stephen Byars.

Just twenty-six days after he paid off the mortgage to Andrew McKee, Byars faced a new set of criminal charges. This time, he was charged with remaining in the commonwealth for more than twelve months—a violation of the law of 1806. The case dragged on all spring, and finally, on May 16, the court again heard charges concerning Stephen Byars's residency. The court had only recently approved his residency, so the decision was likely fresh in the minds of court officials. The case against Byars was determined to be without merit and dismissed by the court.[68] A small group of proslavery ideologues had begun to push the Albemarle community harder regarding enforcing state law and the more rigid policing of free blacks but had not yet prevailed.

After so many years of legal battles considering his fitness for residency in Albemarle, Stephen could have been wary about any contact with the local court system. He could have chosen to keep a low profile, running his hostler's business near the university, and only having regular contact with customers and trusted neighbors. But that is not how Stephen Byars lived. He lived as if he saw himself as a member of the Charlottesville community. When he had grievances that could be aired and adjudicated by the court, he used the courts. In 1846, Stephen lost on appeal a chancery court suit that had been in the system for a couple of years. The extant records do not indicate exactly what the dispute was about, but Byars initially sued the white attorney and Albemarle resident George W. Trueheart seeking payment, likely for services rendered. The free man of color Stephen Byars did not hesitate to take a white customer to court if there was a financial discrepancy. The court ruled for Byars; Trueheart was ordered to pay an undisclosed amount to Byars. Trueheart, an attorney, immediately filed an appeal. Trueheart ultimately won the suit on appeal, and Byars in 1846 was ordered to pay Trueheart's court costs. Although Stephen Byars lost the case, he demonstrated confidence in the local legal system.[69]

Stephen Byars and his family lived out the remainder of the antebellum period as quiet and respectable property-owning people of color. They continued to own their small plot of land just outside Charlottesville. They ran their business that catered to both the university community and travelers headed east and west on Three Notched Road. The 1850s for the Byars family represented a quiet time. They had no contact with the court system. No local whites filed further charges against them for violating anti–free black laws. The Civil War began, and still the family remained in the county of their birth. In 1866, in the early days of Reconstruction, Stephen Byars had his last contact with the court system. Then an elderly man who had lived to see all African Americans in Virginia win their freedom, he was living out his twilight years in comfortable but modest circumstances on that same two-acre plot of land.

On September 1, 1866, William Cole, a freedman, came by Byars's stable. Cole brought a pig with him, which he sold to Byars for ten dollars. Unfortunately, William Cole did not own the pig. He had gone to the house of the white resident Slaughter W. Ficklin and stolen both the pig and a jug valued at five dollars. As far as the legal code was concerned, stealing and knowingly purchasing stolen property amounted to the same offense. As a result, the county court charged Byars with theft of the pig. Both William Cole and Stephen Byars were arrested and jailed on September 29. Byars, however, had a real advantage that the recently emancipated Cole lacked. He was an elderly property owner who had lived almost his entire life in Albemarle and had long ago developed a reputation as an honest and upright person. Byars called upon his white acquaintance George L. Crank to come and help him post bail. That same day, Byars and Crank each filed twenty-five-dollar recognizances guaranteeing Byars's appearance at November court to answer the charges. Byars was admitted to bail and freed pending trial.[70]

On November 5, Stephen Byars returned to the courthouse for his trial. The commonwealth's attorney had charged him with "knowing the pig to have been stolen . . . [and] purchasing the pig worth ten dollars from William Cole." Byars pleaded not guilty, arguing that he in fact had not known that the pig was stolen. Indeed, his actions and his situation differentiated him starkly from his codefendant William Cole. Cole had stolen not only the pig but also that five-dollar jug and had been arrested with the jug in his possession. He had clearly stolen the pig. Times were difficult for newly emancipated people of color in Albemarle right after the war. Cole may have been desperate for food, and he stole what he needed during those first couple weeks of September 1866. In separate criminal trials, Cole was also charged with stealing two bushels of wheat from Ficklin on September 10 and twelve pieces of bacon from Thomas L. Farish on September 12.[71]

The accumulated weight of the theft charges against William Cole were reinforced by his lack of the reputation and personal connections that had for so long helped Byars in freedom. No one came to Cole's defense. Slaughter W. Ficklin testified that Cole had indeed stolen the pig and the jug and that Byars did not know where the pig came from. The court acquitted Byars of the one charge against him. Cole, however, still faced four separate charges. On the first count, stealing wheat from Benjamin Ficklin, the commonwealth declined to continue prosecution of the case, citing a lack of evidence. On the second charge, stealing bacon from Thomas Farish, William Cole was actually acquitted on October 13. For stealing the pig and jug from Ficklin, however, the evidence against Cole was hard to ignore. On this charge, the court on November 5 found Cole guilty and sentenced him to twenty lashes at the public whipping post. Cole, having committed a crime and lacking any visible personal connection to the white community, received a punishment that doubtless reminded him of his years as a slave. Byars, thanks to his innocence as well as his good reputation and strong connections to the community, went home a free man once again.

Stephen and Ginney Byars, William Swingler, James Munroe, and Randolph Jones all found themselves confronted with the realities of the 1806 removal law. They had all achieved their freedom, or had been born to parents who won their freedom, after that law went into effect. All worked hard, and in so doing they earned reputations and made connections that could overcome anti–free black legislation. They also lived in a society in which whites on the local level showed very little interest in applying the expulsion law. In the decade-plus leading up to the Civil War, free people of color witnessed an increase in proslavery agitation as antislavery activity in the North increased. The people of color discussed in this chapter all shared that common characteristic: they were not free before the removal law went into effect. All fought the law in court. Twelve were successful, two were found guilty—one of whom was ostensibly returned to slavery after the court's verdict—and four or more simply emigrated. And emigration was an option exercised not only by free blacks who were living in violation of the 1806 removal law.[72]

For instance, Daniel Goings, the son of the free man of color Benjamin Goings Sr., was born circa 1779 in Albemarle County. He was born free to free parents well before passage of the 1806 removal law. Daniel Goings also was connected to a very well-known and extensive free black family. Daniel's uncle was the Revolutionary War veteran Sherod Goings Sr. Many members of his extended family maintained close personal relationships with their white neighbors. By the turn of the nineteenth century, Daniel Goings was in his early twenties; he owned a small farm consisting of just over eighty acres but lived on his father Benjamin's land in his own modest dwelling. By 1811, he had managed to purchase one horse, his only taxable personal property. No entry exists for Daniel Goings in the marriage register, but the Fredericksville Parish tax collector in 1814 listed him as the head of a household in which he and his son lived. Two years later, he had purchased a second horse.[73]

Daniel Goings was forty-three years old when his father, Benjamin, died in 1822. Benjamin Goings, as a propertied man of color with a large family, understood that a proper will would be the best avenue for ensuring that his property was apportioned as he wished. He fell ill in early April, and on April 15 four white neighbors came to Goings's farm to transcribe the will. By June, Goings was dead. Relying upon his own reputation in the neighborhood where they lived, Benjamin Goings had appointed two other white neighbors as executors. His will bequeathed his property first in life estate to his wife, Betsy. At her death, he gave his son Daniel Goings one hundred acres of land. The remainder of the estate at that point was to be sold at auction to the highest bidder, with the proceeds divided equally among seven of his other children.[74]

Benjamin Goings died a successful free man of color in Albemarle County. In addition to owning a two-hundred-acre farm worth about $170, he also owned one slave worth $150. In his will, he stipulated that his slave Milly was not a family member but allowed her to choose which of Benjamin's children she would like for a master. On July 1, the executors completed their inventory and appraisal of Benjamin Goings's estate. Besides the acreage and Milly, he also owned three horses, sundry household items, goods, and livestock valued at nearly $500.[75]

Daniel Goings's father had provided him with an excellent example of how to succeed in the rural slave South. Benjamin Goings had maintained close personal relationships with a number of his white neighbors. He had accrued property, acted respectably, and cared for a family. At his death, he left taxable property to each of his children. Daniel Goings was the chief beneficiary of this will, receiving one hundred acres and thus becoming the owner of 180, including the eighty acres he had owned before his father's death. He picked up where his father had left off, working as a free black small farmer in a community almost twenty miles northwest of town. His farm adjoined property owned by his relative Charles Goings, his brother James Goings, and his white neighbor Matthew P. Walton. His original eighty-acre plot had increased in value to nearly three dollars per acre. The one-hundred-acre plot his father had left him had likewise increased greatly in value, to over six dollars per acre. According to real estate tax records, Daniel Goings in 1830 owned nearly one thousand dollars' worth of real estate.[76]

In 1833, when the county commissioner conducted the state-mandated colonization survey of free blacks, Daniel Goings had admirably filled his father's shoes, continuing the family reputation for sobriety and respectable behavior. He was a relatively prosperous farmer. He supported his own immediate family, as well as siblings and their families. According to that colonization census, Goings was a fifty-four-year-old farmer living near Buck Mountain in the northwest corner of the county. His older brother James, then sixty-six, and a number of other younger family members also lived on his property. Interestingly, the surveyor noted that one Patsy Beckett, a four-year-old mulatto girl with no familial relationship to the Goings family recorded, was residing with Daniel Goings. Patsy Beckett represents the first small clue unearthing an additional fascinating side of Daniel Goings's life.[77]

By 1840, little had changed for Daniel Goings. He continued to work his own land in the foothills of the Blue Ridge Mountains. In that year, however, the census taker's notes on Daniel Goings's household revealed something very striking about the home. The census report states that Daniel Goings was a free colored head of household with an age over fifty-four. Goings was listed in county records as a mulatto, and his children were all described as of light or very light complexion. Living on his farm with him were four other free colored males of various ages, three colored women of various ages, and one white woman aged thirty to forty. This woman's race explains why extant records did not mention a wife, even though Goings had children. Daniel Goings was apparently living openly in what amounted to a common-law marriage with a white woman. No white neighbors ever filed charges against Daniel for cohabiting with a white spouse. No vigilante mob seems to have intervened to protect white womanhood.[78]

Daniel Goings, despite his obvious successes in Albemarle, began to make major changes starting in 1842. In that year, he sold off his older property, the eighty-acre parcel, to his white neighbor Matthew P. Walton. On March 7, 1843, Goings made the seventeen-mile trip into Charlottesville to meet with the clerk of the county court. Daniel Goings was now sixty-five years old, and for the first time in his life, he applied for his freedom certificate.

The county clerk complied after Daniel paid the fee. It turns out that Daniel Goings was selling land and obtaining freedom papers in order to move out of the area. He would take Evelina Beckett, who appears to have been a white woman, with him. Patsy Beckett, who was recorded as living in his house in 1833, would have been his oldest daughter, and she accompanied her parents and siblings to Ohio sometime in 1843.[79]

Daniel Goings moved his family northwest into the free state of Ohio but continued to own the one-hundred-acre farm he had inherited from his father. Less than three years after the move, Goings returned to Virginia to visit his siblings and inspect his Albemarle property. The records do not indicate whether this was his first trip back to Virginia, but it was an extended stay. Daniel Goings, by removing to a free state and then returning to Virginia, found himself in technical violation of residency laws for free blacks. Yet Goings did not act concerned or avoid contact with local whites.[80]

While staying with his relative William Goings, Daniel became very ill. Convinced that he was dying too quickly to secure a lawyer's services, Goings on January 19 called on two free colored neighbors, Lucinda and Delila Taylor, to come to William Goings's and witness Daniel's will. Daniel appointed Michael Goings his executor and ordered that Michael "collect whatever money was due him in the County of Albemarle" and to pay his debts in the area. Two days later, Daniel Goings apparently having lapsed into a coma, Lucinda and Delila Taylor summoned white neighbor and justice of the peace Thomas R. Dunn to the Goings residence. Dunn met with the Taylors and with Daniel and then drafted a nuncupative will—a will "made [orally] in contemplation of imminent death" and attested to by witnesses.[81]

Daniel Goings expired that same afternoon. In his will, Daniel asked his executor Michael Goings to use any monies left in his Albemarle estate "as his said Executor should think best to the support and maintenance of Eveline Becket of Rockaway County, Ohio and her six children they being children of the said Daniel Goings, namely Patty, Nancy, Rachael, Elizabeth, Benjamin, and Mary Agnes Becket." Daniel Goings had just ordered his executor to use the one-hundred-acre farm he had inherited from his father, Benjamin Goings, to benefit his mixed-race family living in Ohio. This might well entail selling the land. Daniel Goings's siblings, including Mary Brock and Jesse Goings, did not find this will to their liking; they did not want the family farm to be given to anyone other than themselves and other family still living in Albemarle County. They quickly filed suit contesting the validity of the will—hoping, no doubt, that it would be more vulnerable to challenge than one drawn up in a more orthodox manner.[82]

The suit questioning the legality of Daniel Goings's will dragged on for more than a year, as lawsuits typically did in old Virginia. Finally, in August 1847, the argument came to an end. The court agreed with the executor Michael Goings that the will was valid and ordered it to be entered into the public record. Mary Brock, Eleanor Frazier, and Jesse Goings were ordered to pay court costs stemming from their objection to the will.[83]

The court, in upholding the validity of Daniel Goings's nuncupative will, also implicitly suggested that his removal to Ohio and return on a visit, though illegal, were of no concern. No white person ever demonstrated suspicions about Daniel Goings. Even the census taker in 1840 did not seem disturbed by a white woman living as if married to a free man of color—a domestic fact that would have been common knowledge in the neighborhood. Daniel Goings, through respectable family connections, through his property ownership, and through his own face-to-face relationships with black and white neighbors, had become something very different from a troublesome free black. White neighbors saw him as a property-owning and respectable farmer with extensive familial ties to the county.

His removal with his white wife and mulatto children to Ohio was likely not the result of pressure from the white citizenry in Albemarle. No one appears to have seen his relationship with Eveline viscerally as an immediate threat to the racial order. Instead, Daniel Goings may have moved to Ohio for the sake of his children. As long as Eveline Becket and Daniel Goings lived as if married and acted with discretion, they would have no problem maintaining their respectability. But seeking public or legal recognition of their relationship, which obtaining freedom papers for the children would have entailed, might actually have drawn the attention of the wrong people. Even so, Daniel Goings's return visit to Albemarle demonstrates just how important personal, face-to-face relationships were. Friends and neighbors all recognized him as the property-owning farmer and neighbor Daniel Goings, not as a free black who had moved to an abolitionist-filled free state and was now returning with dangerous ideas. On the contrary, Daniel Goings had always behaved in the proper fashion. He was an integral, if legally inferior, part of the interracial Albemarle community.

In the final analysis, all these people demonstrate just how important conforming to behavioral norms was. But behaving properly did not mean acting totally subservient, as if a slave. In reality, respectable behavior was a bundle of attributes that whites, too, were expected to conform to if they were to be viewed as trustworthy and respected members of the neighborhood, community, or county. Embedded within this behavioral system was indeed a sense of social hierarchy, one that had a powerful racial component. Whites remained at the top of the hierarchy, black slaves at the bottom. But there existed de facto statuses between black slave and free white citizen. Some slaves were allowed to live as if free, hire themselves out, and even work to purchase their own freedom. This class of slaves-at-large functioned as the first step up the social hierarchy above the ordinary slave. Next was the status of free blacks. But even within the free black realm, there existed a number of gradations. The more successful, well-behaved, and respectable free people of color such as Daniel Goings and Stephen Byars experienced greater freedom than a propertyless and new-to-town male free black apprentice who lacked community ties might have. They, too, occupied another de facto status that allowed them to gain informally some of the privileges of whiteness.

Albemarle County, from its founding to the Civil War, was a county dedicated to slavery. The county was home to thousands of slaves, who made up close to half of the population at any given time. The county was also home to a small but ever-increasing class of free blacks, growing from fewer than two hundred in 1780 to over six hundred in 1860. All residents of Albemarle—white slaveholder, white worker, slave, free person of color—lived and worked in a place where daily contact was the norm. Social and economic activity that involved both whites and blacks represented a major part of lived experience for most Albemarle residents. Free people of color and even slaves had names and faces, a sense of knownness that attached to them. This highly personal face-to-face culture created the space in which the likes of James Munroe, Stephen Byars, William Swingler, and Daniel Goings maneuvered and sometimes thrived. These free people of color often acted and lived in ways that contradicted notions of a strictly enforced color line in which blackness was equated with slavery and only whites could be free.

4

"I'll Show You What a Free Negro Is"

Black-on-White Violence in Albemarle

So far, this study has examined the life experiences of a number of people of color in Albemarle, men and women, young and old. Whether male or female, light-skinned or not, all of these people successfully navigated the social system in a rural antebellum southern county. None acted as if they lived in a police state that saw their presence as a threat to the racial and social order. They did not hide; they participated openly in the community. Their face-to-face interactions with area whites often displayed a fairly high level of familiarity and even intimacy and at times even demonstrated a rough sense of practical equality. These free people of color rarely complied with residency and registration laws. Yet they did not act as recluses, avoiding whites and community institutions. All saw the judicial system as a useful tool for settling disputes. They did not live impoverished and pathetic lives in semi-seclusion from the white and slave communities. Yes, the racially based slave system of the antebellum South was predicated upon a racial and social hierarchy, and free people of color found themselves located near the bottom end of that scale. But they did not live quiet and marginal lives avoiding white surveillance.

Though denied the vote and unable to serve on juries, Albemarle's free people of color participated rather fully in the social and economic aspects of county life. They often visited the same bawdy houses as whites. The two races mingled at houses of entertainment, engaging in gaming and drinking. They shopped in local mercantile establishments and attended estate auctions throughout the county. Free people of color had credit extended to them by neighbors and businesses and occasionally themselves acted as creditors. They entered into contracts with neighbors, both black and white.

They demonstrated great freedom of movement within and without the immediate vicinity, traveling to Charlottesville and hamlets throughout the county, as well as locations as far away as Richmond, Lynchburg, and even other states. And they also routinely bought and sold land.

Clearly, property was seen as a very important tool to protect freedom and ensure that freedom's benefits were passed on from generation to generation. Most of the people this book has examined managed to chart an upward trend in property ownership over a two- or three-generation period, some with much more success than others. But property ownership was not the only key to a secure and comfortable life in the slave South. Indeed, for all of the people examined so far, property may have been of secondary importance. Most vital for a secure existence in Albemarle was being known, preferably as someone who was hardworking and respectable. In such a local and personal environment, avoiding contact with whites would have constituted a self-imposed, self-reinforcing imprisonment. Participating in the community and developing a respectable reputation, by contrast, helped ensure that free people of color would live safely and comfortably in the community.

The Battles, Goings, and Barnett families endured and even succeeded in Albemarle because they were not strange free blacks living on the edges of society. They were community members who in public behaved appropriately. They were cognizant and respectful of the social hierarchy. They worked hard and deported themselves properly. Respectability was defined by a diverse group of social qualities. One need not demonstrate every characteristic to achieve respectability. These qualities included being known in one's neighborhood (having a name attached to a face), working hard, living publicly as a family (husband, wife, and children), behaving with discretion, and faithfully honoring financial and personal obligations. As highlighted in chapter 1, the lives of the Revolutionary War veterans Shadrach Battles and Charles Barnett demonstrate that a free person of color could lack one or more of those qualities and still fare well. Other free black Battles and Barnett family members were commonly known as hardworking and faithful community members. All honored financial and personal obligations. Their personal qualities enhanced by enduring ownership of real and personal property, these free people of color managed to exist comfortably in the slave South. Here, "being known by your neighborhood" refers to the ability of community members to identify an individual by both name and geographic location. For example, county records sometimes make just such an indication: "John Goings of Shadwell." Not only did people know John Goings's name, but they could situate him residentially, understanding what neighborhood he lived in and also implicitly evincing knowledge about who his neighbors were.

As aggregate evidence from around the South suggests, successful free black property owners were a minority. Most free people of color in Albemarle and elsewhere owned little property and shared assets within an extended family. Together, these extended families farmed land that was often mediocre at best; additionally, some worked as skilled craftsmen, while others hired themselves out as common laborers. Some owned small plots of land, and others likely rented the land they worked. Poor whites living in rural areas faced similar problems, and many likewise lacked the ability to pull themselves out of poverty. Those free people of color who did not manage to so acquire and pass on property to descendants represent the majority of free blacks in the rural antebellum South. Do their lives suggest that the experiences of people such as the Barnetts and Battleses were exceptional? To be sure, not everyone successfully maneuvered in the highly personal culture of rural Albemarle. What about those people of color whose behavior caught the unfavorable attention of white law enforcement or whose property ownership remained far more modest? The patterns that emerge in studying those less successful people of color provide a fuller picture of how free blacks participated in an interracial community.[1]

In November 1845, the free person of color Thomas Goings was arrested and charged with violently assaulting a white man, Richard W. Durrett. Durrett was a farmer in the county who owned over one thousand acres of land. His family had lived in the county since well before the Revolution.[2] On the day of Goings's arraignment, the situation looked dire for the accused. Thomas Goings had been arrested, and a panel of five white justices of the peace had convened as a called court of oyer and terminer to try the defendant. The prominent white attorney Egbert R. Watson appeared as counsel for Goings. The court wasted no time, agreeing that Goings should be tried for the assault. They sent the case to the Circuit Superior Court of Law and Chancery. Watson, acting as attorney for the defense, appealed to the court to have his client admitted to bail. This would have made Thomas Goings eligible for release if he could post sufficient bond guaranteeing his appearance for the court case. The court, however, overruled Watson's request, and instead Thomas Goings found himself remanded to jail to await trial.

No white patron had stepped forward to offer security for Goings. At this point, the court was handling charges of black-on-white violence just as a supposedly rigid racial hierarchy demanded. Under such a system, no person of color, slave or free, could verbally or physically confront a white person; such behavior would threaten the very fabric of society. In fact, Virginia law made it quite clear how such cases were to be handled. In 1823, the legislature passed a law stating, "If a slave or free Negro shall wilfully assault and beat a white person with an intention to kill, on conviction he shall be punished by stripes at the discretion of the jury or court, and moreover, be banished from the United States forever. If such convict at any time shall return, he shall suffer death without benefit of clergy."[3]

What was to follow during the next six months after Goings's incarceration, however, did not conform to those expectations at all. A host of witnesses were called to testify or give information, including a slave, several white men, and free people of color. The court treated each witness mainly as a community member and observer of the dispute. Almost all of the witnesses, white and black, had been together at the time of the alleged assault. No one seems to have thought that such an assembly of people from such vastly different social and racial ranks was unusual or dangerous. Instead, the testimony reveals just how unremarkable such gatherings appeared to Albemarle residents.[4]

On a November night in 1845, two men had just finished harvesting their crops of corn. They were neighbors. One, a white man named Richard Durrett, would become the alleged victim of an assault by Thomas Goings. The other, the free man of color Noah Tate, was Durrett's neighbor and Thomas Goings's brother-in-law. Both Tate and Durrett were property-owning farmers who found themselves that fall with a crop in need of harvesting. Neither man felt he could handle his crop alone, so as neighbors, they decided to team up and hire people to help them with both the harvest and the shucking. Such decisions were common among farmers throughout America. Neighbors shared or pooled resources at critical times such as harvest.[5]

Durrett and Tate hired anyone and everyone they could—friends, neighbors, and any laborer who was available to come to their aid, including slaves hiring themselves out as well as free black laborers. Such gatherings were an annual event wherever corn or wheat was planted in the South. Durrett and

Tate hired several local free men of color, including Thomas Goings and his brothers and also a number of self-hiring slaves.

The yearly gatherings for the harvest and shucking of corn that happened across the county not only functioned as periods of intense labor; they often involved a fair measure of play as well. In particular, the corn shucking was an all-night event, preferably on a cloudless evening with a full moon. Everyone gathered: white farmers, their families, their slaves (if they owned any), their neighbors, and hired help (black and white, slave and free). Usually, some sort of feast was prepared. A bonfire was lit in the early evening, and liquor passed around frequently, the men both black and white alternating between shucking and drinking around the fire.[6]

It was just such a gathering at which Thomas Goings had allegedly assaulted a white man. Noah Tate, the cosponsor of that eventful corn shucking, testified that he was in Richard Durrett's house at the time of the assault. "Durrett came in saying someone had thrown something at his house," he continued, "There had been three dollars of liquor drunk, and Durrett had been drinking, but all seemed in good spirits right up till the affray." Tate's testimony suggests that, for most of the participants, drink may have been the expected reward for a job well done. But Tate further indicated that Durrett had been drinking elsewhere before the shucking and had consumed a lot of liquor. He was surely fairly intoxicated at the time of the alleged assault. The slave Colin corroborated Noah Tate's testimony, indicating that Durrett had been "drinking a good deal."[7]

The court testimony described a fairly typical fall scene in agricultural areas. Everyone gathered, worked hard, and made sure to take time out for celebration. The Durrett-Tate shucking started out following this very traditional pattern. A rough interracial social intermingling existed at these events. But the testimony also suggests how an alcohol-soaked evening could suddenly take a turn for the worse. After Durrett came into the house complaining about someone having thrown an object at his house, he returned to the crowd outside shucking corn next to the bonfire. Noah Tate had followed Durrett out the door, thinking an altercation was likely and telling the gathering to ignore him. Tate, a man of color, felt free to advise a mixed crowd to ignore a white man and demonstrated no qualms about giving damaging testimony regarding that white man's behavior. Tate concluded by stating that after the alleged assault, Thomas Goings and several other free blacks continued to work.[8]

Who was in that crowd that surrounded Richard Durrett when he came storming out of his house? Paschal Gentry, a local white man of some property whose family had lived in the area since the founding of the county in the first half of the eighteenth century, was there, for he gave eyewitness testimony. Gentry, a white man, failed to mention race at all and never once suggested that an interracial gathering of this sort was unusual, troubling, or even worthy of notice. Gentry addressed the altercation, stating that it started after "someone told Noah Tate to go in the house and get some liquor which he did." For Gentry, the sight of a free black man walking into a white neighbor's house to get some alcohol elicited no reaction. Gentry continued, stating that "[Tate] had been there [in Durrett's house] a little while when Mr. Durrett's son called out and said his father was knocked down." Again, Gentry seemed unsurprised. He did not rush to defend his fellow white, whose racial superiority had supposedly just been questioned. His testimony suggested that Mr. Durrett found himself on the ground more because of his heavy drinking than from any assault. Gentry, however, did explain just who was in the "crowd" that surrounded Richard Durrett when he started bellowing about someone's throwing an object at his house. It was "Tom, Billy, and Jim Goings [who] surrounded Durrett."[9]

Thomas, William, and James Goings were all young free men of color who had been hired to work the Durrett-Tate corn shucking. They were brothers, sons of the Revolutionary War veteran Sherod Goings Sr. Thomas Goings and his brothers, hired by their white neighbor Willis Dunn, had spent the daylight hours together repairing a schoolhouse, leaving this work in the afternoon. Only the testimony of the slave Colin ever referred to the Goingses or to Noah Tate as free people of color. Every other witness, white and black, described the incident through the names of each individual actor: Mr. Dowell, Noah Tate, Tom Goings, and so on. No one, however, applied "Mr." to anyone not white—the hierarchy still existed. The Goings brothers, young men who had already worked a full day, came to the corn shucking expecting to have a good time. The ex-slave John Spencer, remembering his youth as a slave in King George County, Virginia, said, "They always selected a bright moonlight [night] for the shucking. A week or more from the time, the news began to spread around when it was going to be; and as soon as it was dark, the neighbors began to drop in. . . . The shucking would last until late in the night, but after all the corn was shucked, they had a feast." Another slave remembered that they "would pass de jug around too. Den dey sho' could work and dat pile'd just vanish."[10]

Tate, Durrett, the Goings brothers, and everyone else in attendance was at Richard Durrett's house for the same reason, and all went according to plan for much of the night. The witness William Dowell's words capture the conviviality of the corn shucking. The corn was shucked, liquor was consumed by all, and "all seemed friendly and in good behavior until the quarrel." So what went wrong that November evening? According to Dowell, "someone unintentionally threw a piece of corn or an ear against the window of Mr. Durrett's house." Next, "Durrett came out and inquired who done it." Dowell described the assault as happening immediately after Durrett asked who had thrown the corn—"when Durrett was knocked down by the prisoner [Thomas Goings]."

William Dowell, a white man who had just witnessed a free black man confronting a white man at that white man's house, did not sound any alarm, as he would have if he had feared that the racial order was being challenged. He did not rush to defend Durrett's superior status, nor did he seek out a sheriff to arrest the free black Thomas Goings. Instead, Dowell stopped shucking momentarily and walked over to get the piece of wood with which Goings had allegedly hit Durrett. Dowell "took the piece of scantling and threw it into the fire, knowing it would be necessary to have it in court [to convict Goings of assault], [and] thought the matter would not go any further." William Dowell saw Thomas Goings as a neighbor who had engaged in a drunken argument with another neighbor, Durrett. Dowell felt that liquor, and in particular Richard Durrett's belligerent drunkenness, was the root cause of the dispute, and after "Noah Tate seemed to make peace," everyone calmed down and returned to the corn shucking. Even Thomas Goings's behavior after the altercation suggests that no one was concerned about a perceived threat to the racial order. Goings did not flee in terror. He simply sat down and returned to shucking corn for Tate and Dowell.[11]

The one enslaved person to testify in the assault case, a slave named Colin, the property of Elizabeth Salmon, was the only witness to mention the race of any of the participants. And the details his testimony provides flesh out the story more completely. Through the eyes of Colin, the easygoing interracial quality of the corn shucking becomes visible, yet so does the social hierarchy that slaves and free people of color sometimes chafed under. Colin's account also brings to light again the importance of familiarity and reputation to black freedom. His testimony was the only one to dramatize the events that unfolded that November night. He vacillated between a dramatic interpretation that painted Durrett in a favorable light while simultaneously describing Thomas Goings as a bit of a brute and what was more likely the reality: that the confrontation between Durrett and Goings happened in a haze of alcohol and after both men had had a long day.[12]

Colin acknowledged, as every other witness did, that someone threw a piece of corn that hit Durrett's house. Colin's memory of Durrett's reaction, however, was different from others': "Durrett came to the corn pile with a shovel in hand, threatening and demanding to know who threw the corn." Suddenly, race for the first time inserted itself into the testimony in the case. According to Colin, a free black named Taylor shouted in response: "Dammit I did not do it." Colin elaborated on Durrett's remarks, stating that Durrett "offered a dollar to anyone who will tell him who threw the corn." Colin next testified that Durrett said that he "intends to no longer have free negroes working here."

At that moment, the Goings brothers stopped shucking corn and approached Durrett. A series of unfortunate drunken actions and statements had suddenly escalated into a confrontation oozing with the potential for violence. For Durrett and the Goingses, the party was suddenly over. Colin continued, stating that "the defendant Thomas Going [*sic*] walked up to Durrett, said he 'never seen a free negro and that he'd show him [Durrett] what a free negro was' and struck him [Durrett] with some scantling he picked up from the ground which knocked him [Durrett] down." In dramatic fashion, Colin elaborated on the piece of wood used—"a stout piece of wood about four or five feet in length and tolerably thick."[13]

Thomas Goings, in confronting Richard Durrett that November evening, had shown that he felt completely free to assert his freedom without stint. He simply did not recognize Durrett's claim to superiority. His literal blow to Durrett's head was for Thomas Goings also a figurative blow at the pretensions of a drunkard that were based solely on race. Most notably, Thomas Goings willingly confronted a white man and does not seem to have imagined that such inflammatory words and deeds would provoke a violent white response—and in fact, they did not draw any sort of response from the whites at the gathering. As individuals who happened to be situated in the upper reaches of the racial hierarchy, they did not see a dangerous and violent free black threatening their control. Instead, they saw a neighbor who happened to be socially inferior engage in fisticuffs with another neighbor who, though their social equal, had committed an insulting act. They all saw the affray as a "boys will be boys" event that had been fueled by alcohol. Every person involved, for those white witnesses, was also a person with a name connected to a face.

For Thomas Goings, the months that passed between that November night and the day in May 1846 when the verdict was announced were difficult ones. Yes, Thomas had found counsel, which in itself was evidence of a measure of community inclusion. A well-connected white lawyer agreed to defend him—for a fee, of course—in a case in which he was charged with assaulting a white man. But Thomas may have lacked more intimate connection to a large number of whites who could or would vouch for him. As a result, the arraignment for Thomas Goings was the beginning of a months-long incarceration. His lawyer's appeal to have him admitted to bail was summarily rejected by the officers of the court. This alone would amount to a form of punishment—six months in jail between his arraignment and the conclusion of his trial, because the Circuit Superior Court of Law met in a given county only once every six months.

Thomas Goings had little to encourage him when he entered the courthouse on that spring day. He had been charged with a felony, his appeal to be admitted to bail had been denied, and he had spent six long months in jail. At a minimum, local precedent suggested that Goings could expect at least fifteen lashes at the public whipping post, if not years of incarceration in the state penitentiary. After all, this was a case about a free black assaulting a white man, a white man who was on his own property at the time of the alleged violent attack. His clubbing of Durrett could easily be seen as a brutal challenge to white male mastery; witnesses even testified that Goings said he struck the blow to vindicate his rights as a free black man.[14]

But on May 20, 1846, the local court did not follow state law in the trial of Thomas Goings on charges of assault and attempted murder of a white man. After initially forming a called court of oyer and terminer as state law directed in criminal cases involving free back defendants, a jury was instead convened to adjudge the case and ruled that Thomas Goings was "NOT GUILTY." No angry white mob waited outside the courthouse after the verdict, even though Thomas Goings had "forgotten his place." How could this outcome have occurred? The judge and jury who acquitted Goings may have felt that he had been punished enough already, having served six months in the county jail. But the combined weight of the testimony in the case suggests something else. Richard Durrett's doctor had testified that "he examined the wound, and has found two gashes running parallel and extending from the top of the forehead to the top of the head, also another running across the two above mentioned."[15]

But Dr. Mallory had gone on to undermine fatally Durrett's claims about the assault: "[Dr. Mallory] thinks it very strange that the weapon alleged to have been used (which he has never seen) could have produced such a wound." But Mallory was not yet finished sabotaging the case against Thomas Goings. He even suggested that most of the pain Richard Durrett continued to suffer from had nothing to do with the alleged assault: "Mr. Durrett complains a good deal from pain on the back of his neck produced from corn which loosened his teeth but did not otherwise injure them." According to Dr. Mallory, Richard Durrett's discomfort stemmed from eating corn, not from a beating at the hands of a free black. Offering a neat coda to his testimony, Dr. Mallory dismissively stated: "think he [Durrett] will recover."[16]

The combined testimony failed to paint a picture of a violent assault that threatened racial hierarchy or white male mastery. Instead, the testimony indicated, first, that Richard W. Durrett was a heavy drinker who was acting foolishly. Second, most witnesses felt that tempers had flared momentarily and resulted in a drunken tussle best forgotten. Last, the testimony suggests that all witnesses viewed the key participants, Noah Tate, Richard Durrett, and Thomas Goings, as known quantities, neighbors, people who interacted on a regular basis. Thus, the white witness William Dowell had decided to quickly destroy the evidence, tossing into the bonfire the piece of wood that Goings allegedly had used as a club. No threat to the racial order was seen as having occurred. The Goings brothers, as young itinerant laborers in the county, were part of a rough and rowdy culture. Thomas Goings's response to a heated argument had allegedly been to club his adversary with a large stick. He was ultimately acquitted because all who were involved in the case saw the assault, if it actually happened at all, as a commonplace event at a gathering of common men, especially one that involved consumption of liquor—particularly since no serious injuries occurred.

Another participant in that November 1845 corn shucking also provides evidence about the nature of Albemarle's racial hierarchy and the highly personal social network within which it was situated. Thomas Goings's brother William, one of the free men of color who had initially surrounded Richard Durrett, had far less positive contact with the judicial system. William Goings, too, participated in this tough, predominantly lower-class culture. He and an extended family of Goingses lived together on a cluster of family farms in the county. William, like his brother Thomas, was well-known in the area. He, too, had a confrontation with a white man. But this incident was vastly different, and his fate was decided not by the color of his victim, but in part by his own reputation. In fact, William Goings spent his free life in Albemarle slowly destroying the family reputation for respectability that his father, Sherod Goings Sr., had worked so hard to establish, starting in the eighteenth century.

On July 5, 1850, Albemarle authorities charged William with murdering a white man, Woodson K. Hall. According to state law dating back to 1831, a black man like Goings should have been tried in a court of oyer and terminer within ten days. But William Goings was not arrested and jailed until March 1851, even though he almost immediately became a prime suspect, and he received a jury trial as well. For eight months after the murder, William Goings continued to live as a free black farmer in northern Albemarle County.

Interestingly, though the case involved a free man of color openly possessing a firearm and then allegedly using that firearm to commit a premeditated murder of a white man, the neighborhood and the county did not find themselves polarized along racial lines. All who testified spoke of the homicide as tragic, but characterized the incident as one involving a conflict between neighbors. Demonstrating rather clearly that the trial would not proceed as a swift and retributive reassertion of racial order, sixteen white men were called as witnesses for William Goings. They included a list of surnames that had appeared at the Thomas Goings trial and were clearly familiar both in the neighborhood and to generations of Goingses: Dunn, Gentry, Dowell, Catterton, and others. Nine witnesses were summoned to testify for the prosecution, including two free blacks and a slave.

Yet in this trial, unlike that of Thomas Goings, nearly every piece of testimony, from either white or black witnesses, made mention of race. The first witness to testify for the commonwealth was Brightberry Gardner, a white yeoman farmer and neighbor of both William Goings and Woodson K. Hall, whom Gardner identified as a farmer with a family who also owned a small general store in the neighborhood.[17] Gardner testified that Woodson Hall had disappeared on Wednesday, July 3. By Friday, Gardner, Hall's wife, and a man referred to in the testimony only as Mr. Campbell had all become very concerned about Hall. They went to Hall's store and broke in to see whether he was there. They did not find him. Now Gardner "felt uneasy and proposed to him [Campbell] to make a search around deceased's house in the thicket, was accompanied by Mr. Campbell, Mr. Gentry, and [a] coloured fellow named Spinner." Whereas in the 1845 trial, no one except one slave ever mentioned the race of Thomas Goings and other free blacks, now in 1850, color appeared explicitly. Gardner continued: "[We] were working & conversing about blacks & recollect the report of a gun."[18]

Yet the picture these white men painted of their rural neighborhood in Albemarle is far from one of racial separation and antagonism. For instance, the free black Garland Spinner helped the two whites with the search for Hall. Further, Gardner's testimony sheds light on the racially integrated residential pattern found in their neighborhood. Following a set of tracks left by a man and a dog, the search party came to a plot of land owned by Zachariah Brock. They searched Brock's field but found nothing. Gardner "thought [the tracks were left by] Hall, as he had a dog." Adjacent to Zachariah Brock's field, the search continued. The free man of color Garland Spinner, "after turning about 10 or 15 paces cried out 'here he is,' [and the party] discovered from the wound on the left side that [Hall] had been shot." Neighbors, both black and white, came together and formed an impromptu search party that found Woodson K. Hall's body.[19]

The search party then split up to inform local authorities about the crime. The records do not say who sat with the body until the next evening, waiting for the county coroner to arrive. In the meantime, Gardner had time to assess the evidence at the scene of the crime. In his testimony, he gladly offered a general theory: "There were three or four shots in the body . . . from the appearance of the wound & c. supposed the assassin stood in the path. . . . The bushes [where the body was found] were thick but very stubby. Could see a man through them, almost at any distance from his knees up, from the path, saw no evidence of a scuffle . . . seemed to have been going in the direction of the prisoner's house." The next evening, the sixth of July, the county coroner, Dr. Bibb, arrived, examined the body, and removed one slug from Hall's body. Gardner's testimony also situated the crime scene spatially in the neighborhood: "Prisoner [William Goings] lives in the woods on the land belonging to Zach Brock. Prisoner lived about 1/2 mile from the place body was found. Hall rented some land from Brock & had a cornfield about 200 yards from where body was found." Hall, a white man, had rented land from a free person of color.[20]

Fascinatingly, Brightberry Gardner failed to sound any sort of cautionary note in his testimony about a free black possessing a firearm. As early as 1806, the Virginia legislature had weighed in on free black gun possession, stating that "a free Negro is not to carry any firelock of any kind without a license. For a second offense he shall in addition to forfeiting all such arms be punished with stripes, at the discretion of the justice not exceeding thirty-nine." That law had stood for more than a quarter of a century when the Nat Turner Rebellion in Southampton County shocked the nation. In the wake of that bloody but unsuccessful slave revolt, the Virginia legislature in 1832 replaced the 1806 act with a stricter law, declaring that "free Negroes are not to carry firelocks of any kind, under penalty of thirty-nine lashes. Permission heretofore granted authorizing justices to permit slaves and free Negroes to carry firearms is in some cases repealed."[21]

Clearly, some white Virginians after Nat Turner's uprising were deeply concerned about blacks possessing weapons, but even the legislature left wiggle room for county-level officials by only repealing permission "in some cases." Gardner's failure to acknowledge any danger in William Goings having a gun suggests that Goings represented just such a case. A survey of local criminal presentments supports that theory. Despite evidence that some free blacks openly possessed guns, no person of color was ever charged or tried under that statute up to that time. Gardner and other Albemarle whites may have seen the law as applying to dangerous free blacks who lived elsewhere in the commonwealth, not to the likes of well-recognized neighbors Zachariah Brock and William Goings.[22]

Someone, however, did mention state laws and William Goings's apparent violation of them: John Goings, who also lived in the neighborhood, on his father Henderson Goings's farm. Henderson was William Goings's brother. Woodson K. Hall's body was found at the base of the mountain upon which Henderson Goings's farm was located. In his testimony, John Goings stated that he knew Woodson K. Hall and had seen him only a week before he was murdered. John Goings was summoned because of an encounter he had had with the defendant, William Goings, earlier that week: "On Wednesday preceding the murder, I was on my way to Mr. Davis about 100 yards from where the body was found. I met the prisoner [William Goings] with a gun. He told me 'Howdy' and asked me not to tell any one that he [*sic*] had seen him with a gun. I made no stop. I said I saw he was squirrel hunting."[23]

But that was not the only meeting John Goings had with William Goings that week and not the only one in which William brandished a firearm: "On Friday the day dec'd was killed I was at work in Mr. Davis field with his Mr. D's sons," John Goings testified. "On going to the spring I saw Prisoner [William Goings] setting down near the fence near Zach Brock's with a Gun. He was about 200 yards from where body was found and near the road a person could see any one passing from where I was, along the road. Prisoner told me again not to tell anyone that he had a gun." John Goings continued, suggesting that William Goings had possessed a firearm for quite some time and was seen regularly using it: "I heard the gun fire in the direction of the place where Hall was found. And I observed 'there was someby [somebody] with empty gun in his hand looking up the tree.' Alluding to a squirrel or something begin [being] killed. Prisoner has told me not to tell white people about his having a gun over & often at least 20 times."[24]

Commenting on William Goings's longtime firearms possession, John Goings also demonstrated at least a basic knowledge of laws concerning free blacks, stating that "colored people were not allowed to carry a Gun." By the time of this 1850 trial, the tenor of race relations had indeed changed in some ways. Both white and black witnesses made explicit mention of the race of some of the people involved in the case. John Goings's testimony suggests that the gap between state law and local practice may have narrowed at least as far as gun possession was concerned. But his testimony also reveals that daily interaction between whites and free people of color was the norm. John Goings had spent the previous week employed by his neighbor John Davis, working Davis's fields with Davis's two sons.[25]

John Goings's testimony also suggests that the gap between state law concerning racial control and actual local practices still remained and offered a surprising amount of flexibility. Both John Goings and William Goings understood that free people of color were no longer allowed to carry firearms. But William Goings had not stolen the gun. He had not surreptitiously come into possession of it, and he had owned it for quite some time. John Goings stated that he had seen the defendant with a gun "a hundred times." And John Goings also knew where William Goings had managed to get the weapon: "He got the gun from Linkard Shiflett." A white neighbor had sold the gun to a free black man.[26]

Surely, if John Goings had seen William Goings carrying and using the gun at least one hundred times, and had had dozens of conversations with

Williams about squirrel hunting and his illicit gun possession, others in the neighborhood besides John Goings and the white area resident Linkard Shiflett also knew that William Goings had the gun. At the time of the shooting on Friday, John Goings had heard shots fired but assumed it was someone out hunting. The sound of occasional gunfire was routine in rural areas. Local residents, white and black, regularly hunted for food.[27]

The day after the shooting, John Goings was out and about in the neighborhood. He came across Woodson K. Hall's wife and children. He termed them "much distressed," and "after hearing that Hall was killed, circumstance of having seen the Prisoner with Gun occurred to me & encited suspicion. And I told my mother about it first. Was summoned before the Justice committing Prisoner. Told him (Mr. Chapman) about it."

Reading through the combined testimony of several witnesses, William Goings begins to look as if he was a troubled or unpopular character in this northern Albemarle County neighborhood.[28] The white blacksmith Michael Catterton lived in the hamlet of Nortonsville, in the northern part of the county, over twenty miles from Charlottesville and only about two miles from William Goings's house. The court summoned Catterton's slave Bob as a witness. Bob testified that on the day that "Hall was killed, Prisoner [William Goings] came to where me and other men gernally [generally] slept at an outhouse or cabin to stay all night." Conditions for slaves such as Bob, living in a rural outpost such as Nortonsville, often were not pleasant. Bob and a number of other slaves and hirelings lived together in a shack next to Catterton's blacksmith's shop. These were cramped and crude accommodations: "I was fixing the pallet to lie down when Prisoner observed 'there was one damned Rascal out of the way.'" Bob said he responded, asking William Goings whom he was talking about. Goings then said: "I [Bob] would hear in a day or two." William Goings's oblique utterances to Bob sounded nearly like a confession. At least according to Bob's account, William also acted guilty: "before P. came to bed he sat out on the porch and seemed to be very restless & uneasy."[29]

By Sunday morning, William Goings was officially a suspect. He left Bob's Nortonsville cabin early in the morning and headed to the home of his white neighbor Ezekiel Wilhoit. A buzz about the murder had raced around this rural northern Albemarle neighborhood. A frenzied investigation ensued. On Tuesday morning, a Mr. White went to Goings's home to search for a key piece of evidence, the gun. Rumors had been circulating the neighborhood for days that William kept the gun hidden "between the logs of the House inside of the planks or weatherboarding." Once again, William Goings's possession of the firearm was something of an open secret in the area. What had been quiet common knowledge in the neighborhood was transformed into loud gossip and corroborating evidence in the wake of the murder.

White said that when he arrived at William Goings's home, Goings was asleep on top of some barrels outside. Mr. White immediately approached Goings and began to question him about the gun. Goings told White that "it was somewhere there." White repeated the question, but Goings replied that he "did not know what he [White] was talking about." White testified that William fleetingly admitted to him that he indeed possessed a gun, then denied it. As Goings lay sleepily on those barrels, White quickly searched the home and stated that, although he had heard that Goings kept a gun on a rack, White found only some buckshot.[30]

A crime such as murder, when occurring in a rural community like this one in northern Albemarle, would create quite a stir at any time. But this crime, with a free black man allegedly murdering a propertied white man and using a technically illegally possessed gun to do it, should have set off particular alarms. The combined weight of testimony and other archival evidence suggests that alarms did not sound because the community, both black and white, saw William Goings as a difficult but nonetheless familiar resident.

The community also knew that this was not the first time William Goings had had a confrontation with Woodson Hall. The white resident Willis Dunn testified that about a week before the shooting, he was sitting near the defendant and heard William tell "his own brother that Hall had prohibited him [William] from coming inside of his lot & that he (Hall) had better mind how he managed or he [William] would be the worse for him." At the time, the barely concealed threat of black-on-white violence elicited no panicked response from Dunn or anyone else who may have overheard that conversation.[31] Weeks before the murder, William Goings and Woodson Hall appeared to the community as disputatious neighbors, with Goings making vague threats implying violence.

According to John Goings, William had also had a conflict with his relatives. John Goings's own "mother [Agnes] & the women folk of the family [were] not on good terms" with William before Hall's murder. Chancery court records suggest that they may have been angry with William Goings over the suit he had filed at the beginning of 1850 that concerned distribution of property from the estates of two recently deceased relatives, his father Sherod Goings Sr. and his uncle Charles Goings. Existing records do not elaborate on why he filed suit, but the court ordered the land from both estates sold at public auction for the benefit of the heirs. For John's father, Henderson Goings, this may have represented a loss of land considered vital to the family's economic well-being.[32]

Henderson Goings and his family owned seventy-five acres of reasonably good farmland upon which they grew corn, oats, potatoes, and wheat. He and his wife, Agnes, owned over one hundred dollars' worth of livestock and nearly twenty dollars' worth of farm equipment. In a good year, Henderson, Agnes, and their children could produce upward of one hundred dollars in revenue through home manufactures and the sale of meat from slaughtered animals. As small farmers in the slave South, white or black, Henderson and Agnes Goings were by any definition successful.[33] William Goings, even before the murder trial, could hardly be described as successful. He may have watched Henderson's farm and family grow and thrive while he remained desperately poor and in debt despite inheriting land from their father, Sherod Sr.

As early as 1842, William Goings was becoming known in the community as something of a credit risk. In that year, he mortgaged his inherited land to guarantee payment of a fifty-seven-dollar debt to his white neighbor David Ballard. At that time, William Goings was viewed by at least one white person in the community as deserving of some confidence: the deed of trust on William's land was held by the white Albemarle resident Thomas Douglass. Since William Goings never appeared on county land tax lists as the owner of any property, it seems likely that he failed to pay Ballard and lost his inheritance. And Brightberry Gardner's testimony had said as much: "prisoner lives in the woods on the land belonging to Zach Brock [a free black property owner]."[34]

Surely William's forfeiting of both the literal land inheritance and the reputation bequeathed by their father created tension between the two sons. Henderson and William's relationship may have taken a turn for the worse when William lost his plot of land. Henderson Goings, however, understood how to behave and succeed in a rural community and achieved a measure of respectability. He successfully followed his father's example and may even have exceeded Sherod's successes. William Goings, however, was a failure by just about any measure. William, perhaps angered by the disparity between their lives and his own personal failures, may have used that lawsuit as a way to gain another opportunity for success.

William Goings may have been doing something similar with Woodson K. Hall, who owned and farmed a field next to William Goings's house. Hall also ran a mercantile business in the area. His shop was likely a key source of necessities for all the local residents, black and white. Establishing face-to-face relationships with all of his clientele, Hall extended lines of credit to many of his customers. After his murder in early December 1850, Hall's family set about the grim business of having his estate inventoried and appraised. That process yielded an account listing the names of borrowers and the amounts they owed. A number of free people of color who lived in the area were on that list. Hall's estate records also included a second account book listing all insolvent notes due to him. These were debts that were long overdue and probably uncollectable. Again, a number of local free people of color appeared on the list, including William Goings.[35]

Already a somewhat truculent neighbor, William Goings had repeatedly failed to honor financial obligations. Woodson K. Hall's accounts show that Goings had piled up debt for quite some time and had failed to pay any of it back; Hall had moved him to a list of people who no longer deserved a line of credit.

Just who was William Goings? In 1814, he was a twenty-one-year-old father who owned one horse. William continued to own little more than that one horse for the next two decades.[36] William Goings was born free in Albemarle in the 1790s, but never once appeared at the courthouse to register his freedom during his first three decades of life. Finally in 1828, he registered in Charlottesville. Other than his yearly appearance on the Fredericksville Parish personal property tax lists as a free mulatto owner of one horse, William Goings for the next few years returns to obscurity. By the 1830s, he resided in the northwestern portion of the county on a plot of land near the white farmer John Dunn's residence and near a number of other Goingses. Goings's family had grown to include five children by 1833.[37]

The 1850 murder case was not William Goings's first brush with the legal system in the county. Back in October 1847, Goings had been charged with "selling ardent spirits without a license." In the 1840s, whites and blacks alike often found themselves facing legal troubles as a result of alcohol production and sale, which remained common facets of life in rural agricultural communities such as Albemarle. The Charlottesville newspaper publisher James Alexander remembered that "all the stores in town sold ardent spirits and kept open doors on Sunday mornings till 10 o'clock to traffic and trade with the slaves." Everyone, white and black, slave and free, was given the opportunity to spend disposable income on spirits such as peach brandy and corn whiskey.[38]

Liquor consumption was a habit that crossed class boundaries as well. Planters were known to rise in the morning and pour themselves a julep, "a large glass of rum sweetened with sugar," before making daily rounds of the farm. They would return for breakfast and wash it down with hard cider. From lunchtime on, rum toddies were the beverage of choice for many planters. The lower sorts, including poor whites, free blacks, and slaves, were described by some local white elites as "averse to labor, much addicted to liquor, and when intoxicated extremely savage and revengeful."[39]

But by the 1830s, temperance had begun to emerge in Albemarle as a powerful reformist urge to oppose distilling, liquor sales, and drinking. By 1830, both the University of Virginia in Charlottesville and the county had active temperance societies. The temperance movement, combined with a general increase in denominational religious activity in the area, began to have an effect on Albemarle. Activist local ministers and devout elites in particular started to complain about vice and disorderly behavior. They saw liquor consumption as the root cause. By the 1840s, local law enforcement had responded, beginning to put more effort into controlling or eliminating vice. Arrests for gaming, selling liquor without a license, brawling, keeping houses of public entertainment, public drunkenness, and using profane language were more frequent from that point on.

A number of local whites as a result ran into legal troubles after 1830. Free people of color such as William Goings were not excepted from this rising crusade against vice. When William Goings was arrested in October 1847 on misdemeanor charges of selling "ardent spirits" without a license, his neighbor Mace P. Hall, a relative of William Goings's later nemesis Woodson K. Hall, appeared as a witness for the commonwealth. Goings, by selling his own whiskey, had become direct competition for the Hall store. The Halls, then, had a grievance against William Goings that may have continued up to the time of Hall's murder. Goings, in killing Hall, may have had that long train of friction on his mind. Hall's recent warning to William Goings about staying off his land, then, was only the last of a number of provocations between these two neighbors.[40]

Some testimony suggested that William Goings had planned a confrontation with Hall, if not the murder itself, possibly as much as a week in advance of the actual crime. He had waited in the woods along a path he knew Hall often took. When Hall appeared, Goings pulled out his gun and shot Hall repeatedly. But days after the crime, investigators had yet to find the murder weapon. Without the weapon, Goings would remain the prime suspect, but all of the evidence continued to be circumstantial and unlikely to result in a conviction, even for a free person of color accused of shooting a white man.

Brightberry Gardner had testified that the gun was not discovered at the time Hall was found, with his coat off and "smeared with blood." According to Gardner, Hall still "had on his shoes, shirt and pantaloons, his coat was lying near him." The day after the coroner arrived and conducted his examination, search parties in the area finally found what they were looking for. On the west side of the mountain where Goings and Hall lived, they found a pistol in the bushes, "near him [Hall], loaded." This may have been the same gun that several witnesses testified they had seen Goings carrying in plain sight along that well-traveled footpath in the neighborhood.[41]

The murder weapon had been found. All evidence pointed squarely at William Goings as the perpetrator. Despite the fact that a free black man had killed a white man, the community did not polarize along racial lines, with whites demanding justice and vengeance. Free people of color in the area did not feel it necessary to go into hiding. Instead, whites and blacks alike had worked to find Hall's body, discover the murder weapon, investigate the crime, and testify at the trial.

Even at court, no neat racial divide appeared. Nearly twenty white men who resided in the area were listed as witnesses for William Goings. Not a single free black relative or neighbor of Goings appeared to testify on his behalf. Whether testifying for the commonwealth or for William Goings, the witness list represented a laundry list of family names prevalent in that rural northern Albemarle County neighborhood. Almost all, whether black or white, were at most modest farmers. Only George Gentry and John Gentry, witnesses for William Goings, stand out as men from elite families in the county. William Goings's neighborhood was populated predominantly by nonelites, and his trial revolved mainly around their testimony.[42]

The trial concluded on May 27, 1851, almost eleven months after Woodson K. Hall had been found shot to death. The free man of color William Goings, a suspect from the beginning of the investigation back in July of the previous year, had at first been jailed but was later released on bond; he had spent several months free, awaiting trial. The county constables picked him up in March 1851 and confined him to the jail in preparation for the trial. The evidence against William was overwhelming. The murder weapon had been located, and witnesses verified that it was indeed one of the guns they had seen William Goings brandishing shortly before the murder. William Goings had an obvious motive, mired in debt to Woodson Hall and known by the community to have a grievance against the Hall family. Members of his own family testified against him. Witnesses stated that they had seen Goings in the vicinity of the murder shortly before the crime. One witness, the slave Bob, testified that William Goings had basically confessed to him, muttering, "there was one damned Rascal out of the way."[43]

Given the brutality of the crime and the overwhelming evidence against William Goings, a guilty verdict seemed inevitable, and it came. But remarkably, on May 27, 1851, the jury found William Goings guilty only of second-degree murder. By being convicted of a lesser charge, Goings avoided capital punishment. Despite his apparent violation of the racial order, the community felt no need to send Goings to the gallows. Instead, the court sentenced him to eighteen years in the state penitentiary. True, the community sent William Goings to jail for what might well amount to the remainder of his life. But Goings had murdered another member of the community. His violent behavior had severed those cords of community inclusion that created a space for comfortable living. William Goings had failed spectacularly to behave in a respectable manner. Whatever remained of his reputation disappeared with the murder. In the eyes of the community, he had become untrustworthy and violent.

Even so, Goings received what seems to have been a fair trial. He was not threatened with extralegal violence. Whites did not see in Goings's murder of Hall a terrible portent of race war. They likewise essentially ignored the evidence that Goings possessed a gun in clear violation of the statutes. The court also did not pursue any sort of charges against Linkard Shiflett for selling the gun to Goings. No one in Albemarle evidently evinced concern about a person of color in the neighborhood possessing a gun. Even as a convicted murderer, William Goings benefited from being a known person in Albemarle. Convicting Goings of only second-degree murder, the jury appears to have judiciously examined all the evidence in the case and determined that Goings had sought out Hall in premeditated fashion, but only to confront him. The shooting had not been planned, but was the result of what must have been a heated conversation. The murder was still, first and foremost, a dispute between neighbors.[44]

Was the failure of the court to make an issue of William Goings's firearm possession simply an exception to some general policy of tight enforcement of proscriptive laws concerning free blacks? Or does the Goings case suggest that the law concerning free black gun possession was actually routinely ignored? A survey of criminal cases in the county over an eighty-year period suggests the latter. Only two cases exist between 1789 and 1865 that concern free black firearm possession.

The first case, in 1842, involved an alleged assault on a white man that involved a free black. Benjamin Johnson was charged with having "assisted in an assault against the said yeoman William Hayes . . . having a gun in his possession at the time of the affray." The altercation had initially arisen between William Hayes and another white farmer, William W. Wallace, and Johnson had intervened in some way on Wallace's behalf. Three days after he was charged with the crime, Johnson appeared in court and filed a one-hundred-dollar recognizance, promising that he would be "of good behavior toward the Commonwealth and all its citizens." Two white yeomen, James H. Bailey and Samuel Wallace (likely William W. Wallace's brother), came in with him and also filed one-hundred-dollar recognizances as surety for Johnson's keeping of the peace.[45]

Apparently, the gun-possession charge was dropped. Johnson was not arrested, much less incarcerated. The court records do not indicate how or why the charges evaporated or what Johnson might have told the court, but the case was discharged after Johnson, Bailey, and Wallace filed recognizances. Evidently, the only reason the court entertained the charge at all was as a result of the assault, not of the gun possession. The court saw nothing unusual in the conflict—rural neighbors, black and white, interacted on an almost daily basis and sometimes fought. Benjamin Johnson, after participating in an assault on a white man, was treated by the court in exactly the same fashion as a white person charged with assault would have been. He was a free man and as such was simply required to file a peace bond guaranteeing his good behavior. The court's primary concern seems to have been the general one of maintaining the peace of the community.[46]

The only other instance of a free person of color charged with carrying a firearm in violation of the law occurred in 1857. This case, too, came to the attention of the court not because white residents were alarmed by a free black possessing a gun, but because a pair of actual assaults had occurred. First, on the night of June 19, the white resident John W. Wheat and his free black neighbor William Farrar assaulted William F. Plunket, a white man. Apparently, these three men had some sort of running dispute. The court entertained Plunket's complaint in June, making Farrar and Wheat file fifty-dollar peace recognizances and additional fifty-dollar securities, standard practice in assault cases. But Plunket returned in September with more complaints. That time, Plunket alerted the court that "he had reason to believe that William Farrar a free negro kept & carried about his person fire arms to wit a pistol." Worse still, Plunket charged that Farrar, along with his accomplice John Wheat, had assaulted him yet again on the evening of September 17.[47]

Once again, it was the assault that precipitated the charges. Slave patrollers and constables did not sound any alarms or step up enforcement. First the court ordered William Farrar to file a one-hundred-dollar recognizance guaranteeing his appearance in court a couple of weeks later. The white resident John T. Barksdale secured the funds for Farrar. Then the court tried him, but only for assault. The weapons charge simply vanished. Farrar was found guilty by a called court and sentenced to twenty lashes at the public whipping post. Farrar immediately filed an appeal and, with the help of James W. Widderfield, a white man, filed another recognizance guaranteeing his appearance at the appeal. The court once again ignored state law and allowed the appeal.

Even in 1857, a free black who illegally possessed a firearm and who participated in two assaults on white men did not set off alarms. Local whites who knew William Farrar came to his aid legally and financially. The gun-possession infraction was simply ignored by the court. Since this was Farrar's second arrest for assault on Plunket in several months, he was sent to the whipping post. But a gun-owning (if not gun-toting) free black man, working in concert with a white man, had allegedly assaulted another white man not once, but twice, and all he suffered was twenty lashes. Neither the court nor the community acted as if Farrar's actions were unusual or alarming.[48]

Further evidence helps to highlight just how permissive Albemarle may have been concerning free blacks possessing guns. As discussed earlier, back in 1806, the free man of color Zachariah Bowles had petitioned the county court for permission to "make use of firearms." The court complied, permitting Bowles to carry and use a gun. He was not alone. In 1829, the court granted permission to "keep and carry a gun and powder until further notice" to the free man of color Henry Barnett. Being known by the community as respectable property-owning residents may have played an important role for both Zachariah Bowles and Henry Barnett. As documented earlier, Zachariah Bowles was a successful free black farmer who owned his own land. Henry Barnett owned over one hundred acres of land on Mechum's River, eleven miles west of Charlottesville. Alongside those two, who sought formal permission, however, there were numerous free men of color who owned guns without ever seeking permission.[49]

Perhaps the most powerful evidence about the casual acceptance of free black gun possession in Albemarle comes from a different source. William Goings was not the only member of his family to openly possess a firearm. A sibling, Charles Goings, also owned a gun. Charles Goings, like William Goings, may have benefited from being born into a family that already owned property and was widely known and respected in the county. Charles, however, managed to make sure that this reputation endured. In 1825, Charles had reached his majority. He was a twenty-four-year-old man of color. His uncle Joshua Goings gave him a ninety-five acre plot of land located nineteen miles northwest of Charlottesville. Charles Goings thus became an independent and propertied farmer. He lived in the same hilly and poorer farming region occupied by certain other free blacks: Sherod Goings, William Goings, Henderson Goings, and Zachariah Brock, among others.[50]

When Commissioner of the Revenue Ira Harris came to Charles Goings's farm to conduct the state-mandated colonization census in 1833, Harris listed Goings as a thirty-two-year-old farmer who had been born free in Albemarle and lived alone on his farm. That same year, however, personal property tax returns indicated that Charles lived on his farm with at least two sons. Two years later, Goings, to formalize the status of his growing family, married the free woman of color Matilda Middlebrook in a Methodist ceremony. By 1840, he was the head of a farming household that included one free colored female between the ages of ten and twenty-four and two free colored female children under ten years of age. Throughout the 1830s, Charles remained a modest but reasonably successful farmer. He owned little more than his land, a horse or two, and a few head of cattle. Charles Goings never once had his freedom registered. He felt no need to obtain paper proof of his free status. But he was an active participant in the community who evinced no fear of his white neighbors. In addition to working his farm, Charles Goings performed labor for other area residents. The executor accounts for his white neighbor William Catterton's estate record a number of payments to Charles Goings for services rendered.[51]

Charles Goings died before he turned forty-seven years of age. No will is extant, but his estate was inventoried and appraised in May 1847. At that time he owned one rifle, one shotgun, two cows, and one mare. The inventory and appraisal, as was the custom, were admitted to public record in Charlottesville. Apparently, no one took particular notice of the fact that Goings owned not one but two firearms and did so fairly openly and without permission from the court.[52] White and black neighbors mingled at the public auction of Charles Goings's estate, and the white Albemarle resident James E. Chapman—a justice of the peace, no less—purchased Goings's rifle for $5.05. His white neighbor William Blackwell bought the shotgun, paying $2.50. Chapman, Blackwell, and other white bidders at the estate sale did not see Charles Goings or any of the Goings family as social equals, but neither did they see those free people of color as suspicious, marginal, or dangerous, despite Charles's ownership of firearms. Goings was a property owner and behaved respectably throughout his life. To those white men, he was a known and trusted neighbor. For them and for Charles Goings, black freedom had a face.[53]

The experiences of Thomas Goings, Noah Tate, William Goings, Charles Goings, Henry Barnett, Zachariah Bowles, and Zachariah Brock all demonstrate that property ownership, being commonly known in the area, and preferably having a respectable reputation could offer a person successful enjoyment of life as a free black in Albemarle. There was no single recipe for success, but the path to failure was marked rather clearly. These free men of color all interacted regularly with their white neighbors, and often these meetings were conducted in a spirit of neighborly familiarity that lessened the social distance between white and free black. These men felt comfortable speaking their minds with their white neighbors. They saw the Richard Durretts and Woodson Halls of the county first as neighbors and only secondly as white superiors.

Likewise, white men such as Richard Durrett, Woodson K. Hall, James Chapman, and William Blackwell saw the free people of color they knew first as neighbors with a name attached to a face. For those white neighbors, these free men of color thus became not dangerous and foreign free blacks, but named and known figures. This personal relationship was of primary importance and regularly superseded rigid notions of racial hierarchy. Hierarchy was an ideal that reflected the attitudes of white people toward unknown, foreign free blacks, not the relationships among neighbors. The court system in Albemarle also supported this view of events and social relations, adjudicating cases involving free blacks in a mostly impartial manner. Albemarle's free people of color, far from being slaves without masters, instead functioned as propertied masters of lesser worlds.[54]

5

Bawdy Houses and Women of Ill Fame

Free Black Women, Prostitution, and Family

On July 9, 1821, the free woman of color Fanny Barnett came to the Albemarle County courthouse in Charlottesville to file a fifty-dollar recognizance guaranteeing her appearance at the next month's county court to answer charges of a "breach of the peace and for a riotous and unlawful assembly." The white resident Benjamin Austin acted as surety for Barnett, filing his own fifty-dollar bond for her appearance. Also charged for the same offense that day were the white men Edmund Wade, Joshua Grady, and Bennett Wheeler. Two whites—Andrew McKee and Solomon Ballard—posted security for those men. Finally, two white women, Nancy Riley and Betsey Wingfield, found themselves similarly charged with a breach of the peace. The indictment described all of them, white and black, as "not of good fame, nor of honest conversation, but evil doers, rioters, disturbers of the peace."[1]

Although the details of the disturbance no longer remain in the records, the above indictment contains within it the outlines of a picture of one side of life in the little nineteenth-century town of Charlottesville. The people named in the court papers regarding the indictment were all neighbors, living and working close to one another. Andrew McKee, a white man, worked as a hatter. The blacksmith Joshua Grady, also white, cohabited with the free black woman Betsy Ann Farley. Nancy Riley and Betsey Wingfield were unmarried white women. Fanny Barnett, age thirty-five, was a free woman of color who owned little or no property.[2]

This episode in the summer of 1821 reveals far more, however, than simply disorderly interaction between free blacks and whites of the lower and middling sorts. Each of those charged managed to find a white man to come to the courthouse and pledge security for him or her. The whites Benjamin Austin, Solomon Ballard, Bennett Wheeler, and Andrew McKee clearly did not see Barnett, Riley, Wingfield, Grady, Wade, and Wheeler as "evil doers not of good fame" who were not to be trusted. Those recognizances, with the financial obligation inhering in them, demonstrate a certain level of trust among all of these people, including both a free black woman and a poor white man living with another free black woman as if husband and wife. Further, the incident represents the first documented contact among Fanny Barnett, Nancy Riley, and Betsey Wingfield. Justices of the Peace Opie Norris and John R. Jones, in filing the complaint, described the participants in the affray as "not of good fame, nor of honest conversation."

Surely involvement in disorderly conduct on a village street typically would not be enough to warrant such official opprobrium. Two legislative petitions from 1815 and 1818 suggest that at least for several years prior to 1821, town trustees had attempted unsuccessfully to control illicit activities (prostitution, gambling, and the like) on the outskirts of town. The first petition, rejected by the General Assembly in 1815, sought to extend town boundaries by a mile in order to bring "some houses of ill fame" within town jurisdiction "for the purpose of suppressing riots." Three years later, town trustees once again petitioned the legislature, complaining of the "pernicious and evil consequences" of "large collections of negroes [gathering just outside of town] on the Sabbath . . . at houses and tippling shops."[3] The legislature once again rejected the petition.

Fanny Barnett, Nancy Riley, and Betsey Wingfield—the three women involved in that 1821 affray—were no strangers to the neighborhood the Charlottesville trustees had sought to control. That criminal presentment in 1821 was only their first brush with the law. There would be others—and those paint a clearer picture of why the court condemned them in 1821. Just two years later, in October 1823, Betsey Wingfield and Nancy Riley would be tried by a called court. This time, they were "charged with keeping a house of ill fame, keeping a home for the entertainment of lewd and idle and dissolute persons of both colors." The presentment against them stated rather plainly exactly what was going on at that house of entertainment. It termed the residence a "bawdy house" where Wingfield and Riley "unlawfully and wickedly did keep and maintain and with said house for filthy lucre and gain, divers and dissolute persons as with man as woman, both black & white, and whores." Nancy Riley and Betsey Wingfield, poor and unmarried, were prostitutes who ran a business, managing a whorehouse in plain view on a street at the edge of the village of Charlottesville.[4]

Indeed, Wingfield and Riley, described in the indictment as "spinstresses," were "not of good fame." Their business, in addition to providing prostitutes for patrons, also served as a house of entertainment where white and black customers were found "drinking, tipling, cursing, swearing, quarreling & otherwise misbehaving themselves." The strong language of both indictments and the charging of a white woman and a black woman for the same offense suggested that these women would be dealt with harshly. Their behavior seemed to challenge bourgeois morality, gendered notions of behavior, and antebellum racial doctrine.

Both women were found guilty of the charges of committing "whoredome and fornication . . . to the total demolition of the public morals," but the justices chose only to fine them ten dollars apiece. The light punishment received was similar to what it would have been in cases of prostitution in which no cross-racial contact was involved—but this offense occurred in Albemarle County, a rural agricultural community, and it involved white women and free black women, as well as men of both races.[5]

The free woman of color Fanny Barnett's connection to Riley and Wingfield, however, remains hidden from view for more than a decade after that 1823 conviction. Barnett was born sometime between 1775 and 1785 in Albemarle, the daughter of a Frances (more commonly called Fanny) Barnett, a clothes washer. The elder Frances remains nearly hidden, only appearing twice in county records: on the 1813 property tax lists and in the U.S. Census of 1820. The census listed her as a free black female head of a household containing three free colored females under the age of fourteen and one free colored female between the ages of twenty-six and forty-four. Throughout her life, she remained poor. Sometime in early 1822, Frances Barnett died, orphaning several minor children (William, Jane, Elizabeth Ann, Mary, and Easton Barnett), as well as their older sister, Fanny. Francis had little to leave to her children at her death. No mention of the father or fathers of her children was ever made, but it seems likely that he or they were white; all of her children are described as of a "light" or "very light" complexion.[6]

The younger Fanny Barnett had reached adulthood by the time her mother died. The county overseers of the poor quickly bound out all of Fanny's siblings, who were under the age of eighteen. Fanny, however, was already in her thirties, a free woman of color. The younger Fanny for decades followed a life pattern similar to that of her mother. She owned no real estate and little or no personal property. And like her mother, she may have continued to have sexual relations with one or more white men. By 1830, she had at least three children, if not more. Three years later, when the county commissioners conducted the countywide colonization census, Fanny Barnett was listed as a head of household residing in Charlottesville who worked as a clothes washer. Living with her were daughters Mary Barnett, an eighteen-year-old seamstress; Martha Barnett, a fourteen-year-old seamstress; James Barnett, a twelve-year-old boy; and Septimia Barnett, an eight-year-old girl.[7]

The trend continued for yet another decade. By 1840, Fanny Barnett remained virtually without property, unmarried, and overseeing a household that included at least three children. She was now in her fifties and seemed destined to live out a life of obscurity. But in 1841, the records reveal the first hint of just what her life actually may have looked like. In October of that year, Fanny Barnett walked to the county courthouse with the white carpenter Allen W. Hawkins and the free woman of color Marinda French. Barnett, French, and Hawkins filed recognizances in the amount of two hundred dollars guaranteeing the appearance of Fanny's daughter Septimia in court. Septimia had been charged with a breach of the peace toward the free woman of color Betsy Randolph and her daughter Elizabeth.[8]

At the November court that year, Septimia Barnett appeared, fulfilling the recognizances her mother, French, and Hawkins had filed. The court agreed that some sort of physical confrontation had indeed occurred and that Septimia Barnett had caused it. She was ordered to file a peace recognizance in the amount of two hundred dollars guaranteeing her good behavior for one year. Fanny Barnett and Marinda French tendered themselves as security for Septimia in the amount of two hundred dollars each. The two women of color clearly knew each other well, and French willingly pledged a fairly substantial amount of money in support of Fanny and her daughter. But how does the white carpenter, Allen W. Hawkins, fit into this story? Hawkins remains a shadowy figure in the historical record. He married one Elizabeth W. Burch in May 1839. This was his second marriage, the first having happened in 1836. Hawkins worked as a carpenter and builder in Charlottesville.[9]

Thanks to his recent marriage, it would seem unlikely that Allen W. Hawkins's 1841 recognizance for Fanny and Septimia Barnett had anything to do with an ongoing sexual relationship, as Hawkins's new wife lived in

Charlottesville. An affair with a free black woman would have been very difficult to carry out without his wife having knowledge of it, and he would presumably be reluctant to give security publicly for a colored lover. At a minimum, however, Hawkins and Barnett were neighbors who knew each other well. For the white Hawkins, Fanny Barnett was not a dangerous free black whose existence challenged notions of racial hierarchy. He may have encountered her sometimes in a house of entertainment in or at the edge of Charlottesville. The possibility remains that Barnett and Hawkins had then, or had once had, a more intimate relationship. Either way, for Allen Hawkins, Fanny Barnett was well-known, someone he considered reliable enough to pledge a substantial two-hundred-dollar security for.

Just four years later, in July 1845, Fanny Barnett again faced charges. This time, the commonwealth's attorney for Albemarle demanded that she file a recognizance for her good behavior and also find someone to pledge surety for her bond. On July 5, she was found guilty of "keeping a bawdy house" and ordered to file a peace recognizance for her good behavior. Barnett pledged fifty dollars to guarantee her good behavior for one year, "especially ceas[ing] to keep a bawdy house." Once again, the white Charlottesville resident Allen W. Hawkins willingly came forward and pledged another fifty dollars as surety for Barnett's peace recognizance. Over twenty years earlier, Betsy Wingfield and Nancy Riley, intimate associates of Fanny Barnett, had faced similar charges. Now, a pattern seems to emerge. Back in 1823, Fanny Barnett may have been working as a prostitute in the bawdy house run by Riley and Wingfield. Now, in 1845, Barnett was running her own house. But she was not doing this alone. This time, it was a family affair. On that same day in July 1845, Fanny's twenty-year-old daughter Septimia was also found guilty of "keeping a bawdy house" and ordered to file a bond promising her good behavior for one year. Yet again, Allen Hawkins appeared to pledge fifty dollars' security on Septimia's bond.[10]

Until 1845, Fanny and Septimia Barnett, in spite of their work in bawdy houses in the Charlottesville area, remained poor and propertyless people of color. Neither Fanny Barnett, her mother Frances, nor her children had ever appeared on the land tax books for the county, and Frances Barnett had only once appeared on personal property tax lists, all the way back in 1813. In that year, she was taxed $1.50 for one tithable (taxable person), probably one of her sons, but no property was listed under her name. Conditions for the Barnetts, however, were about to change. A mere three months after the court found Fanny and Septimia Barnett guilty of keeping a bawdy house, the Barnett household became landowners. In October 1845, Fanny Barnett and daughters Martha and Septimia purchased a half-acre tract of land on the road between Charlottesville and the university—on Main Street, at the edge of Charlottesville proper.[11]

In all likelihood, this property was one on which they already resided or was only a short distance from the dwelling house they occupied at the time. The half-acre lot adjoined the property of the white men John Pollock and Andrew Leitch, as well as that of the free black Jesse Scott. The records remain silent as to how a household of free women of color could raise the five hundred dollars required for the purchase. Perhaps prostitution and illicit entertainments proved sufficiently lucrative. Or perhaps they received help. The deed of sale suggests how this might have occurred. The Barnetts did not deliver payment to George Carr, the white man who held the property in trust. Instead, their old acquaintance Allen W. Hawkins delivered the five hundred dollars to Carr and signed the deed of sale. Regardless of the provenance of the money, the property would remain in the Barnett family for decades. The deed of sale actually conveyed the property to Fanny Barnett as a life estate. At her death, ownership of the property would pass to her daughters Martha and Septimia.[12]

This deed clearly suggests that Allen Hawkins was more than a neighbor or friend to Fanny Barnett and her daughters. Although Hawkins was now married to a white woman who lived in town with him, it seems likely that Hawkins and Barnett had had a sexual relationship in the past, if not one that was continuing at the time. The wording of the deed, in which Hawkins pays for the land but the deed goes to Fanny as a life estate, suggests that both Fanny and Allen were interested in providing for the children. Hawkins's interest in Septimia and Martha may have arisen because he was their father. Freedom registrations, though far from conclusive, are consistent with this theory. Fanny Barnett's registers describe her as a "mulatto" or "light mulatto." As discussed above, Fanny likely had a white father. So, probably, did her daughters Septimia and Martha. Registers for the daughters describe both of them as "light mulatto," "very light mulatto," or "very bright mulatto." The addition of the intensifiers "very light" and "very bright" to the description frequently meant that the person registering was nearly white in appearance. Interracialism apparently ran in the Barnett family and may have occurred across generations.[13]

Who was Allen W. Hawkins? Extant records provide at least a thumbnail sketch. He was white, trained as a carpenter and builder. The Charlottesville newspaper editor James Alexander, in his reminiscences about antebellum Charlottesville, wrote that Allen Hawkins had built the Farmers' Hotel on Random Row in town for its owner. Fanny Barnett lived in the Random Row area. Hawkins clearly was aware of the disorderly activities that took place nearby. In 1834, he appeared as a witness for the commonwealth in a case against the whites Bernard and Nancy Riley for keeping a "disorderly and riotous house." Nancy Riley was the same woman for whom Fanny Barnett apparently had worked before striking out on her own.[14]

Hawkins, as a resident of one of the highly interracial sections of town, continued to have firsthand day-to-day experience with the mix of slaves, free blacks, and whites in and around town. In August 1843, he served on a grand jury that charged the free woman of color Patsey Goings with "permitting an unlawful assembly of slaves." Goings was found guilty and fined one dollar.[15]

Goings, born Patsey Cole, had married the free man of color Robert Goings in 1840. She continued to work at the edge of town, participating in the rowdy interracial culture that thrived there. Patsey Goings's life represents perfectly the gap between law and social practice in Albemarle. In 1842, a county grand jury had presented her and a number of other free blacks on charges of remaining in the commonwealth without permission. The technical outcome of the case remains unknown, but Patsey Goings did not leave the area. All of the people named in the indictment remained in Albemarle for at least another decade. A year later, in 1843, Goings was convicted of allowing slaves to assemble, a crime supposedly deeply threatening to the racial order, but paid only a small fine. As late as 1857, she continued to reside there with her family.

Meanwhile, Allen Hawkins continued to consort with non-whites. Living among free blacks and slaves, it was a normal part of his daily routine. Free blacks were neighbors, acquaintances, fellow businesspeople, clients, and possibly even friends for white people such as Hawkins. In January 1845, Hawkins and his white wife conveyed a quarter-acre tract of land to the free woman of color Louisa Goings. They were conducting business with a neighbor.[16]

To sum up, Hawkins was married but probably carried on a long-term sexual relationship with a free woman of color that produced children, whom he provided for. He participated in a legal system that punished African Americans, slave and free, for assembling and acting without white supervision. He owned at least one slave, but he conducted business with free blacks, including selling land in his neighborhood to them. Hawkins did not occupy an elite social rank, but was located comfortably in the middling range of propertied whites in the county. His concern for slaves "going at large," acting as if free, and assembling must not have been too great despite his having served on a grand jury that indicted Patsey Goings for allowing slaves to assemble. Three times between 1845 and 1847, he was charged with "permitting a slave to go at large and hire himself."[17]

In the first of these trials, concerning his slave Fleming, a number of white neighbors testified on Hawkins's behalf. Despite all the support, he was found guilty and fined ten dollars. This relatively small fine was not exactly the kind of stiff sentence expected in a community assumed to be very concerned about maintaining a strict racial hierarchy. In June 1846, Hawkins was again tried for letting his slave Jarrett "go at large and trade as a free person." This time, he was cleared of the charges. Apparently, however, Hawkins continued to let his slaves conduct business for themselves at their own discretion. Only a year later, Hawkins and his slave were back in court, facing similar charges. In the second trial concerning Jarrett, Hawkins was again convicted and fined ten dollars.[18]

Hawkins's experiences with free blacks in Albemarle demonstrate that at least some white residents did not act as if day-to-day interaction with free blacks and even slaves represented a danger to the racial hierarchy. Each situation with a free person of color was addressed in context. Who were they? What were they doing? How did they fit into the community? Did their presence and actions benefit or threaten the community and the white individual asking this very question? Within white Albemarle, one could find both vigilance and nonchalance toward blacks—a white communal mind divided on how to handle people of color. Thus, a man like Allen Hawkins could maintain a free black mistress and their children, let certain of his slaves go at large and hire themselves, conduct business with free black neighbors, serve on juries that convicted and punished free people of color for transgressing community standards, and himself face occasional fines for ignoring laws concerning slaves.

Fanny Barnett and her daughters in the 1840s lived in a growing village that had a rather open sphere of interracial activity. Slaves, free blacks, and whites intermingled as they conducted business in town or as they played at the edge of town. The Barnetts, as single, free women of color in the rural slave South, saw little reason to hide from the authorities. They continued to operate a bawdy house and continued to appear on the streets of the town, interacting with whites and blacks. Fanny Barnett's encounters with legal authorities had been negative. She only saw the courthouse when she or someone in her family had been charged with violating the laws. But Barnett did not see the law merely as a tool of oppression, a system to be avoided at all costs. Instead, she saw the local legal system as a reasonable venue for the airing of grievances and the handling of disputes. In May 1847, Barnett met with a justice of the peace at the county courthouse and filed charges against on old acquaintance, Marinda French, whom she charged with assault.[19]

The court ordered French arrested and then summoned a series of witnesses to appear before the court for the commonwealth, including Fanny Barnett, Martha Barnett, Mary E. Custis, and Minerva Kinney. All these women were unmarried free women of color who lived in the same area in Charlottesville, along Main Street, between the center of the village and the university. The court also called witnesses for Marinda French. Harden Massie, a local doctor, was summoned by the court to bring in his slave Nelson as a witness for French; Nelson had been moving freely about Charlottesville when the incident occurred. Officers of the court handled the affray in the usual fashion, simply requiring both of them to file peace recognizances guaranteeing their good behavior for a year.[20]

Those peace bonds help to paint a clearer picture of just what happened. The incident had started when Marinda and Mary Jane French assaulted Fanny Barnett on a street in Charlottesville. Mary E. Custis had stepped in to defend Barnett, battling with the Frenches. Custis now had to file her own fifty-dollar peace bond. Fanny Barnett acted as her security. Barnett was in her sixties at the time of the conflict, a property-owning, single free colored woman. The other women were all young, single, free people of color who did not own property. This battle may have broken out between employer and employee; these women may all have been workers in Barnett's bawdy house.[21]

The interracial nature of life in a small antebellum town in the slaveholding South becomes even clearer through census reports. According to the census for Albemarle County in 1850, Fanny Barnett was a free colored head of a household. The census lists her as sixty-five years old, with a light complexion. Living in her house with her were her daughter Martha, a thirty-year-old mulatto; her daughter Septimia, a twenty-three-year-old mulatto; and her grandchildren James and Millie A. Barnett, ages five and three respectively. The report lists Septimia Barnett as possessing twenty-five hundred dollars in real estate. Their neighbors were John Harlow, a thirty-five-year-old white stage driver, and Lewis Sowell, a forty-six-year-old white wheelwright who owned three thousand dollars in real estate.[22]

By 1860, Fanny Barnett had lived a full and successful life as a free woman of color in the slave South. She was seventy-eight years old. She had retired from business and even begun to let her children take control of some of her property. On the eve of the Civil War, Fanny no longer was the head of a household. Instead, she had moved into her daughter Septimia's home in Charlottesville. This family of free black women demonstrated impressive economic success. Fanny owned one thousand dollars' worth of real estate and one hundred dollars' worth of personal property. Her daughter Septimia, now a thirty-one-year-old woman, owned two thousand dollars' worth of real estate and six thousand dollars' worth of personal property. Septimia's sister Martha, age thirty-seven, also lived in the same household. Martha owned one thousand dollars' worth of real estate and one hundred dollars' worth of personal property. Together, Fanny and her two daughters owned an impressive four thousand dollars' worth of real estate and over six thousand dollars' worth of personal property. They did all this despite starting life as propertyless free women of color.[23]

These women, once considered by the court as of "ill fame and not of honest conversation," continued to amass property and live in a highly interracial area of Charlottesville. Described as nearly white in most records, they lived adjacent to property owned by Samuel Leitch Jr., an immigrant from northern Ireland and a man of similar economic standing.[24] Leitch's actual residence was located several blocks away, on the east side of Court Square. He had immigrated to Charlottesville in 1819, and he conducted business in the area until well after the Civil War. On the other side of their house lived a poor free black woman, Rachel Isaacs, a seventy-seven-year-old clothes washer who owned no real property and only twenty dollars' worth of taxable property. Betsy Barnett, a sister of Septimia and Martha, lived several doors down. She was forty-one, a clothes washer, with a $30 personal estate. She lived with her two boys, John and James. They lived next to James Lewis, a propertyless black carpenter, and Marinda French, that longtime acquaintance of the Barnetts. Marinda had apparently worked with Fanny Barnett and later with Septimia as a prostitute in the interracial bawdy houses around Charlottesville. Now she was forty-five and owned $1,500 in real estate and $150 in taxable property. She, too, was listed as a clothes washer.

How could four free black women whose only officially recorded occupation was "washerwoman" all manage to own real estate of fairly substantial value, along with sizable personal estates?[25] As discussed earlier, Fanny Barnett probably had a long-term sexual relationship with the white carpenter Allen W. Hawkins. Her daughter Martha had successfully pursued a similar relationship. James E. Dawson, a white man, died in June 1859. His will stipulated that his estate was to go to his son, Roderick Random Barnett, the son of Martha Barnett. Dawson further ordered that if his son Roderick failed to live until he turned twenty-one, then the estate was to be divided between Martha Barnett and his sister Lucy A. Richardson and her heirs. Dawson's white family members initially opposed the will, but by July, the dispute had been settled amicably, and the will was entered into probate as written.[26]

Marinda French most likely followed a similar path to property ownership, utilizing the connections she had forged with white men in the brothel to secure real estate and personal property. But the experience of Marinda French also reveals some of the dangers inherent in living in the rural South as an unattached free black woman who somewhat openly engaged in interracial sexual liaisons. She did manage to accrue a sizable estate, but she also failed to follow the example of the Barnetts and move toward respectability and stability. Marinda French seemed to live up to the charge of failing to be of "honest conversation." In addition to her work as a prostitute and her involvement at least once in public violence on the streets of Charlottesville, Marinda French never successfully became a fully known personage in the area. The records even display some confusion as to what her name was. Some call her Marinda French; some give her name as Marinda West. Yet others call her "Farinda," "Varina," or even a mixture of all three, "Vairinda." Likewise, she apparently continued to consort with the rowdiest class in Charlottesville, an often drunken and disorderly mixture of poor whites, propertyless free people of color, and even slaves.

On January 20, 1859, she purchased pork from two slaves, Tom and Henry, who frequented Random Row and the other interracial areas in and around town. At the time of the sale, this transaction was not unusual for Albemarle County. Slaves raised their own produce for market, were routinely paid for overwork, or earned additional income through hiring. Virginia slaves often raised their own horses and hogs, too.[27] Thus, slaves, free people of color, and whites all did business with one another on a routine basis. A week and a half later, however, Marinda was arrested and charged with purchasing stolen property. Tom and Henry were slaves owned by James H. Burnley who frequently conducted themselves without white supervision. They had stolen a pig valued at ten dollars from one Horace B. Burnley, a close relative of their master. They had then slaughtered the hog and peddled the meat on the streets of Charlottesville.[28]

A county justice charged her with knowingly trafficking in stolen goods. In fact, he further alleged that Marinda French still had the stolen meat, which was "concealed in the dwelling house of said Marinda French." Justice James Lobban filed a warrant ordering the county sheriff to "enter in the day time, the said dwelling house of the said Marinda French, and there diligently search for the said meat." Later that same day, a county constable executed the search warrant and found the stolen pork. French was immediately arrested and jailed, with a trial date set for the next day, February 2. The trial, in a called court of oyer and terminer, was a fairly quick affair. French was found guilty of "receiving stolen pork" and sentenced to "receive thirty lashes on her bare back at the public whipping post." French, having pled not guilty, continued to fight the verdict; she immediately filed an appeal. Technically, state law did not allow for appeal of oyer and terminer verdicts, but the county court granted French an appeal anyway. Next, she filed a recognizance with the court guaranteeing her appearance the next day at her appeal. The local white merchant John H. Bibb posted surety for French.[29]

Sadly for Marinda French, the court was unmoved by her pleas. No one came forward to testify on her behalf, not even John H. Bibb, who the day before had been willing to make a financial pledge in her name. The court once again found her guilty and ordered her to pay court costs amounting to a little over three dollars. She was ordered to find security in the amount of one hundred dollars guaranteeing her good behavior for a year. Last, the court sent her to the public whipping post, where she received thirty lashes for stealing. For the peace recognizance, French did not turn to John H. Bibb, who only a week earlier had been willing to pledge security for her court appearance. This time, John T. Barksdale, a local white man, pledged one hundred dollars guaranteeing her good behavior.[30]

Marinda French, also known as Marinda West, Varina West, Farinda West, and Vairinda French, had failed to make herself a fully known figure. She had simultaneously failed to gain a full measure of respectability in the eyes of the community. She continued to consort with the least respectable classes in the area. Back in 1847, in the assault case, French had only one witness who came to her defense—Nelson, a slave owned by Harden Massie. She had failed to move toward respectability by separating herself in some way from the "ill fame" of the bawdy houses.

County records reveal little else about French's family, but they do suggest that French may have had children by both white and black men. Her daughter Frances Victoria, born in 1840, was described in public records as being of dark complexion, as was her youngest child, William. Her oldest daughter, Mary Jane, shows that Marinda likely had sexual relations with at least one white man; Mary Jane's 1850 freedom certificate describes her as of light complexion.[31] On that same day in November 1850 that Mary Jane came to register her freedom, so did her mother. Six other single free black women, including Frances Ailstock, Margaret Jane Ailstock, and Minerva Kinney, also appeared at the courthouse to register their freedom (as did fourteen other people of color). These women may well have been coworkers of Marinda French's from the bawdy houses and houses of entertainment on the outskirts of Charlottesville. Fanny Barnett, then a proprietress of one such house, came that same day.[32]

The fifty-year-old black laborer David Hite also registered his freedom that day. Hite and the free black women may all have come to the courthouse together. Was Hite a business partner? Was he involved in a relationship with French or one of the others? Did Hite do work for one of the bawdy houses? All that is known about him is that he was freed in 1839, lived near the university, and worked as a laborer along Main Street, picking up work wherever he found it. Neither Hite nor French would ever become widely known or respectable enough to attain solid standing within the social culture of Albemarle.[33]

White southerners across the region at times paid closer attention to the peculiar institution and the racial hierarchy upon which the system rested. That all-important gap between law and social practice at the local level, a gap that created great opportunities for some free people of color, would sometimes narrow. The gap had shown hints of occasional contraction at moments before, but a comfortable middle ground occupied by many free blacks remained intact at the local level. State laws that circumscribed free black life in Virginia often remained unenforced, and those who could achieve recognition and respectability in their communities continued to live unmolested lives, even if some whites believed laws concerning slaves and free blacks required more vigilant policing.

For those whites who sought tighter policing, the 1806 removal law—which stated that all free blacks freed after May 1, 1806, had to leave the state within one year—became a tool of choice. This law, virtually ignored in most counties and municipalities for forty years, became the subject of greater constabulary scrutiny. Not only were cases filed against free blacks for violating these laws, but those charged were sometimes actually arrested. A few free blacks took the hint and removed themselves. Marinda French's acquaintance David Hite represents one such example. Freed by deed in 1839, Hite clearly lived in Charlottesville in violation of the 1806 law. But no charges were ever brought against him until early 1851. In fact, for more than a decade, David Hite lived in the vicinity of Charlottesville and never once felt it necessary to obtain a freedom certificate. That all changed in late 1850: David Hite registered not once but twice, in the last two months of 1850, visiting the courthouse at the beginning of November and again one month later.[34]

For Hite, neither of the freedom certificates would prove terribly useful. He had been freed well after the passage of the 1806 removal law and possibly freed by someone from outside the immediate area.[35] Lacking a fixed address, performing what was likely only menial labor for a host of employers, and participating in a rowdy lower-class interracial culture, Hite had failed to make himself sufficiently well-known. Hite's freedom in 1850 was faceless. This would come to haunt him. Just three months after he registered his freedom for the second time, an Albemarle County grand jury filed a presentment explicitly naming eleven free blacks who continued to remain in the commonwealth in violation of the 1806 removal law. David Hite's name was on the list. Later that year, in June 1851, the court issued a summons for Hite, commanding a sheriff or constable to apprehend him so he could face the charges in court. For the next six months, nothing happened. Perhaps the authorities searched for Hite but never found him. More likely, they were not trying very hard to find him. Finally, on January 28,

1852, shortly after the court issued yet another summons for Hite's arrest, the constables gave up the search. A sheriff returned a note to the court, stating, "The defendant has left the county and I am informed that he lives in Washington."[36]

The experiences of David Hite demonstrate the dangers inhering in failure to establish oneself in the eyes of the white community. A free person of color had to become a face with a name and reputation attached to it. But Marinda French demonstrates that the reputation needed to be in some way respectable. French was more of a known quantity than David Hite, but she was known only as a free woman of color of ill fame, disorderly, and not of honest conversation. Although she was never driven from the county, sent to prison, or forcibly sold into slavery, she did encounter difficulties with the white authorities in Albemarle, problems that stemmed from her behavior and reputation. In the more vigilant racial climate of the 1850s, Hite's lack of connections in Albemarle forced him to flee the county, and French's questionable reputation and at times questionable companions sent her to the public whipping post. During the 1850s, Marinda fared far better in Albemarle than Hite, despite receiving thirty lashes in 1859. Over the course of the decade, she went from being a propertyless, house-renting free black prostitute to being a clothes washer with fifteen hundred dollars in real estate.[37]

The Barnett family, however, represents the blueprint for successfully navigating the highly personal social culture of Albemarle. Fanny and her daughters, like Marinda West, started out as free black prostitutes working in bawdy houses at the edge of town. This rowdy interracial sphere seems an unlikely place to begin establishing a solid reputation. But that is exactly what Fanny Barnett did. She went from prostitute to manager of her own bawdy house, from being propertyless to owning over a thousand dollars in real estate. And she did this through her own hard work, but also with the help of a white man, Allen W. Hawkins. Whether Barnett simply befriended or manipulated Hawkins, encouraging him to act as a family patron, or the two actually had an intimate and loving companionate relationship remains unknown. What is important is the ways in which she engaged the larger community around her. And not all of those interactions were the result of her relationship with Hawkins. Her first significant act was to acquire property. Property ownership was important for free blacks and highly demonstrative of the essentially economic freedoms available to them. White southern notions of freedom were deeply intertwined with notions of property ownership. Fanny Barnett and other free blacks, by possessing title to land, staked a clear claim to individual freedom, to economic freedom, and to inclusion in the free society of Albemarle.[38]

But as Marinda French's experiences demonstrate, acquiring property was not enough—Fanny Barnett needed to achieve respectability as well. Barnett's second important decision—one that distinguished her from Marinda French—was to begin to move away from immersion in the disorderly lower-class interracial entertainment culture. Instead of continuing as a prostitute in one of those houses, she ran her own. As a property-owning businesswoman, even if her vocation was technically illicit, Fanny had to do business with merchants and other commercial establishments in town. These businessmen came to see Fanny Barnett not as an untrustworthy free black prostitute, but as a woman of property to whom credit could be extended. For instance, Thomas W. Fry, a modestly situated white property owner, sold firewood in and around Charlottesville. Wood was essential in the nineteenth century both for heating and as fuel for the kitchen. Barnett, running a house of prostitution and raising a family, surely needed plenty of wood to keep customers comfortable and her family warm and fed. She turned to Fry for firewood. At Fry's death in 1849, his accounts showed Fanny Barnett owing him nine dollars for wood. He felt at ease extending a line of credit, however small, to a regular customer who happened to be a free woman of color.[39]

Her move away from that rowdy universe inhabited by the likes of Marinda French also entailed behaving differently. The last thirty years of Fanny Barnett's life are a testament to the advantages accrued by conforming to the dictates of respectability. For Fanny Barnett, freedom indeed had a face, and her efforts paid off in a move toward acquiring a face that would engender social acceptance. In 1850, when the characteristically flexible and permissive racial hierarchy appeared momentarily to have contracted, Fanny Barnett was not among those caught up in a law-enforcement dragnet. For one thing, she had been born free prior to May 1806, so she was not in violation of the law. But ten other free blacks in 1850 who were not in violation of the 1806 removal law would nevertheless find themselves charged with illegally remaining in the commonwealth (none had cases that went to trial). Fanny Barnett, a property-owning woman of color, and all of her children, would not be charged or even asked to produce to the court verification of their legal freedom and residency.[40]

The Barnetts had successfully weathered the flurry of activity in 1850 aimed at more tightly policing free blacks. They were not jailed, nor were they subjected to frivolous legal action concerning their residency in Albemarle. Their experiences after 1850 demonstrate that the more easygoing culture had not vanished. In 1851, Septimia was about twenty-three years old, a substantial property owner, and running a successful bawdy house. In early January, she came to the courthouse to finalize a deed of sale for a quarter-acre tract of land adjacent to Charlottesville that she was purchasing from the free black Henry Mann of Greenbrier County, Virginia. Mann, also known by other surnames, including Goings, Middlebrook, and Barnett, was representing another free colored former Albemarle resident, Thomas Goings. The two men may have been related. Goings had picked up his family and moved to a free state, settling in Clinton County, Ohio. His wife, Louisa, had received a plot of land from Allen W. Hawkins back in 1845, but Louisa had since died, so the property fell into Thomas's hands. Through his agent Henry Mann, Thomas Goings sold the land to Septimia Barnett, who paid six hundred dollars for the parcel that had originally been owned by Hawkins, who may have been her own father.[41]

This transaction highlights the generally more difficult climate some free blacks may have faced after 1850. Henry Mann, though still living in Virginia, had moved to a mountainous, lightly populated county in the western portion of the state, where slavery was not significant. Goings had completely separated himself and his family from the slave South, moving across the Ohio River to a free state. He was living in the southeastern portion of Ohio, where a number of fellow free blacks from Albemarle had settled. This trickle of migrants had started in the 1840s but accelerated slightly after 1850. A few free blacks apparently no longer felt comfortable or even secure in Albemarle, so they moved to a free state. But this deed of sale also points to the ability of some to navigate the trickier racial climate in the new decade and to do so with great success.[42]

On the first of April, just three months after purchasing land from Thomas Goings, Septimia Barnett had an encounter on the streets of Charlottesville with the white county resident Henry Pollard. The existing records do not reveal just what the conflict was about, but Pollard drew a pistol and fired it at both Barnett and William Johnson, a white man. Perhaps he had been an unsatisfied customer at Barnett's bawdy house. A circuit court grand jury delivered two separate presentments (one for each victim) and summoned witnesses the next month. Three years later, in 1854, the court decided not to prosecute, and the charges were dropped. Perhaps Pollard, fearing punishment, had apologized and compensated Barnett and Johnson off the record or had left town.[43]

Septimia Barnett continued to prosper in Charlottesville, despite her status as an unmarried free woman of color who ran a house of prostitution. She amassed real estate and increased her personal wealth. In November 1852, she again purchased land from free blacks who had left the area. This time, she bought another plot of land at the edge of Charlottesville, for four hundred dollars. Julia Ann Mann (the wife of Henry Mann) of Greenbrier County, Virginia, sold her the lot, which bordered the property of the white merchants John A. Marchant and John Pollock. Mann had earlier purchased the plot from the free woman of color Elizabeth Randolph. Barnett's success in increasing her personal net worth seems to have been in some ways directly linked to the departure of other propertied free blacks from the area. This transaction once again demonstrates the highly interracial nature of life in and around Charlottesville even in the years after 1850.[44]

Septimia continued to purchase land, most often from free blacks who had migrated out of the area; occasionally she bought property that had been repossessed by creditors and offered for quick sale. On November 25, 1854, Septimia Barnett continued her shopping for additional real estate by bidding at a public auction of properties owned by George Moore, a white man. She purchased a small plot of land in Charlottesville for $160. This lot was located just up a hill from the Random Row area and bordered Little Commerce Street, essentially a cart path a half block to the north of Main Street.[45]

Apparently, Septimia Barnett did not have the available cash to finalize the purchase at the time of the auction in late November. Instead, she secured help from a local white neighbor, Rice G. Bailey. In addition to being a neighbor, Bailey may have had a more personal connection to Barnett; Bailey had hired Allen Hawkins to do major work for him in the past. Bailey became a trustee in the transaction, agreeing to pay the purchase price for the land and not to charge interest, with Barnett paying him back later. Septimia Barnett understood that simply being known by Bailey was not enough; he would hardly have accepted the trusteeship had he not witnessed her proper and respectable business behavior. She paid the purchase price back to Rice G. Bailey two and a half months after the public auction. For Bailey, Septimia Barnett was a respectable neighbor, someone who would settle a financial obligation in a timely manner. He may also have known that she was the daughter of Allen Hawkins. Regardless, he felt he could trust her. It was personal relationships such as this one that allowed Septimia to live comfortably in Charlottesville.[46]

Septimia likely walked a fine line, as her mother had before her. On the one hand, she was an independent property-owning free woman of color in the slave South. Her family had managed to carve out a niche in which they could thrive and that in some ways defied notions and expectations about the role of women and free blacks in the natural social hierarchy. But it was her occupation that made navigating the social culture of Albemarle at times fraught with difficulty. Running a house of prostitution guaranteed that a rowdier class of individuals would come into close contact with the Barnett family. It also promised to draw the attention and ire of crusaders and reformers, who were increasingly prominent in municipalities across America by the 1830s.

As Septimia's encounter with Henry Pollard had suggested in 1851, anyone—especially a white man—could become a dangerous adversary. In another vignette of interracial contact in Charlottesville, a mere three months after Septimia took possession of the land title from Rice Bailey, she ran into trouble on the streets of the town. Not only did Septimia Barnett own multiple tracts of land; she also owned slaves, and slaves who were not family members. She and one of her slaves—a girl named Susan—were accosted on the street by the local white William W. Roach. Roach threatened both of them, "declaring that he would shoot Septimia or her servant girl Susan." Barnett, rightfully concerned about her own safety, came to the courthouse to report the incident and plead for the court's protection. The court ordered Roach to file a two-thousand-dollar peace bond guaranteeing his good behavior for a year. Free women of color such as Barnett viewed the court system as a reasonable venue for airing grievances, even if their complaint was against a white person.[47]

What had caused Roach to explode and threaten a local resident with a violent and murderous act? The records remain silent. His only other appearance in county court records is as a defendant in another criminal case, likewise involving violence against a free black woman. Perhaps Roach, like Pollard before him, was a dissatisfied customer at Barnett's bawdy house. On the other hand, he may have been a reformer who opposed drinking and prostitution, though his near absence from the record casts doubt on that idea. The interracial nature of the activities that took place at the Barnett establishment and elsewhere in the Random Row neighborhood may also have angered Roach, though that would have differentiated him from many other local whites. Septimia Barnett, a free colored property- and slave-owning single woman, may have represented for Roach a threatening symbol of the failure of the gendered, racial social hierarchy. Unfortunately, Roach remains a fleeting presence in the archives.

Back in 1845, however, the commonwealth's attorney had pursued a case against the same William Roach, charging him with destroying the property of Elizabeth Kinney, who had recently died. She was a free woman of color who worked as a clothes washer on Ridge Street, just a few blocks from Random Row. Elizabeth Kinney also owned at least one nominal slave, her husband, John Kinney. As a property owner, she had wisely prepared a will that emancipated her husband, John; appointed him her executor; and left the estate to him. Sometime in late spring, William Roach destroyed some of the estate property. The records do not indicate just what Roach damaged or destroyed. As with the case involving Septimia Barnett, the records also do not explain Roach's motivation. If his actions sprang from an intense animus toward successful free women of color, local legal authorities did not countenance his bias. In both cases, they saw not a white man properly taking justice into his own hands and reasserting the community racial hierarchy, but a violent man who vandalized private property and threatened to shoot property owners. In 1845, the commonwealth's attorney had charged Roach with destroying property. Ten years later, the court required him to file a two-thousand-dollar recognizance guaranteeing peaceable behavior.[48]

The extremely large sum for the peace bond suggests that the court sought to drive Roach from the area. Apparently, the ploy worked, because no record exists suggesting that Roach managed to secure such a large peace bond. Many Albemarle residents would have been unable to prove they had property worth so large a sum, let alone find somebody to post security for them on a bond of that value. So Roach vanished from the county records, while the families of those women of color remained in the county, in plain view. Septimia Barnett and Elizabeth Kinney, Roach's two targets, had much in common. Like Barnett, Elizabeth Kinney was a successful free black woman who owned land and property. She also managed to earn enough income to purchase her own husband.[49]

The Kinney family, however, differed from the Barnetts in one key respect: they never accumulated a personal estate anywhere near the value of Barnett's, and they remained without any prominent white allies or patrons. That did not mean that the Kinneys lacked connections to the community, however. They were in fact quite well recognized. It was this familiarity that ensured their continued undisturbed existence in Albemarle. Elizabeth Kinney died in early 1845, only about fifty years old. Her younger husband, John, until her death technically her slave, found himself a free man when her will was recorded at the courthouse. She had also appointed him as executor of her estate. As such, he would need to find an individual or group of individuals willing and able to pledge security for him in that role. Both John and his deceased wife, however, were well-known in the community. John Kinney turned to three local white men for help. Together, the three men willingly pledged a combined one thousand dollars as security guaranteeing John Kinney's proper performance of the duties of estate executor. Such a serious financial commitment demonstrates powerfully that these white men did not see Kinney—newly freed slave though he was—as a dangerous or marginal free black. He was a community member, whose behavior had demonstrated his fitness for their trust.[50]

John Kinney successfully completed his work as executor of his deceased wife's estate. He acted as a respectable and trustworthy member of the community and as a result took unmolested and uncontested possession of Elizabeth Kinney's estate. Despite his immediate successes, however, he had a real problem. Since had been a slave at the time of his wife's death, he became a free black long after the 1806 removal law went into effect. For Kinney, remaining in Albemarle would put him in technical violation of that law. Before obtaining permission to reside permanently in Albemarle, Kinney would first need to obtain proper freedom papers. Just over a month after he was freed and his wife's will was recognized as valid by the county court, John Kinney returned to the courthouse. He formally had his freedom recorded, paying the registration fee of twenty-five cents and receiving in return a certificate.[51]

Next, he filed an application with the county court seeking permission to remain in the commonwealth. He did not want to stay in the area in violation of the 1806 removal law, and he certainly entertained no thoughts of leaving the state. But to successfully usher such a request through the court process, Kinney would have to endure a two-month period in which his residency request would be posted on the front door of the courthouse. This gave notice to the community that a free person of color wanted to live in the area. Anyone who objected could come forward and testify against Kinney and his request. No one came forward to complain about him, but Kinney believed he would need more than that. He sought out local whites willing to state publicly that he was a respectable man valued by the community. It did not take long for Kinney to find people willing to do just that. In June, a majority of the magistrates for the county gathered. They heard his motion of application for residency and considered the testimony of white Albemarle residents. More than three-fourths of the magistrates present approved Kinney's application. The court found that John Kinney was "a person of good character, peacable, orderly and industrious, and not addicted to drunkenness, gaming or any other vice," and they granted him permission to remain in Virginia. Laissez-faire whites continued to represent a majority in Albemarle.[52]

John Kinney, a former slave who had been married to a free black woman, was now a free propertied resident of Albemarle. Five years later, census takers visited Kinney's home on Ridge Street. John was fifty-two; he lived with Susan, his daughter by Elizabeth Kinney, now a twenty-one-year-old woman. He also lived with one Mahala Tyree, a twenty-two-year-old woman of color. She may well have been his common-law wife, because there was a new addition to his family, a one-year-old girl named Julia A. Kinney. The Kinneys, both before Elizabeth died and after, were free blacks of modest means. They were known well enough and behaved properly; the family lived in relative comfort. And they lived in a close-knit community that included members of both races. The Kinncys lived next to John Bowyer, an old white blacksmith who could neither read nor write. They also lived next to the white laborer James Bragg, also illiterate, and virtually propertyless. Any free person of color who managed to live in relative comfort in Charlottesville or the surrounding county would almost by necessity have frequent interactions with slaves and free people, whites, blacks, and mulattoes. Both the Kinneys and the Barnetts were known to local whites by name, sight, and reputation.[53]

The Kinneys were a free family of color that did not have a single powerful white patron, did not have an ongoing sexual relationship with a white male benefactor, and were propertied but not well-to-do. They were a lower class of free black, but remained well connected to the community. The

Barnetts, however, represented something of a free colored elite. They had at least one white patron, Allen W. Hawkins, with whom Fanny Barnett apparently had a long-term sexual relationship. Between Fanny and her two daughters, they amassed a sizable estate, both real and personal. And they did all this while running a technically illicit brothel. This bawdy house would drag them to court yet again. In July 1857, Septimia Barnett was called to testify in a case that involved an interracial assault. Based upon the testimony of the white resident Chiles M. Brand, the free woman of color Margaret Ailstock was charged with "on June 30 whipping and beating white woman Jane Clarke in a most cruel and unlawful manner."[54]

At first glance, this shocking and very public assault would seem to have been a dangerous challenge to both the racial and the social hierarchies of any antebellum rural southern locale. One might expect the local white citizenry to demand harsh retribution for this defiant attack on southern white womanhood, while any sensible free black would keep out of the way, working hard to remain uninvolved in such a potentially explosive case. But neither of these expectations came to fruition in Albemarle. Ailstock indeed was quickly tried in a court of oyer and terminer, found guilty, and sentenced to receive ten stripes upon her bare back at the public whipping post—not as harsh as most punishments at the post and certainly not a punishment demonstrative of a community alarmed by the threat of black-on-white violence.

Ailstock, however, immediately appealed the case and filed a two-hundred-dollar bond guaranteeing her appearance at the appeal hearing. The court, in allowing the appeal, did not follow state law, which denied oyer and terminer defendants access to the appeal process (this was not the first instance of the county ignoring state law). She managed to recruit a white resident and sometime county official, Andrew J. Farish, to post his own two-hundred-dollar bond as surety for her. Even the free black Ailstock, after assaulting a white woman, was commonly known and trusted enough in the community both to be allowed to file an appeal and to receive white support. On July 6, Margaret's appeal was heard. Three whites again testified on behalf of Ailstock, while Clarke and Barnett again testified against her. The original verdict was upheld, the appeal denied. But the sentence was modified. She was now ordered to receive the lashes not on her bare back, but over her clothes. She was ordered to pay court costs and to pledge two hundred dollars as a recognizance guaranteeing her peaceable behavior. This time, the white resident Elijah Garth acted as security, filing a two-hundred-dollar bond promising that Ailstock would keep the peace for a year.[55] Ailstock was convicted largely on the testimony of the white victim, Jane Clarke, and that of the free woman of color Septimia Barnett. The judge apparently discounted the testimony of several whites, including William Cox, Richard Bailey, and Mary Bates, in support of Margaret Ailstock.[56]

Ailstock's public assault on a white woman did not cause local whites to rally together and demand tighter control of supposedly dangerous free blacks. No one called for harsher punishments of violations of a racial hierarchy. The punishment meted out to Ailstock may have been somewhat more severe than she would have received if she had assaulted another free black woman. But the attack did not cause alarm; she was not jailed, maimed, or worse. Even the public whipping was about as mild as such treatment could be. More typically, the few free blacks who were sent to the whipping post received at least fifteen and most often thirty-nine lashes on a bare back, "well laid on."

Why did the court, although ultimately rejecting Ailstock's appeal, allow her to appeal at all? Why did it also decide to soften the punishment by allowing her to leave her clothes on? Once again, the justices of the peace failed to record their thoughts on that day. The victim, Jane Clarke, appears to have been a woman of little or no property who lived and worked in the Random Row area, where that rowdy mixture of whites and blacks resided, worked, and played. As Fanny Barnett's experience as a young prostitute in the Riley bawdy house suggests, unattached young women of both races who lived in places such as Random Row often worked as prostitutes.

Jane Clarke, as far as the county court was concerned, may have been a woman of ill fame, who, although white, was not respectable and lacked community connections. She left scant evidence of her existence and residency in Albemarle. Since Septimia Barnett came into court as a witness for Clarke against Ailstock, Clarke may have worked in Barnett's bawdy house—a white woman working for a black one. Ailstock, too, was likely a woman "not of honest conversation." Young and unmarried, Ailstock also may have worked for the Barnetts. Orphaned at age eight, Ailstock had been bound out to a white man by the county overseers of the poor. She had been trained in spinning and weaving, but at age eighteen, when released from the apprenticeship, she had immediately connected with the Barnetts. On November 4, 1850, she came to the courthouse a free adult woman seeking her freedom papers. With her came her older sister Frances Ailstock, who had finished her apprenticeship seven years earlier. Also coming to the court for the same reason that day were Marinda French and Fanny Barnett.[57]

Thus, Septimia Barnett in 1857 knew both the victim and the defendant. Clarke may still have worked in the Barnett brothel, and Barnett may now have simply been helping an employee and acquaintance who happened to be white. Maybe Ailstock was a former employee who had left the Barnett establishment on less than favorable terms. Even if neither Clarke nor Ailstock still worked for Barnett, they all seem to have worked together in the same illicit trade. Septimia Barnett continued to follow in her mother's footsteps, seeking both economic safety and success, as well as a sense of security about her social station in town. Questions surrounding the participants' motives in that 1857 case will remain unanswered.

Septimia's move toward social respectability, however, is not a matter of pure speculation. After all, sometime in the year before Ailstock's court case, Allen Hawkins, Septimia's likely father and a man who had been an invaluable patron for well over a decade, died. For Septimia Barnett and her mother, this could have been problematic. If Hawkins's role as a white patron to the Barnetts was his most significant contribution to their lives, that connection suddenly vanished. But neither Fanny nor her daughters Septimia and Martha demonstrated any obvious concerns. They did not decide to move to Ohio or some other free territory. They remained in Albemarle, conducting life much as they had before 1850 and as they had while Allen Hawkins still lived. Not only did they remain, but they found ways to improve their situation, ever gaining respectability in the eyes of the community.

By 1860, Septimia Barnett had taken over as the head of the Barnett household. Septimia was now thirty-one years old and still lived in the Random Row area of Charlottesville. She owned two thousand dollars' worth of real estate and an amazing six thousand dollars' worth of personal property. Her mother, Fanny, now an elderly woman, lived with Septimia, as did her sister Martha Barnett. The archives suggest that the Barnett family continued to operate a brothel at least until the late 1850s, if not longer. But it was not their occupation that determined the Barnetts' social standing in town. That status was determined by two basic factors. First, they were familiar to many in the white community. Likewise, they needed to develop reputations as people whose behavior contributed to the neighborhood in some way. Simply being light skinned or having a white benefactor was not an important factor if a free black sought to escape the legal disabilities associated with skin color. Connections to many whites in the community and a reputation for respectable behavior, however, were the linchpins to success.

A year later, the Civil War began. The county was never the site of any concentrated military maneuvers or engagements, though it suffered from the loss of its young men and the privations brought on by an ailing southern wartime economy. Otherwise, life in this rural and agricultural slave society continued in many of the same ways it had before the war. In 1862, as if a war over slavery was not occurring, Septimia Barnett and her sister Martha completed their fascinating march away from "free mulatto" status. In that year, the sisters both applied to the county court, claiming that they were of mixed blood and should be officially declared "Not Negros." This classification, created by the legislature in 1832, allowed light-skinned free people of color to be declared not black, if they could provide evidence that they had less than 25 percent African ancestry, a proposition best proved by support for their application from whites.[58]

With a war raging in America that was sending shudders through the racially based slave system, it is hard to imagine that communities would entertain discussions of the minutiae of racial classification. Anyone long known as black or mulatto presumably would remain so. But this was not the case—Septimia and Martha felt secure in applying to be declared "Not Negros." The court heard their application, listened to the testimony of local whites, and made a determination. The court declared "Septimia and Martha Barnett, mixed blood Albemarle residents, both daughters of free woman of color Fanny Barnett of Charlottesville, both to have less than one fourth negro blood and therefore certified as 'not a negro.'" Their move away from the disabilities associated with blackness and their inclusion in a more respectable Charlottesville community had just been codified by the court.[59]

Septimia's new status may have served to enhance her business activity. She continued to engage in real estate sales. Six months after she was declared "not a negro," Septimia sold the parcel of land she had purchased in 1852 from the free black Julia Ann Mann. She sold the lot to the white man George Moore for four hundred dollars, the same price she had originally paid for it. Moore was the same man who had watched Barnett purchase one of his properties at a public insolvency auction a decade earlier. A month later, in January 1863, Barnett again sold land to Moore. This time, Moore and his neighbor Peter Harman paid Barnett over one thousand dollars in inflated Confederate currency for a quarter-acre tract of land, the same tract that she had purchased from Thomas Goings back in 1851. By 1863, Barnett had received some schooling—she actually signed the deed selling land to Moore and Harman.[60]

Barnett, now legally not black, firmly occupied a de jure status somewhere between free black and white citizen, and she had achieved this in the rural Upper South. Not only did she continue to make money playing the real estate market, but she continued to position herself and her family to the best of her ability. For women, this process could be difficult. If a female property owner married, her property would become her husband's unless the deed made a specific stipulation. On Christmas day 1863, Septimia sold land to her sister Betsy Barnett for one thousand dollars. The property was the same that Barnett had purchased in February 1855 at public auction. The deal, as part of her effort to maintain female ownership of Barnett property, conveyed the property only as a life estate for Betsy. At Betsy's death, the property would go to her children. Septimia mimicked her mother's decisions, making sure that property passed smoothly from generation to generation and that it would never be surrendered should the female purchaser marry. Betsy Barnett, also known as Betsy Ann or Elizabeth Ann, though she was the younger sister of the no-longer-Negro Septimia, was still known and recognized as a free woman of color, the daughter of Fanny Barnett. By selling the land to her sister in life estate, Septimia followed the same protective strategy her mother Fanny had begun years earlier—working hard to ensure that family property endured across generations in the hands of female Barnetts.[61]

Less than a year and a half later, the Civil War ended in defeat for the Confederacy and for white Virginia. A general emancipation ensued, and slavery was dead in central Virginia. As residents of the state, both black and white, stumbled through the chaotic and confusing postwar reconstruction, Septimia Barnett quietly continued to utilize her energy and her connections. In December 1869, Septimia Barnett bought two tracts of land, one in Albemarle and the other in Augusta County, just across the Blue Ridge Mountains. The Albemarle property was known as "Westview," a 500-acre farm situated in the eastern portion of the county, on Redbud Creek. In Augusta County, Septimia purchased the "Pelter Property," a 337-acre tract of land at Mountain Top. Septimia Barnett's real estate investments no longer only involved lots in Charlottesville. Suddenly, she was dealing in much larger and more valuable tracts. She purchased the Pelter Property in Augusta County for $2,201. More impressively, though, she purchased Westview in Albemarle for $8,000.[62]

Where did Septimia manage to get over ten thousand dollars? How did a woman who at the start of the Civil War was a free black owner of a house of prostitution manage to move so quickly toward whiteness, respectability, and significant property holding? The deed of sale for the two tracts of land sheds some light on the situation. The Pelter Property was located in the area of Rockfish Gap, the main regional east-west passage over the Blue Ridge Mountains. It had been deeded in 1867 to three brothers: James, Dabney, and Dr. John Minor. Westview, in Albemarle, originally had been deeded to James Minor and William W. Minor. William had died and by his will had conveyed his interest in Westview to James Minor. The Minors next took out a deed of trust on both tracts of land. Someone in the Minor family was deeply in debt, because the trustees immediately prepared to sell both tracts to the highest bidder. On September 30, 1869, the Pelter Property was advertised, as was the Westview property one week later.[63]

Unfortunately for the Minors, the trustees were sure that the sale of the two tracts of land was "not likely to bring cash enough to defray the costs of the said sale and the execution of the trust." Septimia Barnett was in fact a creditor of the beleaguered Minors. At that public auction in the fall of 1869, Barnett purchased the land, paying just over four hundred dollars in cash to the trustees, in compliance with the auction advertisement and the sale agreement. The deed of sale further stipulated that "the residue of the purchase money," nearly ten thousand dollars, "should be credited as a payment of so much cash on the claims held by the said Septimia Barnett against the said James and Dabney Minor or against said James Minor." After paying four hundred dollars of the purchase price, the remainder was applied to the large sum James Minor owed Septimia. Apparently, even this sale did not free the Minors from debt to Septimia Barnett. They still owed her just over thirty-seven dollars. James Minor immediately executed to her a new bond payable in gold "which is endorsed as a credit at its gold value."[64]

A little over two years later, Septimia Barnett continued to be financially involved with the extended Minor family. On April 13, 1872, Septimia Barnett filed her own deed of trust. She owed Catharine Emmerson more than two thousand dollars. As security for this large debt, Septimia gave her title to the 540-acre Westview farm to John L. Cochran as trustee. Cochran would hold title to the land until Barnett repaid Emmerson in full. Catharine Emmerson had been born as Catharine Minor, the sister of James, Dabney, and Dr. John Minor. The deed of trust does not explain why Septimia owed money to Emmerson. Other Minor family documents likewise do not shed light on the continuing connection between Septimia Barnett and the family. As she had for well over a decade, Septimia Barnett continued to practice a two-pronged economic strategy in Albemarle County. First, she continued to conduct business with elite white families. The extent of these transactions, and at times the great financial sums attending them, suggest that their connection was more than a casual business relationship. The Minors knew her well and trusted her.[65]

But Septimia remembered the difficult position in which she had started life, one that was exacerbated by the community's categorization of her as a person of color. Septimia's other economic strategy concerned her extended family, in particular those still classified as people of color. In August 1874, Septimia's mother, Fanny, died, having lived well into her eighties. Upon her death, a parcel of land that Allen Hawkins had deeded to Fanny as a life estate became the property of the sisters Martha and Septimia. At this point, Septimia was already a property owner of considerable means who had achieved something approaching legal whiteness even before Emancipation. This parcel of land was not a foundational property for her portfolio. But Septimia recognized that the property could continue to be used for the benefit of the larger family and handed down through the generations. With that in mind, Septimia filed a deed stating her "desire to convey all of her interest in said property to Darris S. West, wife of John West, for her life, and after her death to her children." For one dollar, an entirely symbolic purchase price, Septimia deeded her half interest in that house and lot on Main Street.

Who was Darris S. West? West had been born Darris S. Barnett in 1852, the daughter of either Septimia or Martha. In 1860, Darris S. Barnett was listed as living in Septimia's household, along with Martha Barnett and her grandmother Fanny. She was eight years old then and listed in that census as a mulatto girl. In 1874, Darris West was a young woman in her early twenties who had recently married the free man of color John West. By this deed, Septimia sought to protect the next generation of the Barnett family, particularly the female component. This was a strategy that the Barnetts would practice at least until the 1880s. And it was a family strategy, not solely Septimia's. For instance, Martha Barnett in May 1881 sold to John West a half interest in another property on the north side of University Street in Charlottesville for three hundred dollars. John West acted as trustee for his wife, Darris, and their children. Martha Barnett, like her sister before her, sought to use property to protect two succeeding generations of Barnett women.[66]

What do the life stories of these three free women of color and their friends and family actually reveal about life in antebellum Albemarle? First, their lives demonstrate clearly that contact between whites and blacks was a common occurrence in this rural county. Moreover, interracial interactions of this kind were seldom seen by local whites as fraught with peril. Instead, free blacks participated freely in the local society and culture, and most were not viewed as dangerous or liminal free people of color. Instead, they were seen as community members who were trustworthy and hardworking. This easy and open racial interaction continued through and beyond the Civil War; it did not end in the wake of either Gabriel's abortive 1800 rebellion or Nat Turner's bloody 1831 Southampton revolt.

Second, these women demonstrate that interracial sex was a regular feature of life in Albemarle County. Contrary to much of the scholarship on interracial sex, the evidence for Albemarle suggests that a rural or small-town locale could actually be as permissive as an urban area. Prosecutions for prostitution occurred infrequently, and the punishments meted out were mild. This culture of personalism, which was founded on daily face-to-face interaction, actually allowed interracial houses of prostitution to exist and sometimes flourish in and around Charlottesville at least until the 1850s.

But these women's life stories demonstrate that interracial sex was not the only path to success for free women of color. Some of them went from being prostitutes of ill fame to being legally white property owners controlling significant capital. They achieved results in part by having sex with white men and in part by maintaining long-term relationships with some of them. But they also changed their status by maneuvering successfully and gaining credibility within the local society and culture. They were known personages who strove to behave respectably, who worked hard, paid their debts, and became trusted fixtures on the local scene. Their white benefactors took them only so far. Their own behavior took care of the rest.

Although the Barnetts ultimately managed to achieve great multigenerational success, their lives also suggest that life as both a free black and a woman in the antebellum rural South remained fraught with difficulties and obstacles. The Barnett women worked hard to make each female in their family into a property-owning and respectable member of the community. But they also diligently renewed freedom certificates, unlike the free blacks discussed in the first two chapters—men such as Shadrach Battles, Charles Barnett, and Elijah Battles. Clearly, the female Barnetts' actions suggest that independent womanhood for free blacks was an exceptional status that defied gendered expectations of the time. The Barnett women wanted a long and clear paper trail documenting their free status and their ownership of property. The three Barnett women wanted more than a locally permitted move toward a kind of social whiteness. They felt it necessary to transform this situational whiteness into something more concrete. Thus, two of them petitioned the court requesting to be considered "not a negro." After the court granted their wish, their journey, in some ways, was complete.[67]

6

An Easy Morality

Community Knowledge of Interracial Sex

Richard Thomas Walker Duke Jr., writing his memoirs in the early twentieth century, painted a fascinating portrait of Charlottesville and Albemarle County in the antebellum period. Born in 1853, Duke recollected his childhood in an important family in the county. He grew up learning from his father about the histories behind the faces, white and black, that they saw daily. The world Richard Duke remembered was not a world of only black and white, however, nor was it a world of strict separation of the races. His memories illustrate clearly the routine nature of contact among whites, blacks, and mulattos, slaves and free people. Family slaves and free people of color appear as multidimensional personages, in much the same way that prominent whites do. Certainly, Duke's memoirs portray a more benign master-slave relationship than truly existed. The mist of time separated Duke from that childhood, and his "moonlight and magnolias" memories of race relations suggest that he censored the stories and memories that did not depict a blissful pre–Civil War life. Yet a close reading of his memoirs unveils a fine-grained, personal portrait of the non-whites he knew.[1]

Duke's color palette in describing skin color was impressive: black, very black, yellow, ginger bread–colored, mulatto, ruddy, florid. His careful renderings of the skin tone of the people he knew demonstrate the highly personal nature of Albemarle's culture. For Duke and other Albemarle residents, face-to-face relationships shaped the human landscape. The range of complexions among "Negroes" hints also at the widespread sexual activity between whites and blacks over many years. For instance, in 1833, there were 452 free people of color in Albemarle County, 397 of whom were recognized as mulatto. Nearly nine out of every ten free people of color in Albemarle had white ancestors.[2]

Duke did not simply hint at the occurrence of sex across the color line, however. He addressed miscegenation directly. In a passage fondly remembering the family slaves he grew up with, Duke described Maria as "a housemaid—a rather handsome ginger-bread coloured woman." According to Richard, Maria became the subject of some consternation in the Duke family when "she increased the live stock with a yellow baby—Caesar—whose father she always claimed was John Yates Beal—a student at the University of Virginia." Duke remembered first that a mulatto slave gave birth to a child who was much lighter skinned than she. He even remembered the name and description of the person she said was the father, and his recollections suggest that he did not doubt her story: "If there is anything in likenesses the wench's story is true. Caesar—now an immense six footer is remarkably like a picture of Beal I saw in Charlestown, W. Va. where he lived."[3]

Duke's story about Maria and her "yellow" son Caesar was not an isolated mention of interracial sex. The former Virginia slave Byrl Anderson's early childhood memories included one in which his white father "took me on his knee an' gave me his birthright. He called up an' ole sow that had thirteen pigs all different collors. He said, 'You see them pigs there? They are all of different colors but all have the same mother and are all brothers and sisters.' Then he called up his son and said, 'This boy here is your brother an' I am the daddy of both.'" Anderson's recollection of the results of interracial sex was not unusual. Frank Bell remembered that "dey was many a little white-skinned nigger baby that growed up on ole Marser's plantation." Susie R. C. Byrd, describing one of her ex-slave interview subjects in the 1930s, noted that "Dr. Carter is a squat, light-colored Caucasian featured mulatto. . . . Dr. Carter's two claims to fame are his 'free issue' ancestry which he got by having 'a white pappy.'" Another former slave, Robert Ellett, described himself this way: "I am a mixture of Negro-Indian-French and white blood." Uncle Moble Hopson recollected that "Mammy was uh Injun an' muh pappy was uh white man, least-ways he warn't no slave even effen he was sorta dark-skinned." Even former slaves defined people they knew partly by remembering skin tone. Richard Duke's recollections continually return to the subject of miscegenation, confirming those slave memoirs that suggest that interracial sex occurred often.[4]

Many of these relationships occurred in relatively plain view. Nor were all of them instances of whites having sex with female slaves or the result of the sex trade. To be sure, interracial sex was an important feature of bawdy houses in Charlottesville and elsewhere in the South. But sex across the color line happened in other settings, too. Henry Ferry, recalling his childhood as a slave near Danville, Virginia, remembered that his master's wife never had any children because the master instead slept regularly with his slave Martha. Ferry stated that "Marsa was always goin' down to the shacks where she [Martha] lived. Marse John used to treat Martha's boy, Jim, jus' like his own son, which [he] was. Jim used to run all over de big house, an' Missus didn't like it, but she didn't dare put him out." Neither was this household arrangement kept completely hidden:

> One day de Parson come to call. He knew Marse John but didn't know Missus Mamie. He come to de house an' Jim com runnin' down de stairs to meet him. He took the little boy up in his arms an' rubbed his haid, an' when Missus come, tol' her how much de boy look like his father and mother. "Course it favor its father most," de preacher say, tryin' to be polite, "but in de eyes, de lookin' glass of de soul, I kin see dat he's his mother's boy." Miss Mamie shooed de child away an' took de preacher inside. Never did let on it wasn't her chile. Was pow'ful mad 'bout it, though. Never would let dat boy in de hose no' mo'.

In this passage, the wife's actions evince an implicit knowledge about the child's parentage. A former Tidewater slave, Charles Grandy, remembered "an ole white man name Mack Moss had a colored woman fer overseer an' wife." Sis Shackelford agreed: "Lots o' white men had cullud wives. I knowed lots o' cases." Such common-law marriage arrangements may have occurred with some regularity across the South. Whites and blacks in Virginia were legally prevented from marrying, but they could live together as man and wife as long as the neighbors accepted the relationship. Charles Grandy's memories seem to say that they often did.[5]

Richard Thomas Walker Duke's memoirs suggest that many interracial sexual relationships were visible to far more than the slave community, and they involved whites of all social stations. In a rural and highly personal culture in which almost everyone in the community was familiar with everyone else, ongoing sexual ties between whites and blacks would be very hard to hide. Whites of all social stations, by regularly allowing these relationships to continue, gave local social sanction to them. Duke, speaking about Robert and James Scott, "the best known and finest 'fiddlers' in the Country," commented that "they were the sons of old man Jesse Scott and his wife who was a daughter of Col. Bell." Scott's wife was a woman of "mixed blood," and Duke asserted that her musical sons "evidently had negro blood in their veins." Jesse Scott, himself the product of generations of interracial sexual unions, had married a woman of similar background. Scott's father-in-law, Colonel Thomas Bell, himself was involved in an open interracial union. According to Duke, "his [Bell's] 'woman' was said to be of Indian descent with a very slight admixture of negro. With the rather 'easy' morality of those early days no one paid any attention to a man's method of living & Col. Bell lived openly with the woman & had two children by her. One was Jesse Scott's wife—the other a very handsome young man, of whom Col. Bell was very proud." The Bell children themselves went on to intermarry with other mixed-race residents of the area.[6]

A closer inspection of Colonel Thomas Bell's relationship with that mulatto woman reveals just how unremarkable interracial sex may have been in Albemarle. It also reveals how miscegenation connected wealthy, poor, and middling whites to the free and enslaved black communities in Albemarle. In 1784, Thomas Bell was new to Albemarle County, having come east across the mountains from Augusta County. He purchased two lots on the main street running east-west through Charlottesville and moved into an approximately twenty-year-old log home, a former tavern. These purchases were the beginning of Thomas Bell's important role in developing Charlottesville. Bell first improved the house, building an addition on the west end; he also ran a general store out of the dwelling.[7]

Thomas Bell, through his general store on Main Street in Charlottesville, met numerous Albemarle residents on a daily basis and rose to prominence, developing a highly respectable reputation. Thomas Jefferson, who became his friend, described Bell as a "man remarkable for his integrity." In 1787, Thomas Jefferson was working as an American diplomat in Paris. Bell hired a slave from Monticello, a house servant named Mary Hemings. For the next five years, Hemings remained in Bell's house as a hired slave.

Hemings returned to Monticello shortly after Thomas Jefferson had returned from France, but she asked her master to sell her to Thomas Bell. Jefferson agreed. Bell, however, purchased not only this favored slave from Jefferson; he also bought two of her children, of whom he himself was the father. This was not the act of someone seeking more labor, nor was it simply an act of benevolence, a kind master allowing a slave to bring her children with her: Thomas Bell in 1792 purchased his own children. Mary Hemings, a mulatto slave, and Thomas Bell, a white merchant, wanted to raise their children together, "living openly," as Richard Duke put it. Charlottesville at the time was a small village. James Alexander described the town over thirty years later as having "few houses, and only two or three business places on it." Thomas Bell ran a mercantile business in his own home. Customers must have come and gone with great frequency. They would have noticed Mary, the living arrangements, and later the resemblance of Mary's children to Bell himself.[8]

Although no deed of manumission for Mary Hemings has been found in the public record, the community apparently considered her free and did not behave as if it saw Bell's relationship with a free woman of color as an outrageous violation of racial hierarchy or as an evil and dissolute act. Finally, the white community may have accepted the couple's open cohabitation because they did not claim to have a sacralized union even if they lived as if man and wife. They did not violate religious or secular law concerning marriage, nor did they participate publicly in outrageous and troubling behavior.

The community viewed Mary Hemings as a free woman, and her children with Bell were likewise considered free. This social milieu, however, was predicated upon a steep hierarchy. Robert Washington Bell and Sarah Jefferson Bell, Mary and Thomas Bell's children, were seen as well-behaved, respectable community members, but they did not occupy anything close to the same station as the likes of Thomas Jefferson or even their own father. Richard Duke, speaking about Robert Washington Bell, commented that "Col. Bell was very proud. He sent him [Robert Washington Bell] up North to school and college & he came back a very elegant & charming fellow—tho' of course with no social status whatever." Duke's remarks perfectly distill how this highly personal social culture functioned. Robert Washington Bell, even though he was technically a person of color, could achieve a measure of respectability. Some local whites, although not considering him a marginal or anomalous figure, did see him as living at the lower rungs of the social hierarchy.[9]

Thomas Bell lived as if his relationship with Mary Hemings were perfectly normal. About five years after he freed Mary Hemings, Bell drew up his will. If he were to die intestate, his estate would not go to his common-law wife or to his children, who were technically illegitimate. Bell hoped that writing a will would ensure that his estate would remain in the possession of his immediate family. That he seemingly felt no reluctance to make a written admission of his relationship with Hemings and with his "natural son" and "natural daughter" suggests once again that the relationship was already open.[10]

Thomas Bell ordered that, upon Mary Hemings's death, her life portion of the estate would go to their son, Robert Washington Bell. He also gave jointly to his white nephew William Love and his son, Robert, "all my personal estate I may die possessed of in the county of Albemarle, State of Kentucky, northwest of the River Ohio." Bell did not forget his daughter. He ordered Robert and William to pay Sarah Jefferson Bell, as soon as she turned twenty-one, one-sixth of the personal estate and one-tenth of the real estate that they would inherit. Last, Thomas Bell provided for two of his slaves. First, he ordered his slave Armistead emancipated at age thirty-one. In the meantime, Armistead could choose whether he remained with Robert Washington or William Love. Next, Bell provided for "his old Negroe man Darby." He ordered that Darby was "not to be sold out of the family unless it be his choice." In a few short paragraphs, Thomas Bell had permanently recorded his interracial family's existence and structure in an official document. Bell, in taking a formerly enslaved and now free woman of color as his common-law wife, did not become an abolitionist (even though he did manumit one slave through his will). He still owned slaves, though he seems to have been a relatively considerate master; his household contained free whites, free people of color, and slaves, as did the community at large, with daily, close contact between free and enslaved individuals and between blacks and whites.[11]

Thomas Bell appointed two white relatives and two other white men to execute his will: his nephews Robert Gambill and William Love and his "worthy friends" Wilson Cary Nicholas and Thomas Carr Jr. Bell signed the will in the presence of a number of white witnesses, including Thomas Carr Jr., John Carr, and Peter Lott. Apparently, Bell had a good reputation, and so did Mary. No one voiced any objection to their family arrangements, which were common knowledge.

Robert Washington Bell continued the trend set by his father. According to the recollections of Richard Duke, the Bells had wealthy white neighbors named Schenck. The two families surely knew one another. The Schencks lived across a side street from the Bells, occupying the next lot to the west on Main Street. Robert Washington Bell was an educated and light-skinned man of color whom some in the Charlottesville community may have considered white or at least "not a negro." Tax lists do not identify Robert W. Bell as a free black or mulatto. The census reports list him as white and make no mention of any free blacks living in his household. Duke recalled that the Schencks "had a daughter 'passing fair' who in some way became acquainted with young Bell. . . . One fine morning the Schencks woke up to find their daughter had eloped with this young fellow." Duke seems only mildly surprised that a white woman would consort with a "very handsome young man . . . very elegant & charming." Robert Washington Bell's passing as a white person was not a secretive act. His past was not obscured. Instead, the community, recognizing his father as a member of the social elite with a good reputation, ignored or downplayed the fact that Robert Washington Bell's mother was a free woman of color.[12]

Thomas Bell and Mary Hemings's other child, Sarah Jefferson Bell, had a similar life experience as a member of an openly interracial family. Neither Thomas Bell nor Mary Hemings ever entered a deed of manumission for either Sarah or Robert, who thus, according to the law, were still slaves. Neither of them, however, was ever considered by the community to be a slave. They lived as if they were free, and the community accorded them the privileges of freedom. The Charlottesville community, as they did with her brother, seemed to see Sarah as white or at least "not a negro."

In 1802, Sarah Bell married Jesse Scott, a local man of confusing racial origins. Richard Duke described Scott's family as "not negroes—tho' they evidently had negro blood in their veins." The newspaper editor James Alexander remembered Jesse Scott as "half Indian, half white—married the daughter of Col. Bell." The southern writer Orra Langhorne termed the Scotts "mulattoes, men of fine manners, good musicians, and generally popular." Jesse Scott, though openly of mixed racial heritage, had an outstanding reputation in town. Alexander, speaking about Jesse and the two sons he had with Sally Jefferson Bell, said, "The Scotts have always stood well in this place, and were respected by every one." The Scotts and the Bells represent excellent examples of people who confound notions about a strict color line in the rural Upper South in the antebellum period.

Both the Bell children and the entire Scott family were known to have "mixed blood." They did not work to obscure their heritage or pass as white. Instead, the community treated them as racially ambivalent but socially white. They assiduously maintained a respectable reputation and carved out an existence in Albemarle that allowed them many of the privileges usually reserved for whites. Enjoying such privileges, however, did not mean that these people were white in all respects. They remained legally people of color and still lacked full citizenship rights.

This intermediate status functioned as an outgrowth of both Albemarle's personal culture of respectability and its implicit, nuanced recognition of a spectrum of social stations between black slave and white elite. These included free black, free mulatto, mixed race but not "Negro," and possessed of some non-white blood but legally and socially white. These stations depended not solely on actual somatic condition. A largely white heritage known to the community, or a light complexion, each remained an important factor in achieving a recognized sense of social whiteness or something approaching that status. But behavior, reputation, and respectability were the most important measures. The Scotts traded on both their light complexions and their well-maintained reputations to achieve a degree of social whiteness in slaveholding society.[13]

Orra Langhorne in particular vividly portrays just how all this may have functioned. She said that the "Scotts for many years made the rounds of the fashionable watering places." They enjoyed public entertainments in the presence of and with whites. Jesse Scott, by all accounts, was a topnotch fiddler. He and Sarah brought up their two boys, Robert and James, as respectable young men with great musical training. According to Langhorne, "the taste for music shown by [Jesse's] family had early attracted Mr. Jefferson's notice . . . and had encouraged him [Jesse] to have his children educated." Jesse took the advice from the sage of Monticello to heart. The sons "had attended white school in Charlottesville." The Scotts did not violate any sense of racial propriety, and the community saw them as in many ways worthy of the privileges of whiteness. Langhorne, quoting Robert Scott, summed it up best: "the prejudice between the races was not so strong then as now, and he [Robert] had never heard of any objection being made to the presence of the colored pupils in his school." Scott did not get it quite right. Prejudice in some quarters was quite strong even in the antebellum period. But the racial divide clearly was not policed as systematically as it would be in the era of Jim Crow.[14]

Since 1797, Robert Washington Bell had effectively controlled his father's estate. The house and lots in Charlottesville had gone to his mother, Mary

Hemings, in life estate, but all would ultimately go to Robert and Thomas Bell's white nephew William Love. In July 1802, administration of Thomas Bell's estate was not going well. Debts mounted. William Love, facing several civil judgments against him, mortgaged his share of the estate to creditors. In August 1803, the trustees William W. Hening, John Kelly, and Peter Lott held a public auction at the Eagle Tavern in town and auctioned off Love's share of the Bell estate to his neighbor Cornelius Schenck for $202. For the Bells, this meant that control over what was left of the family estate now lay only in the hands of Robert Washington Bell. Robert, though a charming and respectable person, was not responsible with money. Since the end of the eighteenth century, Robert had been frittering away the sizable estate his father had left him. Fortunately for his mother and sister, he did not yet have control over the house and lots in Charlottesville. The mountain of debt his spending created finally caught up with him in 1813. One creditor, Martin Davison & Company, filed suit against Bell in the fall of that year. The firm sought full payment from Bell but knew Robert actually lacked the cash to pay off his long-overdue account with them. The firm applied to the court to have Bell declared insolvent. Then, his assets would be auctioned off to pay the debt, and Martin Davison & Company would finally receive at least some payment.[15]

Martin Davison & Company was victorious. Robert Washington Bell came to the courthouse and took the oath of an insolvent debtor. The court also ordered him to sign an indenture conveying all real estate that he possessed to his creditors. Robert had squandered much of his father's sizable estate. Finding himself legally insolvent, Robert may have realized that his reputation had taken a turn for the worse. He could no longer count on the goodwill of the community. As a credit risk and spendthrift, he would no longer be seen as trustworthy. Perhaps this, rather than Bell's mixed-race parentage, was why Richard Duke referred to Bell as having "no social status whatever." Although no other documents make reference to Bell's eloping with the Schenck daughter, that scenario seems plausible. With his insolvency about to become public knowledge, Bell may have decided that leaving town with a young lady and starting over elsewhere was the best idea, an option his family might well have opposed.[16]

For Sarah Jefferson Bell, however, her brother's insolvency posed a problem. Robert Washington Bell, according to Thomas Bell's will, would jointly own the family house in Charlottesville after his mother, Mary Hemings, died. Sarah, now known as Sarah Jefferson Scott, and her husband, Jesse, benefited greatly from the Bell properties in Charlottesville. They lived in a sizable home. They interacted easily with whites in town in no small part because Sarah was Thomas Bell's child and Jesse Scott was not considered a person of color. Jesse Scott by 1810 had a fine reputation, but he possessed no land as sole owner. Back in 1804, however, he had purchased from his neighbor Cornelius Schenck William Love's interest in the lots where the Bell house was located. That purchase was the beginning of his property ownership in Albemarle. Thanks partly to his highly respectable reputation, but also thanks to his connection to the Bell house and lots in Charlottesville, he lived well.[17]

In May 1810, Jesse Scott was charged with "unlawful gaming at cards in his own house." This was no simple case where a white community tightly policing the racial hierarchy trumped up charges against a free person of color. Quite the contrary, the case against Jesse Scott offers a revealing glimpse into the interracial community in Charlottesville. The charge itself was unremarkable. Albemarle men, white and black, were regularly charged with illegal gaming. If convicted, the defendant could expect to pay a small fine. Also charged for participating in that same game of cards were white residents Richard Garland and Peter Garner. As far as those men were concerned, Jesse Scott was part of their circle. Going to his house to play cards was not an illicit or surreptitious act, court authorities seemed to agree; Garner, Garland, and Scott did not threaten the racial order by socializing together. The case against these men went nowhere, and the court dismissed the charges in 1811. Jesse Scott's reputation does not appear to have suffered from the incident.[18]

Jesse Scott and his wife, Sarah, lived comfortably in the old Bell house on Main Street, but they sought greater security. With Robert Washington Bell's insolvency a looming issue, they could not expect to remain in the Bell house forever unless they made some sort of financial preparations. Jesse Scott worked hard to save money and accrue property. By 1812, small signs of the Scotts' success began to show. In that year, Jesse Scott owned one horse, an adult slave, and a slave child. Even if these were relatives who were only technically Scott's slaves, he still had saved enough to cover their purchase price. He had also purchased a gig (a two-wheeled riding carriage). Three years later, he had added two cattle to his growing list of personal property. Jesse Scott now owned one mahogany table, a mahogany bookcase, a cabinet, and two carpets worth between fifty and one hundred dollars each. Despite still technically lacking a controlling interest in any real estate, Jesse and Sarah J. Scott were doing quite well. Their growing family continued to lead a comfortable existence in Charlottesville.[19]

Meanwhile, Sarah's brother, Robert, continued his slide into complete insolvency. In July 1813, part of his interest in the old Bell house and lot on Main Street had already been conveyed to John R. Jones as part of the bankruptcy agreement. Bell owed some $328 to William Wardlaw and Nimrod Branham. Additionally, he owed Branham alone over $150. To secure payment to Robert Washington Bell's creditors, Jones auctioned off his share in the old Bell property in November 1813.[20]

By 1820, Jesse Scott, acting on behalf of his wife, Sarah, and his mother-in-law, Mary Hemings, began actively to pursue ownership of the remnants of the Bell estate in Charlottesville. He purchased Robert's remaining interest in the family estate, finally ensuring that he and his wife could continue to live in the Bell house on Main Street. The Scotts now began to pursue a more aggressive program of purchasing land. In 1821, Jesse Scott bought forty-eight acres on the headwaters of Doyle's River in northwestern Albemarle County for two hundred dollars. Scott purchased real estate again less than five months later. This time, he bought a half-acre plot of land lying on the north side of Three Notched Road between Charlottesville and the University of Virginia, about a half-mile west on Main Street from the Bell house. This was an impressive purchase at eight hundred dollars.[21]

Two decades of marriage for Jesse and Sarah J. Scott had proven quite lucrative. In that time, they had refurnished the Bell house; purchased title to the house and lots in Charlottesville; acquired a forty-eight-acre farm in the county; and bought a plot of land in an area of growth, the stretch of road between town and the university. These properties ranged from quite valuable (the downtown lots), to moderately priced (the lot between town and university), to low value (the farm in the county). Jesse Scott and his family were of a racially mixed background, and the Charlottesville community knew it. But the community, for all intents and purposes, considered the Scotts white. For example, the 1820 U.S. Census lists Jesse Scott as a white male, the head of a household containing eight white people: six white men and two white women, one of whom was his wife, Sarah Jefferson Scott. Jesse Scott sent Robert, James, and Thomas, his three sons, to white schools. He entertained white men in his house. He did business with anyone and everyone. And he did all of this in a community that knew that he and his wife were of mixed heritage. The family's upward mobility continued in the 1820s. In 1826, Scott again purchased land, this time another plot on Three Notched Road, on the way to the university. This plot adjoined the original half-acre plot. He paid $235, extending his road frontage to forty feet.[22]

Despite living as a successful, respectable, and socially white man in Charlottesville, Jesse Scott was still married to a woman who was technically a slave. Scott's mother-in-law was a free woman of color who was related to a large slave family at Monticello. In fact, Mary Hemings had a family before she ever met Thomas Bell back in the 1780s. The Bell house on Main Street thus linked prominent Albemarle whites, free people of color, and slaves. Albemarle's intricate social web encompassed every social and racial grouping in the county. Jesse Scott could live as if white, but he did not ignore his non-white and non-free family members. Until 1826, the fact that some of the larger Hemings family, Jesse Scott's kin by marriage, remained enslaved was cause for concern, but not a problem demanding, or allowing, immediate remedy. The enslaved family members lived only a short distance outside of town, at Jefferson's Monticello. The Scott family, especially Jesse, was on speaking terms with Jefferson, so they surely had fairly regular contact with enslaved family members on Jefferson's property.

But by early 1826, the fate of those enslaved family members suddenly came to be of great concern. Thomas Jefferson was in his eighties and in failing health. He had freed only two of his slaves during his life, and there was little hope that he would decide to free them now.[23] To make matters worse, Jefferson's financial situation was chaotic. He was deeply in debt, and a considerable portion of his estate, including slaves, would have to be sold off to pay creditors. Mary Hemings's other children, possibly fathered by the free white carpenter William Fossett, could face the auction block when Jefferson's estate was sold off in February 1827. Mary's son Joseph Fossett was the only person in this particular family to receive his freedom upon Jefferson's death. Jefferson's will left Joseph's wife, Edith, and their children, Mary Hemings's grandchildren, in slavery and subject to public sale. Jesse Scott attended the February sale, purchasing Edith and two of their children for $505.[24]

In addition to working to free his extended family by marriage, Jesse Scott after that 1827 estate sale continued in much the same fashion as before. He remained of ambiguous racial classification, living as if white. The U.S. Census, having recorded the Scotts as white in 1820, classified Jesse

Scott in 1830 as a free colored head of a household of six people of color that included one older slave woman. Jesse, his wife, Sarah, his sons Robert and James, an unnamed daughter, and one female slave lived in the house. Their third son, Thomas, had been apprenticed to a white carpenter. In July 1833, when the county was conducting its state-mandated colonization census of free people of color, the commissioners George M. Woods and Ira Harris went from house to house in Charlottesville and Albemarle County. If they visited the Scott-Bell residence, the lists they signed when their survey was complete do not say so. Neither Jesse Scott, his wife, Sarah, nor their children were listed as living in either Fredericksville or St. Anne's Parish. No Bells made the list either. As far as county officials in 1833 were concerned, the Scotts were at a bare minimum "not negro."[25]

But who was that old slave living in the Scott household in 1830? It may have been Mary Hemings, who lived as if free but may not actually have received a deed of manumission. Perhaps it was Joseph Fossett's wife, Edith, whom Jesse had purchased at the Jefferson estate sale in 1827. On the other hand, this enslaved woman may simply have been an investment made by Jesse Scott, either a slave he had purchased or a hired house servant. A person who appears to be that same slave shows up again in the Scott household in 1840. This could not have been Mary Hemings, who died in 1834, or Edith Fossett; Joseph Fossett was also listed as a free colored head of household in the 1830 census, and his household included five slaves: one adult woman (likely Edith) and four children. Starting in 1832 no free black was allowed under the law to "acquire ownership, except by descent, to any slave other than his or her husband, wife or children." Well after the passage of that law, however, Jesse Scott would continue to purchase slaves not related to him. His status as someone who was "not a negro" allowed this.[26]

Over the next decade, both Robert Washington Bell's insolvency and the purchase of enslaved family members took a heavy toll on the Bell family estate. First, Jesse and Sarah sold the half-acre plot of land on Three Notched Road that they had purchased from the Starkes back in 1826. They must have been desperate for cash, because they sold the property at a considerable loss. The Scotts had originally paid $235, and now they sold it for $150. Two years later, Robert Washington Bell's creditors were still seeking payment of outstanding debts. Bell had died, leaving an estate more fictive than real to his elderly mother, his sister, and Jesse Scott. The estate included his remaining interest in Thomas Bell's estate, so the court appointed a commissioner to sort things out. One lot sold for $87, and an adjacent parcel went for $127. The Bells and Scotts sold a third adjacent lot at about the same time, to persons who built a Methodist church on it.[27]

Unfortunately for Jesse and Sarah Scott, it appears that Robert's was not the only death in the family that year. In the midst of all the legal and financial wrangling concerning Robert's estate, Mary Hemings died. This further complicated the already byzantine family financial situation. Robert had been scheduled to take possession of the family house and lots in Charlottesville—the property that had been in the possession of Mary Hemings as long as she lived. Originally, a controlling interest in the lots and house would have gone directly to Robert, leaving that property open to claims from his creditors. But Robert was already dead, and his will had deeded the property back to Mary Hemings jointly with Jesse and Sarah Scott. The Hemingses and Scotts, who began the nineteenth century with a house and seven Charlottesville lots and had added several more land holdings by 1832, now found themselves with much less land. By July 1834, largely as a result of Robert Washington Bell's insolvency and subsequent death, the Hemings-Scott family owned only four lots and a house in Charlottesville, as well as a lot on Three Notched Road between the town and the university.[28]

The Scotts had indeed given up a considerable amount of money and property over the previous several years. But this was not a story of continuous decline. They had saved part of the family estate and managed to purchase several family members. Moreover, the Scotts not only continued to interact with whites but retained intimate ties to their fellow free people of color. In January 1835, Jesse and Sarah Scott attended the wedding of the free people of color Christopher M. Smith, a native of Petersburg, and Sarah Foster, a local woman whose mother was a propertied female head of household.[29]

In May 1837, Jesse Scott attended an estate sale in Charlottesville with his sons Robert and James. The estate in question was that of David Isaacs, a Jewish merchant and neighbor. Isaacs was a key figure in Charlottesville's interracial community. For almost twenty years, he had lived openly with a free woman of color, Nancy West. As with Thomas Bell and Mary Hemings before them, David Isaacs and Nancy West lived as if man and wife, together in the same house with their children. At the Isaacs estate sale, Robert Scott purchased one book and a six small bowls. Jesse bought a dictionary, old French grammar books, and a half dozen little bowls. James purchased bound copies of Thomas Jefferson's memoirs and correspondence book.

The entire Scott family continued to act as if they were members of the community—and indeed, literate, perhaps even bilingual citizens. No one seems to have thought it strange that free mulattoes were purchasing books at a public estate sale.[30]

Since marrying in 1802, Jesse Scott and his wife, Sarah, had acted as if they were both legally free and socially (if not legally) white. They sent their children to school with the children of prominent whites in town. They may have attended some white social functions as guests, not servants. The white community saw them as respectable and trustworthy neighbors.

Sarah Scott, however, was not free, at least according to state law. Thomas Bell had in fact never entered a deed of manumission for her. His will did not provide for her emancipation. As far as the community had been concerned for the past forty years, Thomas Bell said that he had freed her and that she was his child. That was enough for the community. Her marriage to the free man Jesse Scott in 1802, technically void because of her slave status, was officially recorded in the county marriage register.

In the late 1830s, the Scotts might have been worried that a creditor might discover that Sarah could not legally own property and would use that opportunity to wrest control of the old Bell house from them. In November 1838, Robert Scott "for and in consideration of the regard and affection which he entertains towards the said Sarah Bell," freed his mother, "wholly dissolving the relation of Master and slave." The deed never mentions that Sarah Bell Scott was his mother. Some forty years after her father had first "freed" her, Sarah Scott now possessed an official deed of manumission. She neither left Virginia nor was pressed to do so by authorities under the 1806 law.[31]

By 1840, the extremely long and drawn-out process of settling both Mary Hemings's and Robert Washington Bell's estates finally came to closure. Six years earlier, the Wayts and Winns, as creditors of Robert Washington Bell, had laid claim to portions of the old Thomas Bell estate. Since then, John Winn had died, and wrangling had continued over just how to divide up ownership of lots 23 and 24 in town. After years of haggling, all parties were "willing and desirous to divide said lots." Winn's executor reached an agreement with the other two parties claiming partial ownership of the parcels. Jesse and Sarah Scott, along with Twyman and Mary Wayt, agreed with the executor on how to divide the property. About half of the property went to Jesse and Sarah Scott. As the deed stated, this was "where the said Jesse has for many years resided & where he still resides."

Scott retained possession of the old Thomas Bell house. But he did so for a price: he had to pay Wayt and Winn's executor four hundred dollars. Sarah Scott, Twyman Wayt, Mary Wayt, and the Winn executor Valentine Southall all signed the deed. Jesse Scott made his mark.[32]

At the same time that the Scotts were negotiating the final settlement of the Main Street properties, Jesse Scott remained engaged with other white neighbors. Together with John Pollock, Andrew Sample, and Andrew Leitch, Jesse Scott petitioned the county court seeking permission to open a road through his land and that of Sample and Leitch. This branch road would give his neighbor John Pollock better access to the turnpike road and would connect Main Street to Little Commerce Street in Charlottesville. The town by 1840 was no longer a sleepy little village. It was well on its way to becoming a bustling small town. Both the courthouse and the university drew people in from the countryside, and business opportunities had begun to abound for merchants and artisans who owned property along Main Street. All four men, white and colored, stood to benefit from the new road. The court on the first of June approved construction.[33]

Over the next decade, Jesse Scott continued to have economic success, although his wife, Sarah, died sometime between 1840 and 1845. Scott continued to demonstrate that he was a member of the community. Thomas W. Gooch extended him a line of credit. Valentine Southall, the executor for the John Winn estate, refunded fifty-five dollars to Jesse Scott on account of an error in partitioning lots 23 and 24 back in 1834. The white Charlottesville hat maker Andrew McKee also felt safe extending a line of credit to Scott as a neighbor and customer. In addition to bettering his own economic position, Jesse began to prepare his children for ownership of the Scott-Bell estate. On the day after Christmas in 1840, Jesse Scott, "for and in consideration of the natural love and affection which he bears toward his said two sons," deeded his remaining half interest in lots 23 and 24. The old Bell house would remain in the family for at least another generation. Although Jesse had transferred title to the house and land to his sons, Robert and James, he did not step down as the head of household. He continued to live on Main Street. By 1850, he was a seventy-year-old man who owned twelve hundred dollars' worth of real estate. Robert and James and their families all lived with him.[34]

Neighbors of the Scott family included the white merchant John Marchant. Marchant was a truly wealthy Charlottesville resident, possessing fifteen thousand dollars' worth of real estate. At the time, Marchant was on his way to purchasing most of Charlottesville's manufacturing concerns. In particular, he bought a woolen mill and began a lucrative trade in the county. He processed local wool and produced slave clothing, a product much in demand in Albemarle. Another neighbor occupying a lot adjacent to Jesse Scott's was the white resident Ebenezer Watts. The census described Watts as a merchant owning four thousand dollars' worth of real estate. Watts ran the bookbinding service in town. His services included printing Charlottesville's *Virginia Advocate* weekly newspaper, which was published on the ground floor of Watts's store. Jesse Scott's grandson James Scott Jr. was in 1850 apprenticed to and living with V. E. Shepherd, who at the time was the newspaper's editor. The Scott children continued to be educated with white children in town, and the family lived as if white. In fact, their neighbor Ebenezer Watts's wife ran a school on the south side of Main Street that may have been attended by the Scott children. To white neighbors, Jesse Scott and his family were respectable and well-behaved people.[35]

Jesse Scott for more than seven decades effectively lived on both sides of a color line that in theory separated whites from all people of color. The white community accorded him a de facto status as socially white, even while occasionally acknowledging his racially mixed heritage. By the 1850s, however, Jesse Scott saw that the community was changing. He had watched relatives in his extended family, such as the Hemingses and Fossetts, move north and west, often settling in Ohio. Jesse Scott's status had not changed, but he may have been concerned about his children. What would happen to James and Robert when he was gone, as antislavery agitation nationally potentially created interracial tensions locally? His sons' reputations were tied to his own. When he was gone, they would lose the connection.

Jesse Scott's sons, perhaps at his suggestion, applied to the local court to get legal ratification of their socially white status. The community already saw them as almost white. Because they all had less than one-quarter Negro blood, according to Virginia law, they could petition the court to be declared "not negro." Jesse Scott's parents had been either a mulatto and a white or an Indian and a white. Sarah Scott was very nearly white herself. She had a white father and a light-skinned mulatto mother. James and Robert, therefore, could assert that they were legally not black. Even Albemarle's most famous resident, if he had been alive in 1857, might have agreed. Jefferson, writing to Francis Gray in 1815, argued that anyone with less than one-quarter "Negro blood . . . if he be emancipated . . . becomes a free *white* man, and a citizen of the United States to all intents and purposes." The Scotts sought the help of Jefferson's own grandson Thomas Jefferson Randolph, a prominent local citizen. After Randolph testified on behalf of the Scott brothers and the two Fosters, the court accepted the evidence, including Randolph's testimony. In November 1857, the court affirmed that Robert Scott, James Scott, Susan Catherine Foster, and Clayton Randolph Foster were legally "not negroes."[36]

The Scotts and Fosters had staked a legal claim to a status they had already informally achieved. At least since 1785, the state assembly had demonstrated concern with racial classification. In that year, the legislature passed a law declaring that "every person of whose grandfathers or grandmothers anyone is or shall have been a Negro, although all his other progenitors, except that descending from the Negro shall have been white persons, shall be deemed a mulatto." The law went into effect in 1787. According to Virginia law, the mulatto racial classification carried the same disabilities as free black status. But the law's very existence remains as a reminder that interracial sex occurred with regularity and worked to blur the color line. In 1792, the assembly rewrote the law but still declared anyone with "one-fourth part or more Negro blood" to be a mulatto. Ironically, just two years after the Nat Turner Rebellion, the state assembly again addressed racial classification, this time in a way that wrote certain people into, rather than out of, the white race. In that year, the assembly authorized the county courts to "grant a certificate to any free white person of mixed blood [less than 25 percent black ancestry], not being a white person, nor a free Negro, that he or she is not a free Negro, which certificate shall be sufficient to protect such person against the disabilities imposed by law on free Negroes." The legislature had created for the first time de jure recognition of an already existing de facto socially white status. It was through this legal door that the Scotts and Fosters walked in 1857.[37]

Three years later, the census taker who visited houses on Main Street in Charlottesville stopped at the old Bell house. There he found Jesse Scott, whom he enumerated an eighty-year-old white man owning twenty-five hundred dollars in real estate. Jesse was living in the household of his son Robert Scott, recorded as a fifty-six-year-old white farmer owning five thousand dollars in real estate and four thousand dollars in personal property. Jesse's other son, James, lived next door. The census taker listed James as a fifty-year-old white farmer owning six thousand dollars in real property. Over the course of his eighty-year life, Jesse Scott had been assigned three separate statuses: free person of color, socially white ("not a negro"), and now legally white. Early on, through face-to-face relationships with white neighbors, he had won a reputation as a respectable and trustworthy man. He had provided well for his children, both through management of the portion of the Thomas Bell estate he had acquired through marriage and through his other financial dealings. He had owned slaves, hired slaves, and bought extended family members who were enslaved. He was neither a dangerous free black nor an abolitionist. He would die in 1862 a respected Albemarle resident, widely celebrated for his fine manners and virtuoso fiddling abilities. When he died, he left his children and their families with an excellent estate. James and Robert Scott would continue living in the old Bell house into the twentieth century.[38]

The experiences of Thomas Bell and Jesse Scott were not isolated examples of individuals who dared to challenge the strict racial hierarchy. Sex across that putative color line seems to have been a fairly regular affair in Albemarle County and elsewhere in the slaveholding South. At least one of Thomas Bell's contemporaries in Albemarle, and one with whom he was well acquainted, participated in a long-term interracial relationship. Stephen Hughes Jr., a white man, was born in the southern part of Albemarle County, on his father's nearly one-thousand-acre farm, which stretched south from Biscuit Run a few miles south of Charlottesville down to the Hardware River, which roughly bisected the southern half of the county. Stephen and his brother Edward grew up in the colonial era on this farm with their parents, two sisters, and perhaps twenty or more slaves. As young men in 1775, both brothers were full of revolutionary spirit. They volunteered in the Independent Companies of Albemarle County, a militia group that formed early that year; also signing or marking the militia resolves was free mulatto Shadrach Battles. Four years later, Stephen Hughes signed an Albemarle County declaration of independence along with several neighbors.[39]

After the American victory in the Revolution, the Hughes family settled down in rural Albemarle. Stephen Hughes Sr., now elderly, continued to run his small plantation on the north bank of the Hardware River. His sons, Edward and Stephen Jr., busied themselves establishing their financial independence. In 1788, Stephen Jr. purchased his first plots of land—two lots in the tiny hamlet of Charlottesville, which at that point was little more than a cluster of crude buildings on a dirt road. Stephen set up a blacksmith's shop there and inherited part of his father's estate in 1793.[40]

By 1794, Stephen Hughes Jr. owned two lots in Charlottesville and a one-hundred-acre parcel that had been carved out of his deceased father's plantation. In September 1798, Hughes filed a deed of manumission with the clerk. According to the deed, Stephen Hughes did "emancipate, manumit and make free Chancy & her children Elijah Louisa Hastings Johanna and Sophia." These were not slaves who had been willed to Stephen by his father or who belonged to the still-undivided portion of his father's estate. As Stephen noted in the deed of manumission, these six slaves were "formerly the property of Peter Marks & now mine."[41]

Peter Marks was a friend, neighbor, and contemporary of Stephen's father, Stephen Hughes Sr., and he also owned a house near Stephen Jr.'s blacksmith shop in Charlottesville; either circumstance may explain how the younger Hughes met Marks's enslaved woman Chancy. The deed of manumission does not state why Hughes freed these slaves; it does not mention that she had to buy her freedom from him. Stephen did not suggest that he found slavery to be at odds with the principles he held dear from the Revolution, though deeds may reveal little about motives. He certainly freed no other slaves and continued to own slaves for the remainder of his life.[42]

The relationship between Chancy and Stephen Hughes becomes clearer years later. Stephen Hughes did not follow Thomas Bell's example and very publicly and unashamedly admit to his relationship with Chancy, but he did not struggle to hide it, either. On gaining their freedom, Chancy and her children immediately took Stephen's surname as their own and moved onto a plot of land adjoining Stephen Hughes's farm on Moore's Creek. Stephen may have given them title to the land as a way to be discreet about their relationship. By 1808, Chancy had given birth to two more daughters, Mary and Betsy. A complicated series of financial transactions from 1816 to 1827 suggests rather clearly that Stephen and Chancy's relationship was not hidden from anyone.[43]

Their white neighbors John Pollock, John Wheeler, and James Lewis continued to have close contact with the Hugheses. If they had a problem with Chancy and Stephen's relationship, they did not show it. John M. Perry, however, came to feel differently, at least about Stephen. In late July 1816, he purchased thirty acres of land near Moore's Creek from Stephen Hughes. But less than a year later, in April 1817, John Perry and Jesse Garth complained to Justice of the Peace Charles Brown that they "feared Stephen Hughes Jr. will injure them." The words or events that had precipitated the quarrel are lost to history, but some conclusions can be drawn. The conflict between these neighbors did not happen until after the land sale—the parties may have fallen out over that land transaction. After years of coexistence between the interracial couple and their white neighbors, a conflict arose—not, apparently, over race, but rather over economics.[44]

We will never know exactly what happened in the spring of 1817 that led to the altercation. But this was the only time since Stephen Hughes had freed Chancy and their children that anyone who knew them had any sort of conflict with either of them that spilled over into the public record. The incident, however, changed little for Stephen Hughes and his family. They did not move away or work to obscure their relationship. The court, in handling the petition brought by Perry and Garth, followed the usual course in breach-of-the-peace cases. The court ordered Stephen Hughes to file a recognizance guaranteeing his good behavior and to find someone else to post surety for his keeping the peace.[45]

By 1820, Stephen and Chancy Hughes's children were growing up, interacting with whites and free blacks in the area. Their son Hastings, their oldest child, began to strike out on his own. Now in possession of a twenty-acre plot originally given to his mother by Stephen, Hastings had routine face-to-face interactions with his neighbors. He developed relationships in much the same way that his father had before him. Hastings and his white neighbor John Pollock, a man very familiar to all of the Hugheses, agreed to redirect the creek on Hastings's plot to a mill and distillery on Pollock's land; Pollock had purchased the mill from Stephen Hughes four years earlier. Pollock and other neighbors knew, trusted, and respected Stephen Hughes. He had a family reputation that stretched back to the colonial era. They likewise knew Chancy and the children, including the mulatto Hastings. Now Pollock and Hastings had an opportunity that would benefit both: Pollock needed water to power his mill and run his distillery. Hughes and other area residents needed Pollock's mill to process their crops.[46]

In fact, beyond furnishing water, Hastings Hughes shared ownership of Pollock's mill and distillery. As part of the ownership agreement, Hughes would work the mill to process his own harvest as well as Pollock's. Hastings agreed that he would mill twelve bushels of grain for Pollock on a daily basis. If Pollock needed more processsed, he agreed to pay Hastings a fee per bushel. Hastings, on days when he did not mill twelve bushels of grain for Pollock, would have to pay the same per-bushel fee for each bushel under the agreed-upon twelve. For four years, this relationship benefited both parties. In late 1823, the Hugheses decided to sell Hastings's interest in the mill and millrace. Hastings Hughes had married. Stephen Hughes may have died. Chancy Hughes had inherited Stephen Hughes's much larger farm adjacent to Hastings Hughes's plot. Hastings, his wife, Jinney, and Chancy sold the land that the millrace sat on and their interest in the mill to neighbor John Pollock for $225.[47]

Stephen Hughes Jr. did indeed die sometime between 1822 and 1827, by which date Chancy Hughes had taken clear possession of Stephen's farm. Hastings's decision to sell his interest in the Pollock mill may well have been connected to Stephen Hughes's death. Likewise, Hastings Hughes in 1827 sold the original twenty-acre plot that Stephen had given to Chancy and the family back in 1798. The buyer was the free man of color William Spinner, the son of Albemarle Revolutionary War veteran Richard Spinner.[48]

In the eyes of authorities, the surviving Hugheses were all free blacks. According to the 1810 census, Stephen Hughes was head of a household that included himself and five free blacks. Yet none of them had ever applied for freedom certificates before 1829. Chancy Hughes, even after Stephen died, never once registered. Neither did Hastings Hughes. Only three of the Hugheses, Stephen's daughters, ever registered their freedom. They did so in November 1829. This casualness about registration was commonplace and not limited to those who were known to have white parentage or to those with light complexions. Darker free blacks likewise neglected to register more often than not.[49]

Those Hugheses interacted regularly with their white neighbors. Hastings Hughes, like other people of color, even felt that the county legal system was a proper venue for settling disputes. In 1830, he hired an attorney and sued his white neighbor John Pollock over a debt. The all-white court, far from bristling at Hughes's assertiveness, referred the case to arbitrators, who awarded him a judgment for $35. Pollock's countersuit was also sent to arbitration, ultimately resulting in a $142 judgment for Pollock. Hastings Hughes came out on the short end, but apparently not because of his color.

The Hugheses also maintained relationships with other free people of color. Mary Hughes, Hastings's younger sister, in November 1831, married Madison Hemings in a Presbyterian ceremony. Hemings was a former slave at Monticello and in all likelihood the son of Thomas Jefferson. William Spinner, already well acquainted with the Hughes family, gave security for the marriage bond. As late as 1845, Hastings Hughes still remained in Albemarle, apparently living as if white. In that year, he rented a house and lot in Charlottesville for $154.[50]

Back in 1817, Stephen Hughes Jr. had filed a bond guaranteeing his good behavior for a year after two neighbors alleged that he had threatened them. When he posted the fifty-dollar bond, a white acquaintance of his named Joshua Grady gave security. Grady lived in Charlottesville, working and playing with whites and blacks, both slave and free. Stephen Hughes and Joshua Grady did not come from quite the same socioeconomic stratum, but living and working near one another in the village of Charlottesville may have overcome some of those social differences. By 1817, Hughes knew Grady well enough to ask him to post bond in a considerable amount. Grady knew Hughes to be a respectable and trustworthy man. As it turned out, the two had other things in common. Stephen Hughes lived in something resembling a common-law marriage with a free woman of color. Joshua Grady in 1817 spent much time at taverns, gaming houses, and bawdy houses—highly interracial spheres. By 1822, Joshua Grady had met Betsy (Elizabeth) Ann Farley, a young free black woman with whom he began a long relationship.

Joshua Grady's younger "wife," Elizabeth Ann Farley, was the daughter of Daniel Farley, a well-known free black fiddler in the Charlottesville area. As Lucia Stanton's extensive research into the enslaved families at Monticello has suggested, Daniel Farley may have actually been Mary Hemings's oldest son, which would make him a half brother to Robert Washington Bell and Sally Scott. Born a slave in 1772, Farley at age fifteen was given by Jefferson to his sister on her marriage. By the early nineteenth century, Daniel Farley was living on a small lot on Main Street at the eastern town limits of Charlottesville. Farley's small home and quarter-acre lot were themselves the site of frequent meetings for gaming. Joshua Grady and Daniel Farley probably met while gambling. By some accounts, both men "were frequent transgressors" of antivice laws. According to Lucia Stanton, Farley's property also served as a Sunday meeting place for slaves from local plantations. Once again, whites, free people of color, and slaves mingled with relative ease at a number of sites that allowed for interactions outside the master-slave relationship.[51]

Joshua Grady was indeed regularly involved in the mischief and mayhem that sometimes took place at gaming sites and bawdy houses on the edge of town. In 1810, he was acquitted in a murder trial. In 1811, a free man of color named Peter Barnett who operated with at least one known alias, Peter Fountain, was arrested and charged with felony theft. According to court papers, Fountain had stolen two hundred dollars in bank notes from a mercantile concern in Charlottesville. Fountain was caught when he asked Joshua Grady to make change for him. Apparently, Fountain could not read and did not know the actual value of the notes he tried to pass. He gave Grady one fifty-dollar note but asked him to make change for a twenty. A similar attempt to exchange money sent him to jail. He asked George Branham to change bills, too, and made a similar mistake. In this case, Joshua Grady committed no crime, but the depositions describe a scene that suggested he had frequent dealings with people of all colors in town. In 1817 and again in 1818, he was accused of illegal gaming.[52]

Joshua Grady also knew the free women of color who worked in the houses of entertainment and prostitution that dotted the edges of town. In 1821, Grady, along with the free woman of color Fanny Barnett and his fellow whites Edmund Wade and Bennett Wheeler, faced criminal charges. The court accused them of holding "a riotous and unlawful assembly and failing to keep the peace of the Commonwealth. . . . [They were] evil doers, rioters, disturbers of the peace . . . so that discord and other grievances and damages are likely to arise." The court papers do not reveal just what brought this about. Justices of the peace could have brought the charges after witnessing interracial entertainment. More likely, the defendants were all drinking and carousing in one of the taverns or houses of entertainment, and some sort of fight broke out that spilled out onto the streets of Charlottesville. Failing to keep the peace was a charge most often applied to brawls, assaults, and instances of publicly threatened violence.

As discussed earlier regarding the free woman of color Fanny Barnett, the case itself demonstrates the highly routine nature of interracial relations in Albemarle. First, three white men were included in a charge together with a free black prostitute. Second, the justices did not throw these people in jail. No one, not even the prostitute, was dragged to the public whipping post. The justices applied to these people the standard legal term, "not of good fame, nor of honest conversation," but then simply ordered each of them to file the standard fifty-dollar peace recognizance and to find someone to post an additional fifty dollars guaranteeing their good behavior. Three white men proved willing to stake money on the behavior of this mixed group for the next year.[53]

A white man living in a common-law marriage with a free black woman, Grady continued after 1821 to consort with the often rough and rowdy crowd that dominated the interracial entertainments in and around Charlottesville. He probably had regular contact with a host of other free people of color, a number of local whites of varying socioeconomic status, and even with slaves. His behavior as a frequent transgressor of the law may have damaged his reputation. He and two other white men may have been accused of a crime in 1822 involving interracial sex. That charge, possibly for fornication, was tabled by the county court for several years before being dismissed in 1827.[54]

In 1833, the memories of the bloody Nat Turner Rebellion still fresh in the minds of most Virginians, Joshua Grady would again become involved in a crime that involved both free blacks and whites. At a time that we are told brought heightened policing of the racial hierarchy, one might expect Grady's penchant for publicly fraternizing with free blacks to have been frowned upon by the white community, especially if commingling led to a violent crime. That does not seem to have been the case. Once again, a careful reading of the court documents provides a glimpse into the highly interracial social geography of Albemarle.

On a September evening in 1833, Joshua Grady was at his father-in-law Daniel Farley's house. The former Monticello slave Joseph Fossett, a blood relative of Farley's, was staying at the house at the time. On that night, the interracial gathering was really one of a family having a quiet night together. Farley often used his home as a house of entertainment, running card tables for gambling. But on that fall night, Farley's house was not open for business. Elijah Battles and Elijah Farrar, local men of color, showed up that evening, seeking entertainment. Farrar wanted to play cards, but Farley refused and told the two men to leave.

Battles left immediately, but Farrar argued with Farley for a while before leaving the house. Farrar did not let the issue go—he swore he would whip and kill Farley. Farrar's belligerent ranting suggests he and Battles may have been drinking before coming to Farley's house. Farley stayed inside but told the pair once again to leave. Joshua Grady, sitting in Farley's house and witnessing the altercation, counseled Farley to tell Farrar that he had an old pistol "and would get Fossett to repair it and shute him." Eventually, Farrow quieted down and departed.[55]

Unfortunately for Farley, Farrar returned a short time later, still threatening to kill Farley. Suddenly, Farrar appeared in Farley's kitchen, "warning that he could and would whip Farley . . . swearing that he could whip Farley and he would kill him." Farrar then struck Farley. In the ensuing fight, Farrar cut Farley on the head and chest repeatedly."[56] Joshua Grady, hearing the commotion, came back to the kitchen. Grady and Fossett watched in horror as a close relative was savagely attacked in his own kitchen. Fossett, desperate to stop the brutal assault, tossed a bucket of water on them and then threw the empty bucket at the two men, finally stopping the fight. Fossett had doused the flames of the conflict, probably saving Daniel Farley's life. With the crisis averted, Fossett attended to his friend.[57]

A few days after the incident, Farley, Fossett, and Grady filed a complaint with the local magistrate James R. Watson. Watson then issued a warrant for the arrest of Elijah Farrar for having "unlawfully feloniously evilfully and maliciously cut & stabbed a certain Daniel Farley." Days later, Justice of the Peace John R. Jones had Farrar arrested and jailed. The court charged him with attempted murder and tacked on a second count, unlawful stabbing. On October 12, Farrar, having pled not guilty, was tried by a called court. The panel of white justices, upon hearing all the witness testimony, decided that Elijah Farrar's attack did not meet the standards of attempted murder and delivered a not-guilty verdict. But in considering the second count—unlawful stabbing—the justices believed there was clear evidence that Farrar had stabbed Farley with intent to injure, so they found him guilty and sentenced him to two years in the state penitentiary. A week later, the justices met and amended the sentencing, ordering Farrar to spend half of his prison sentence in solitary confinement on "low and course meal."[58]

No white justice or magistrate mentioned the race of any of the individuals involved in the assault. No one ever complained that a white man, Joshua Grady, treated free people of color as friends and equals. Not a single justice acted as if Grady's participation in this interracial sphere was unusual or troubling. No one complained that Grady was still living with a free woman of color at the time. The white and black participants in that stabbing were all commonly known and had reputations that for white justices promised they were not a threat to any racial hierarchy. Even Elijah

Farrar—who was at that time earning a reputation for violence—was not seen by the community as a horrible threat to safety.

The white lawyers Egbert R. Watson and Nathaniel Wolfe agreed to serve at the trial as Farrar's counsel. Elijah Farrar did spend two years under difficult conditions in the state penitentiary. But by all accounts, he had clearly attacked and stabbed Daniel Farley without legitimate provocation while Farley was on his own property. After the assault trial concluded, life went on as usual in Charlottesville. Joshua Grady continued to live openly with Betsy Ann Farley. All continued to participate in the frequent interracial entertainments that occurred in and around Charlottesville. Even Elijah Farrar would serve his sentence and return to town two years later, falling back into familiar patterns.[59]

Both black and white nonelites in the rural antebellum South as a general rule left little in the way of documentary evidence of their existence. Women of the lower classes were even less likely to leave a clear paper trail, owing to both illiteracy and poverty. Interracial relationships, often involving two people who fit one of the above categories, only occasionally appear in plain view in public records. These unions were not legally or religiously sanctioned, so neither ministers nor county clerks recorded them. It is therefore surprising that in a county with a relatively small population, so many interracial relationships can be ferreted out of the archives. The lack of residential segregation, the low population density, and most important of all, a highly personal social culture that valued intimate face-to-face relationships above all else virtually guaranteed that blacks and whites would mingle in unanticipated ways.

For example, Christopher McPherson, born a slave in nearby Louisa County, would become a highly literate legal clerk and merchant who worked in Charlottesville for a time. McPherson himself was the son of a slave woman and a Scottish merchant living in Virginia. When McPherson received his formal emancipation in 1792, his owner declared him "long since emancipated." The filing of the deed of manumission was simply a formality confirming the lived reality. McPherson's life belied both the stereotypes of free blacks and modern understandings of the lives of free people of color derived from anti–free black legislation in Virginia.[60]

As a slave, McPherson had received two years of formal schooling. His master in 1782 moved to neighboring Fluvanna County, where McPherson worked as "Principal Storekeeper whilst 8 to 10 white Gentlemen were under

[his] directions." As a clerk at the store, McPherson became well-known to the white citizenry. In 1800, now a free man, McPherson applied to and was hired by the Charlottesville lawyer William Waller Hening as a clerk. Hening described McPherson as a man of respectable and trustworthy character whose work was "dextrous and accurate." That same year, the brother of his former master appointed McPherson as one of the executors of his estate. McPherson later moved to Richmond and, thanks to a letter of recommendation from Hening, landed a clerk's position with the High Court of Chancery there. In 1802, he testified in a case involving a white defendant. His testimony, differing from that offered by two white witnesses, was accepted as the true story.[61]

The early Charlottesville resident Thomas West, a white saddler, owned a slave named Priscilla, with whom he had three children. By the early 1780s, he had freed Priscilla; they continued to raise a family. The Albemarle community considered their oldest son, James Henry West, a white man. Thomas West married a white woman in 1794 but died two years later, leaving his entire estate, including a plantation, Charlottesville lots, Amherst County land, livestock, furniture, and slaves, to his son James Henry West. James's sister, a woman of color named Nancy West, was also provided for in a much smaller way. Thomas West left her the annual interest on forty pounds (approximately $133) for a period of seven years. Thomas West's white business associate William Taliaferro agreed to take the minor Nancy in and continue raising her. Another friend, Thomas Bell, agreed to manage Nancy's money.

Nancy West in the 1790s began a relationship with a white Jewish merchant in Charlottesville by the name of David Isaacs. Together over the next twenty years, they had seven children. Charlottesville at that time had fewer than three hundred residents scattered within two or three blocks of Main Street, the east-west road running through town. The relationship between the white merchant and the free woman of color must have been common knowledge by the time their seventh child was born. By 1820, Nancy West had moved into David Isaacs's home. They had ended the public fiction of maintaining two separate residences and chosen to live together essentially as man and wife.[62]

Joshua Rothman, in his excellent study of interracial sex in Virginia, has already extensively documented the West-Isaacs relationship. I seek here merely to situate Nancy West and David Isaacs in a network of interracial relationships in the county. In this context, the West-Isaacs relationship appears as unusual in only one respect. Only three interracial couples were ever presented with charges concerning their relationship: David Isaacs/Nancy West, Joshua Grady/Elizabeth Ann Farley, and Andrew McKee/Matsy Cannon.[63] Only David Isaacs and Nancy West were actually taken to court and endured a trial as a result of their living arrangements. In 1822, the county court convened a grand jury that listened to testimony from two witnesses concerning West and Isaacs. The grand jury then charged West and Isaacs with "umbraging the decency of society and violating the laws of the land by cohabitating together in a state of illicit commerce as man and wife." Almost two years later, the commonwealth's attorney sought to pursue fornication charges against West and Isaacs. Ultimately, the local court balked, passing the case to the General Court in Richmond. The latter court ruled in favor of West and Isaacs, denying the local courts the ability to pursue the fornication charge. Five years after the first witnesses testified against Nancy West and David Isaacs, the Albemarle County Court dismissed all charges against the free woman of color and the white Jewish merchant who lived together in a common-law marriage. The court likewise dismissed the charges against the other two couples.[64]

No one in Albemarle was ever convicted of charges involving interracial sexual relationships and cohabitation that did not involve prostitution. Even those cases of interracial prostitution, so few in number, elicited relatively minor fines. Most people who openly lived together in interracial relationships in Albemarle never faced charges: Thomas Bell/Mary Hemings, Thomas West/Priscilla, Stephen Hughes/Chancy Hughes, Daniel Goings/Evelina Beckett, and Robert Washington Bell/Ms. Schenck. These are merely the relationships that have been documented; surely there were others. Even those few couples that at least faced criminal presentments on one charge or another—David Isaacs/Nancy West, Joshua Grady/Betsy Ann Farley, Andrew McKee/Matsy Cannon, and Samuel Birckhead/Dolly Evans—were either acquitted of all charges or saw the prosecution decline to continue the cases. All these couples continued to live together after their court cases. Local reputation derived from intimate and face-to-face meetings created a rough community consensus about individuals and social relationships that carried far more weight than any law passed in Richmond or the antipathy of some white individuals on the local level.

A pronounced gap existed between law and local practice in Albemarle County at least until the 1850s, if not later. Those anti–free black laws that sought to enforce the racial hierarchy rigidly were important to white Virginians, even to Virginians who lived in Albemarle. But those laws were important for what they said about unknown free blacks who lived in some other town, whom whites read about in the local paper. The free people of color who lived among Albemarle's white citizenry, thanks to the daily face-to-face relationships that predominated, were not seen by most as dangerous. They were regarded as individuals, with names attached to faces.

Certainly, most free people of color were not seen by Albemarle whites as occupying stations in life equal to their own. The racial hierarchy could coexist with a locally or regionally fluid color line. Free people of color could and did interact with whites in myriad ways that contradicted the racist notions behind racially proscriptive legislation. They could as well move toward a social and even legal whiteness by advancing themselves within that highly personal social culture. Richard Thomas Walker Duke hinted at how this culture operated when he stated, "With the rather 'easy' morality of those early days no one paid any attention to a man's method of living."

Duke, writing his memoirs at the height of racial segregation and violence in America, anachronistically assumed that those interracial relationships arose from the lack of morality and character that Albemarle exhibited at that time. His second observation, that no one spent time policing the way their neighbors lived, hints at the reality. "No one paid any attention to a man's method of living" if that man was widely recognized as someone who was trustworthy and respectable. This rule applied to black as well as to white and created the maneuvering room that separated local practice from racist legislation and thought. In that space, free people of color could develop close personal relationships with neighboring whites that would protect them from racially proscriptive and punitive policies and might even afford them the opportunity to climb the social hierarchy to occupy a de facto intermediate position between free black and white citizen.

Conclusion

In 1781, Thomas Jefferson wrote his *Notes on the State of Virginia.* In this lengthy disquisition on American exceptionalism and superiority, Jefferson addressed the issue of race at length. In Query XIV, Jefferson stated plainly his belief in black inferiority. Jefferson "compared them [people of color] by their faculties [to whites]. . . . In reason," he wrote, "[they are] much inferior, as I think one could scarcely be found capable of tracing and comprehending the investigations of Euclid; and that in imagination they are dull, tasteless, and anomalous. . . . This unfortunate difference of colour, and perhaps faculty, is a powerful obstacle to the emancipation of these people [black slaves]." Even as a war dedicated to "life, liberty, and the pursuit of happiness" was coming to a successful close, Thomas Jefferson did not resolve the contradiction between the revolutionary ideals he espoused and his belief in white superiority and by extension in a slave system ensuring permanent black subservience. Jefferson's belief in the inferiority of people of color would only deepen as the years passed. By 1814, Jefferson wrote that free people of color, "by their habits, [were] rendered as incapable as children of taking care of themselves and are promptly extinguished whenever industry is necessary for raising the young. In the meantime they are pests in society by their idleness and the depredations to which this leads them."[1]

Evidently, not everyone in Jefferson's beloved home county of Albemarle agreed with him. On November 9, 1785, Thomas West came to the courthouse in Charlottesville to file a deed. On that fall day, West, "for and in consideration of the sum of five shillings to him [Thomas West] paid by the said James," manumitted his slave James Henry West. At first glance, this deed of manumission tells the reader very little. This individual manumission occurred three years after the passage of the law of 1782 making individual emancipations possible. The deed does not contain any convincing language that demonstrates Thomas West's adherence to revolutionary principles or that contradicts the holding of other humans in bondage. Nor does the document demonstrate that West and his slave had much of an economic motive for the manumission. The small five-shilling payment was perhaps cited as a mere formality. James Henry was probably not making the final payment after years of toiling to earn enough money to purchase himself.[2]

But James Henry West was much more than simply a favored slave who earned his freedom thanks to the beneficence of a kind master. James Henry was the son of Thomas West. West had a relationship with his former slave Priscilla, whom he may have informally freed at some point prior to 1782. By 1793, only eight years after becoming free, James Henry possessed land, owning one lot in Charlottesville. He contradicted Jefferson's concept of free people of color as "pests in society by their idleness." James Henry, at the death of his father in 1796, had become much more than an anomalous former slave. He already owned land, but his economic position was about to change dramatically. James Henry inherited his father's estate, including eight slaves. James Henry West and Thomas West were family. It was this most personal of relationships that led to James Henry's freedom.[3]

Though he was a former slave, and a light-skinned free mulatto subject to the same legal proscriptions as other free people of color, James Henry West's life suggests he escaped those restrictions. He managed to cross the color line, achieving a social whiteness recognized by the Albemarle community as well as by people in locales beyond the confines of that rural county. His father raised him as if he were white. James Henry likely went to school with white children. Thus, even before his father died, James Henry West lived his life as if he were white. In July 1794, he married a white woman named Susannah Harlow in a ceremony that county officials recognized as legal. The white Albemarle resident Benjamin Wheeler, speaking in 1836 about James Henry and Susannah's children, said they were "esteemed, received and accepted as white men, and allowed to intermarry without objection on the score of blood, with white women." But the West family was not engaged in passing, a secretive claiming of whiteness that denied or obscured an interracial lineage. As Benjamin Wheeler suggested, the Wests were known to be of mixed heritage, but their ancestry, behavior, and reputation accorded them many, and perhaps all, of the privileges of whiteness.[4]

The experiences of James Henry West and his descendants were not isolated exceptions. Others, too, demonstrated that people of color could be far more than "dull, tasteless, [and] anomalous" and "incapable of taking care of themselves." Rather, these people of color worked and interacted with the white and black people around them, thereby avoiding some of the legal disabilities associated with darker skin color. Only a few, such as James Henry West and his family, would complete the shift, becoming for all intents and purposes white. A number of other free people of color, however, would achieve a status that came with many privileges of social whiteness without fully separating themselves from free black status and sometimes even without the aid of a benevolent white father. Orra Langhorne, interviewing the Albemarle resident Robert Scott two decades after the Civil War, termed the Scotts "mulattoes, men of fine manners, good musicians, and generally popular." Langhorne noted Robert's "dignified bearing" and courtly manner. Scott told Langhorne that he "had attended a white school in Charlottesville. . . . The prejudice between the races was not so strong then [in the antebellum era] as now [the 1880s], and he had never heard of any objection being made to the presence of the colored pupils in his school." Robert Scott and his brother, James, may not have been the only respected free people of color to be educated at white schools. The Albemarle community's reliance on personal, face-to-face interactions remained the most important factor in determining social status.[5]

Obviously, the notion that blacks, whether slave or free, were unfit for membership in white civilization was not one held by Jefferson alone. Similar ideas about black incapacity for membership in civilized society were common in the period. One Albemarle newspaper, the *Virginia Advocate,* in August 1830 reprinted a satirical news report about an "African Celebration," written as a comical letter to the editor of the *New Haven Register* from the free black "Cesar Strateleg." The article mocked the social pretensions of free blacks and portrayed them as unfit to acquire the rudiments of civilization. These portrayals represent the dominant discourse in the antebellum period on the abilities of free blacks in both the South and the North. But the lives and experiences of Albemarle's black, mulatto, and white residents belie the uniformly pejorative image of free people of color embodied in anti–free black legislation and racist rhetoric.[6]

Even Thomas Jefferson, the "Sage of Monticello" and a purveyor of racist ideas about free blacks, acted in Albemarle as if strict notions of racial difference and a rigid color line did not apply to the sea of familiar faces in the neighborhood of Monticello. Jefferson knew the Scott family and treated them well. According to Robert Scott, Jefferson was "very kind and sociable—kind to everybody." Robert remembered in particular his father Jesse's comments about Jefferson. Robert recalled that Jefferson "had always been very kind to [Robert's] father and had encouraged him [Jesse Scott] to have his children educated." The Scotts, through their face-to-face interactions with Jefferson, ceased for Jefferson to be inferior and idle pests unfit for inclusion in Virginia society. Jesse Scott's sons, Robert and James, attended school with white students. The actions of many other white Albemarle residents over an eighty-five-year period, from roughly 1780 to 1865, demonstrate that Thomas Jefferson was not alone in his capacity to behave flexibly toward free people of color.[7]

The newspaper editor and ardent proslavery ideologue James Alexander also recognized that some free people of color achieved a community-recognized social whiteness. He remembered that Tucker Isaacs, the son of the Jewish merchant David Isaacs and the free woman of color Nancy West, lived as if "not a negro." Tucker Isaacs, legally classified as a free person of color, was also seen as socially white by the community. Alexander remembered Tucker as "a painter, and . . . a good citizen and much respected. . . . His brother Frederick was a printer, and both were educated with the whites in this town." Alexander further described Tucker's brother Frederick Isaacs as "well educated . . . and [having gone] to school with the white boys." Alexander's comments recognize that the Isaacs brothers were not legally white. But his remarks also evince no surprise or anger at the sight of people who were visibly persons of color gaining privileges usually reserved for whites only. Even to a proslavery ideologue such as Alexander, behavior and reputation remained the primary indicators of actual social status. The racially coded legal status of the Isaacses, Scotts, and Wests was of secondary importance.[8]

In remembering the Wests and Isaacses, Alexander mentioned that Frederick Isaacs was a printer. He was educated, "had a natural talent for drawing, and could imitate with accuracy every signature in the Declaration of Independence, even to the palsied, shaking one of Steph. Hopkins, of R. Island." On Main Street near the center of the growing village of Charlottesville, Frederick Isaacs for a time co-owned a building and business with his mother, Nancy West. Together, they published a newspaper, the *Chronicle*, a "quasi-democratic sheet," in 1832 and 1833. No copies of the paper remain. James Alexander remembered that "Fred loved to frolic and drink; one night when he quit work he left a lighted candle on his case, which set fire to it and to the building, and the office was entirely destroyed."[9] Despite that carelessness or ill fortune, many white residents, including Alexander, regarded Frederick Isaacs as a respectable "citizen," not a dangerous free black.

At least until 1850, and indeed longer, this personal culture that assigned reputation and status through face-to-face interactions allowed free people of color room to maneuver and negotiate effectively within their society. They could overcome somewhat their legally codified position of distinct inequality by owning property, behaving respectably, and being known by the larger community, resorting to the courts when necessary. For instance, Tucker Isaacs's ability to copy handwriting so well would come to cause problems that same year. In February 1850, he was arrested and charged with aiding John R. Jones's slave Peter Fossett by counterfeiting a freedom register for someone named James Battles and giving it to another slave named Peter. This act amounted to a direct challenge to the slave system and was a crime whether committed by a free person of color or a white. Five county justices sitting as a called court quickly found Tucker Isaacs not guilty. Presented with an opportunity to tighten white control of the slave system by punishing a free person of color accused of threatening that system, these white justices could have ruled against Isaacs, sending a message to both Albemarle slaves and free people of color. On further advice of the county court, the commonwealth's attorney also refused to continue the case. Perhaps Tucker Isaacs's longstanding reputation in the community gave him room to establish his innocence. Even so, Isaacs and his extended family in Albemarle may have no longer felt secure. Within a few years, Tucker Isaacs and his family had moved out of the state, settling in Chillicothe, Ohio.[10]

Starting in the colonial period, and continuing for six decades after the nineteenth century began, free people of color who became known personages with a name attached to a face carved out a livable and sometimes even comfortable niche in Albemarle County. Sherod Goings, Shadrach Battles, and Charles Barnett benefited from personal connections formed on the Revolutionary battlefield. Others developed reputations through property ownership and by running businesses. Still others, such as Fanny, Septimia, and Martha Barnett, relied first upon familial connections forged in interracial relationships and then upon engagement with the white community to carve out secure space for living. All of these free people of color capitalized on the personal nature of Albemarle's social structure to succeed and to enhance their children's chances of success.

They also provided visible refutation of Thomas Jefferson's doubts about their capacities. Jefferson himself may have noticed that some of the county's most successful free people of color were mulattoes and cited that impression as "proof" of his theory that white "admixture" improved people. Yet what Jefferson called "blood" was in fact both a product and a facilitator of the social and personal connections that made success more attainable for some free blacks in Albemarle. They, and some of their darker brethren and sisters, carved out a significant sphere of freedom in spite of a legal and social system that denied them many of the basic rights and privileges that whites took for granted.

Appendix

Note: In conducting research for this study, I sketched out the lives and connections of as many individuals as possible. Several surnames—for example, Goings, Battles, Barnett, and Bowles—were very common in Albemarle, representing large extended families. The incomplete nature of extant records and the infrequent appearance of some individuals in those records sometimes makes it impossible to connect everyone in these family trees. Where a maiden name is unknown, no surname is given.

FARROW-BOWLES-BARNETT-BATTLES FAMILY TREE

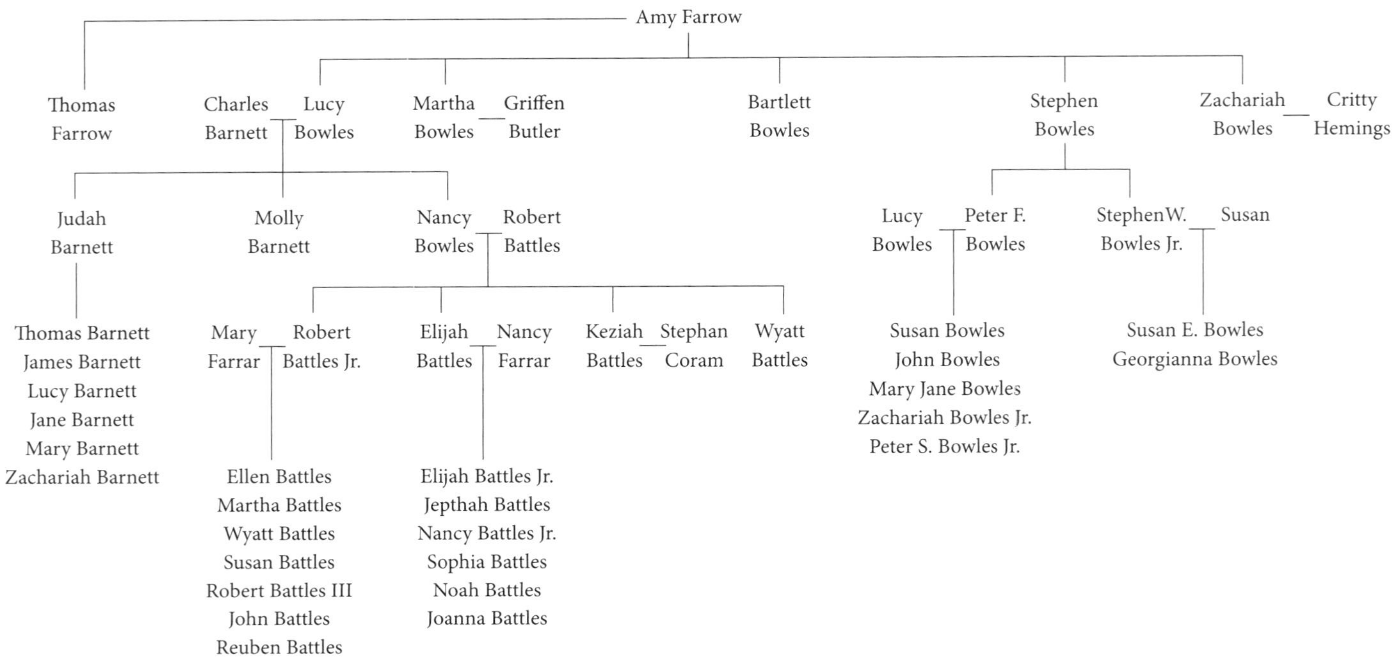

GOINGS FAMILY TREE

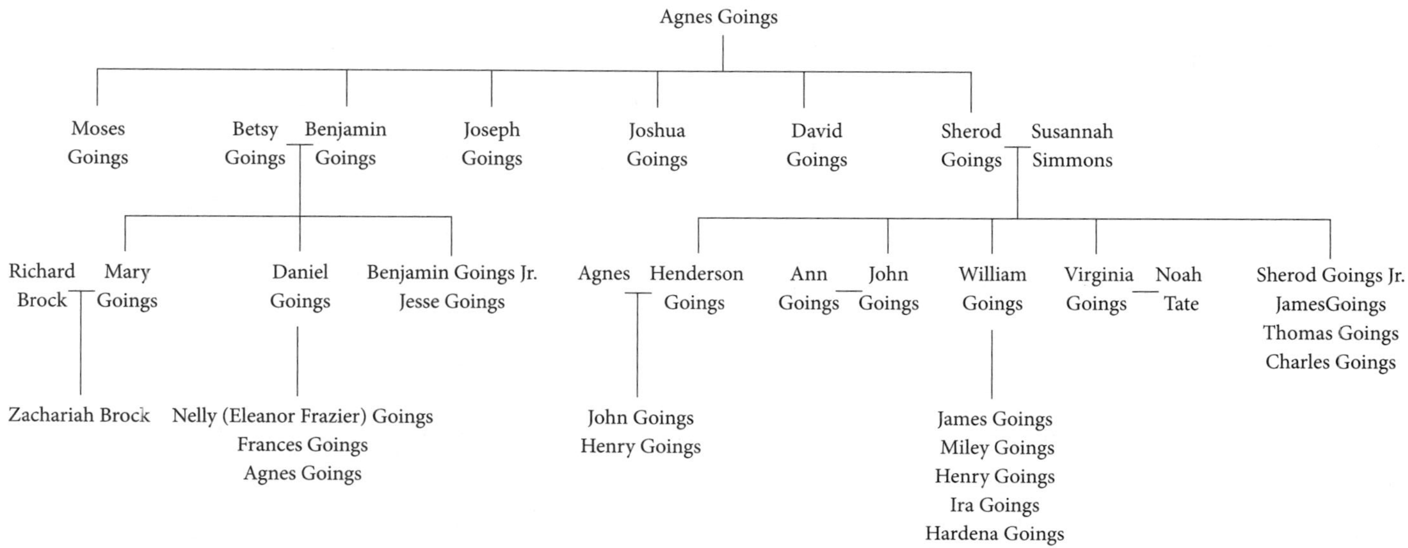

Notes

ABBREVIATIONS

ACCCC	Albemarle County Court Commonwealth Causes
ACCOB	Albemarle County Court Order Book
ACDB	Albemarle County Deed Book
ACLOB	Albemarle County Law Order Book
ACMB	Albemarle County Minute Book
ACWB	Albemarle County Will Book
LoV	Library of Virginia

INTRODUCTION

1. U. B. Phillips, *American Negro Slavery,* 436–41.

2. For free blacks as anomalous, see Berlin, *Slaves without Masters;* Condon, "Manumission, Slavery and Family"; Berlin, *Many Thousands Gone;* Sensbach, *Separate Canaan;* Bogger, *Free Blacks in Norfolk;* Kimberly S. Hanger, *Bounded Lives;* Burckin, "'Spirit of Perserverance,'" 61–81; Schwarz, "Emancipators, Protectors, and Anomalies," 317–38; Fields, *Slavery and Freedom on the Middle Ground;* Ellefson, "Free Jupiter"; and Russell, *Free Negro in Virginia.*

3. Berlin, *Slaves without Masters,* 5.

4. See Rothman, *Notorious in the Neighborhood;* Condon, "Manumission, Slavery and Family"; Franklin and Schweninger, *Runaway Slaves;* Bogger, *Free Blacks in Norfolk;* Hanger, *Bounded Lives;* Lebsock, *Free Women of Petersburg;* Curry, *Free Black in Urban America;* and Berlin, *Slaves without Masters.*

5. Russell, *Free Negro in Virginia,* 60–63; Berlin, *Slaves without Masters,* 20–30. Berlin does not attribute the 1782 law to Revolutionary rhetoric alone. He correctly sees evangelical Christians as another driving force. But he does summarize the period, stating: "Equalitarian ideals motivated most manumitters in the years following the Revolution" (30). See also Egerton, *Gabriel's Rebellion,* 3–12; C. Phillips, *Freedom's Port,* 30–56.

6. For more on manumission in Albemarle County, see von Daacke, "Free Black Families and Freedom." For more on manumission as a complex economic and social negotiation between master and slave, see Whitman, *Price of Freedom.*

7. For the older view on the color line, mulattoes, and miscegenation, see Williamson, *New People;* Berlin, *Slaves without Masters;* Johnston, *Race Relations in Virginia.* For the new scholarship on miscegenation and the color line, see Rothman, *Notorious in the Neighborhood;* Wallenstein, *Tell the Court I Love My Wife;* Lockley, *Lines in the Sand;* Ely, *Israel on the Appommattox;* Hodes, *White Women, Black Men;* Bardaglio, *Reconstructing the Household;* Buckley, "Unfixing Race," 349–80; and Mills, "Miscegenation and the Free Negro," 16–34.

8. See Wolf, *Race and Liberty;* Ely, *Israel on the Appomattox;* Schweninger, *Black Property Owners;* Butler, "Evolution of a Rural Free Black Community"; Franklin, *Free Negro in North Carolina;* and Jackson, *Free Negro Labor.* For two works that focus on wealthy free blacks as rare exceptions, see Madden, *We Were Always Free;* and Johnson and Roark, *Black Masters.* For works that do not focus solely on free blacks but complicate notions of community in the rural antebellum South in important ways, see Kenzer, *Kinship and Neighborhood;* and Burton, *In My Father's House.*

9. For the 1785 law, see Hening, *Statutes at Large,* 12: 182. See also Russell, *Free Negro in Virginia.* Starting in 1832, the state legislature ordered that free black criminal defendants be tried in courts of oyer and terminer, which were previously reserved for slave defendants. See Albemarle County Minute Book (ACMB) 1838–42, 152 (Feb. 14, 1840) (free mulatto Woodson Marks found guilty of felony burglary, sentenced to five years in jail). See also ACMB 1842–44, 210 (July 22, 1843) (free man of color Washington Randolph acquitted of feloniously assaulting free man of color John Kenney).

10. This book is informed by a literature that proposes a more complicated notion of freedom. For examples, see Foner, *Story of American Freedom;* and Patterson, *Freedom, Volume I.* Patterson employs a tripartite model, and Foner constructs a more elastic definition, with at least five categories. This book is also informed by two anthropological studies: Dominguez, *White by Definition;* and S. Moore, *Law as Process.*

1. THE RIGHT HAND MEN OF THE REVOLUTION

1. No complete accounting of Albemarle's population exists prior to 1790, but the first decennial census conducted in that year showed over 6,000 white residents, more than 5,500 slaves, and 171 free people of color living in Albemarle County.

2. Officially, anyone coded as a person of color in Virginia during the time period discussed here was legally a "free negro." However, within that category, persons could be either "black," denoting no admixture of whiteness, or "negro," usually referring to darker-skinned individuals, including some mulattoes; or "mulatto," with a visible admixture of whiteness. "Mulatto" was often further broken down into a

series of categories running from lightest (very bright, Indian, light yellow complexion) to darkest (dark, very dark, negro complexion). Persons coded at the light end often were not categorized locally as "free negroes." Instead, they were counted as whites or counted as whites with mulatto penciled in next to the name. For purposes of clarity, I utilize the terms "free black," "person of color," or "people of color" whenever referring to people classified as "free negro," regardless of actual somatic condition.

3. The extant typewritten version of the 1790 U.S. Census for Virginia includes an 1840 list of Revolutionary pensioners for the county; fifteen white males are listed. See also Woods, *Albemarle County,* 367–71, where he enumerates over one hundred enlistees.

4. Existing records do not indicate whether he was born free or was manumitted, but Smith had been an active participant in the Albemarle community for some time when the Revolution commenced.

5. A.C. St. Anne's Parish Personal Property Tax Book, 1789. The other person in his household remains unnamed but was possibly his brother Granville Smith (also known as Granville Scott), who does not appear as an independent head of household for a few years after that date. See also Jackson, "Virginia Negroes and Seamen," 247–87.

6. A.C. St. Anne's Parish Personal Property Tax Books, 1794–1811. By 1810, Smith's household had four free males over age sixteen living in it (this year he is listed as Johnson Scott). The following year, 1811, Smith's entry indicates that there were only two free males over age sixteen in his house (most likely Johnson Smith and either an adult son or his brother Granville Smith). See also Albemarle County Commonwealth Causes (ACCC), Box 9, Feb. to June 1814, and Albemarle County Court Order Book (ACCOB) 1813–15, 288. Those court papers indicate that the accused, Johnson and Rachel Scott, were also known as Johnson and Rachel Smith.

7. U.S. Census for Virginia, 1810. The "other free persons" was the only category on the 1810 census where free people of color could be counted (most categories were age groupings for white males and females, with one category for "slaves").

8. A.C. St. Anne's Parish Personal Property Tax Book, 1812, 1813. The 1813 tax list has Rachel Smith listed as Rachel Scott on a list of free people of color in St. Anne's Parish who were not listed as heads of household in the personal property tax assessment but were nonetheless subject to the poll tax. See also ACCC, Box 9, Feb. to June 1814, and ACCOB 1813–15, 288. See Whitman, *Price of Freedom,* for an excellent study of the concepts "term slavery" and "virtually free slaves."

9. Albemarle County St. Anne's Parish Personal Property Tax Books, 1811, 1813; ACCOB 1813–15, 288 (Mar. 7, 1814); ACCCC, Box 9, May 9, Oct. 7, 1814. Johnson Smith appears as Johnson Scott in some of the records. His family members are also alternately referred to as Smith or Scott. In particular, the county court papers repeatedly refer to them as having the surname Scott but also indicate that they were known as "Smith."

10. See Berlin, *Many Thousands Gone* and *Slaves without Masters*, for the best examples of this view. I examine that gap between the legislative record and local behavior.

11. ACCCC, Box 9, June 6, 8, 1814.

12. P. Morgan, "Interracial Sex in the Chesapeake." Morgan suggests that often there was a local sociocultural context in which interracial cooperation occurred. See also Howington, *What Sayeth the Law.*

13. A.C. St. Anne's Parish Personal Property Tax Book, 1814. These slaves may have been Johnson Smith's children, or they may have been an older son's children whom he had fathered with a slave woman and whom the family purchased in order to free them.

14. At this time, Fredericksville Parish, the northern half of today's Albemarle, was still part of Louisa County. Thus, the two counties have a history of connection. It is possible that Battles was in fact born in a part of Louisa that later became part of Albemarle.

15. Heinegg, *Free African Americans*, 1: 109–10; Albemarle County Surveyor's Book, 1744–55, 214 (Mar. 26, 1752). Heinegg incorrectly identifies the land as being in Amherst County. The property remained on the southern border of Albemarle after Amherst was created out of the southern half of the county in 1761.

16. In 1761, Amherst County was created out of the southern half of Albemarle (it included present-day Nelson County).

17. Heinegg, *Free African Americans*, 1: 110; Dorman, *Revolutionary Pension Applications*, 4: 44; Albemarle County Deed Book (ACDB), No. 6, 462 (Aug. 21, 1775). See also McLeRoy and McLeRoy, *Strangers in Their Midst.*

18. Heinegg, *Free African Americans*, 1: 110; ACCOB 1783–85, 274 (Nov. 12, 1784). No record of Battles's bond is extant.

19. Albemarle County Record of Marriage Bonds 1780–1806 (Oct. 21, 1786); A.C. Fredericksville Parish Personal Property Tax Books, 1787–92; ACCOB 1791–93, 47 (Aug. 10, 1793).

20. A.C. Fredericksville Parish Personal Property Tax Books, 1790–1800; ACCOB 1800–1801, 250 (Dec. 2, 1850). In addition to Battles, the order listed John Randol, Zachariah Bowles, Thomas Farrow, Griffin Butler, Bartlett Bowles, and William Battles.

21. ACCOB 1800–1801, 275 (Feb. 3, 1801), 279 (Feb. 3, 1801), and 290 (Mar. 3, 1801). See also Hening, *Statutes at Large.*

22. Rawlings, *Early Charlottesville*, 2.

23. Ibid.; Woods, *Albemarle County*, 110, 135.

24. ACCOB 1800–1801, 323 (May 5, 1801). See also ACCOB 1800–1801, 378 (May 9, 1801), for a suit against Battles filed by Margery Parks, who may have been a free woman of color. She even had witnesses: the white merchant John Wineberry and Jonathan Parks. It is not clear whether this was a debt case or what its outcome was.

25. ACCOB 1800–1801, 323 (May 5, 1801). This case, involving county residents who lived miles outside of Charlottesville, highlights the ways in which freedom of movement was possible and expected for free people of color.

26. A.C. Fredericksville Parish Personal Property Tax Books, 1801–7; ACCOB 1806–7, 112 (Mar. 7, 1807).

27. Dorman, *Revolutionary Pension Applications,* 5, 44; Albemarle County Law Order Book (ACLOB) 1809–21, 415 (Oct. 11, 1820); ACDB No. 22, 312–13 (Mar. 4, 1821). Grady was also connected to other nonslaveholding white families through marriage (Woods, *Albemarle County,* 110).

28. ACCOB 1810–11, 62 (Mar. 9, 1810).

29. ACCOB 1821–22, 324 (June 5, 1823).

30. Old Papers Orphans' Indentures, July 3, 1826; ACCOB 1821–22, 325 (June 5, 1823). The suit against Markwood was later dismissed. On apprenticeship as both a system of white social control and a device manipulated by free people of color to their advantage, see Ely, *Israel on the Appomattox,* 117–22; Butler, "Evolution of a Rural Free Black Community," 185–239; and Franklin, *Free Negro in North Carolina,* 122–31.

31. Dorman, *Revolutionary Pension Applications,* 4: 87; Albemarle County Record of Marriage Bonds 1780–1806, Sept. 7, 1785.

32. A.C. Fredericksville Parish Personal Property Tax Books, 1787, 1789; A.C. Fredericksville Parish Land Tax Book, 1789. See also ACDB No. 9, 337 (Jan. 30, 1787), where Battles paid fifty dollars for the land.

33. Albemarle County Record of Marriage Bonds, 1780–1806, Jan. 3, 1791, Dec. 12, 1793. (Walter Key, a white Albemarle resident, witnessed the signing of the marriage bonds.) For George Mann's residency, see Albemarle County Personal Property Tax Books, which lists Mann as living with either William Goings or Benjamin Goings.

34. ACCOB 1795–98, 86 (May 5, 1796).

35. Ibid., 144 (Aug. 2, 1796), 137 (Aug. 2, 1796). See Shepherd, *Statues at Large,* 1: 238–39.

36. Dorman, *Revolutionary Pension Applications,* 4: 87. See also Heinegg, *Free African Americans,* 1: 174–75.

37. For Amy Farrow's will, see Albemarle County Will Book (ACWB) No. 4, 14 (Oct. 21, 1797); for Thomas Farrow's will, see ACWB No. 5, 77 (May 1, 1810). For the division of the farm into two parcels for Thomas Farrow and Zachariah Bowles, see Fredericksville Parish Land Tax Book, 1806. For Lucy Barnett's freedom certification, see ACCOB 1810–11, 58 (Mar. 9, 1810). The Farrows in some documents are alternately called "Farrar." For the sake of clarity and consistency, I have chosen to refer to them as "Farrow."

38. A.C. Fredericksville Parish Land Tax Books, 1810–16.

39. ACDB No. 21, 97 (Jan. 1, 1818). This document was witnessed by Norborne and James Powers, the white men who the following year would come to the legal aid of Lucy Barnett, writing down and witnessing her will.

40. ACWB No. 6, 327 (Feb. 1, 1819). The will states that Critty Bowles is a "granddaughter," but she in fact may have been a niece, the daughter of Zachariah Bowles and Critty (Bowles), a slave at Monticello.

41. Dorman, *Revolutionary Pension Applications,* 4: 87.

42. Ibid.

43. U.S. Census for Virginia, 1850, 189.

44. Albemarle County Record of Marriage Bonds 1780–1806, Jan. 3, 1791; U.S. Census for Virginia, 1850; Dorman, *Revolutionary Pension Applications,* 4: 87.

45. Jackson, *Virginia Negro Soldiers and Sailors,* 31. See also Heinegg, *Free African Americans,* 1: 144.

46. Albemarle County Record of Marriage Bonds 1780–1806, Oct. 24, 1790; A.C. Fredericksville Parish Personal Property Tax Books, 1791–98. See also Heinegg, *Free African Americans,* 1: 144, for a short biographical sketch of Zachariah.

47. ACWB No. 4, 14 (Oct. 21, 1797). The witnesses Usly Topence and Amy Farrow both only "signed" with a mark. For the recording of the will, see ACCOB 1798–1800, 123 (Oct. 21, 1798).

48. ACCOB 1798–1800, 167 (Dec. 4, 1798). For a discussion of where Isaac Miller lived, see Woods, *Albemarle County,* 174.

49. A.C. Fredericksville Land Tax Books, 1798–1805. John Randol, not identified as a free person of color in the documents mentioned above, appears with Zachariah Bowles, Thomas Farrow, and others on an 1800 roadwork order for free black laboring tithables assigned to work on a road north of town being surveyed by John T. Hawkins. ACCOB 1800–1801, 250 (Dec. 2, 1800). The free people of color listed on this order all likely lived in the same neighborhood, with the whites John T. Hawkins, Isaac Miller, Samuel Carr, and others.

50. ACCOB 1801–2, 93 (Nov. 2, 1801).

51. ACCOB 1806, 424 (Oct. 7, 1806).

52. ACWB No. 5, 77 (May 25, 1810). For Lucy Barnett's will, see ACWB No. 6, 327 (Feb. 1, 1819).

53. ACWB No. 5, 77 (May 25, 1810).

54. Ibid.

55. A.C. Fredericksville Parish Personal Property Tax Books, 1810–19; A.C. Fredericksville Land Tax Books, 1810–19. James Lott is listed as living with Zachariah Bowles in the 1813, 1814, and 1816 Personal Property Tax Books.

56. Heinegg, *Free African Americans,* 1: 144; ACWB No. 6, 327 (Feb. 1, 1819); A.C. Fredericksville Parish Land Tax Book, 1820.

57. ACWB No. 7, 250 (Nov. 7, 1822).

58. Ibid.

59. Ibid.; Albemarle County Marriage Register 1806–68, 20 (Mar. 19, 1817), marriage of Stephen Coram and Keziah Battles; Albemarle County Record of Marriage Bonds 1780–1806 (Dec. 12, 1793), marriage of Robert Battles Sr. and Nancy Bowles; A.C. St. Anne's Parish Land Tax Books, 1800–1822.

60. ACWB No. 7, 250 (Nov. 7, 1822). See Woods, *Albemarle County,* 324–27, for a description of Joel Terrell, who owned a major portion of the Carrsbrook plantation (on the north bank of the Rivanna River's North Fork) in the 1820s.

61. ACCOB 1821–22, 182 (Dec. 3, 1822), 185 (Jan. 6, 1823).

62. Ibid., 147 (Nov. 8, 1822). No records are extant showing whether they were actually bound out and to whom they might have been bound. On apprenticeship as a system utilized by free blacks to their advantage, see Ely, *Israel on the Appomattox,* 117–22; Butler, "Evolution of a Rural Free Black Community," 185–239; and Franklin, *Free Negro in North Carolina,* 122–31.

63. A.C. Fredericksville/St. Anne's Parish Land Tax Books, 1819–31. Starting in 1822, the parcels owned by Zachariah Bowles, Lucy/Judah Barnett, and the Thomas Farrow estate all appear on the St. Anne's Parish Land Tax Book. This is probably the result of bookkeeping inconsistency. From the same point on, their personal property tax assessment also appears in St. Anne's Parish, but in 1833, the colonization census puts them back in Fredericksville Parish. See also ACCOB 1800–1801, 243–44 (Dec. 1, 1800), for two deeds of sale between Zachariah Bowles and Samuel Carr; A.C. St. Anne's Parish Land Tax Book, with a note under the entry for Judah Barnett estate regarding "eleven acres off to Samuel Carr."

64. Auditor of Public Accounts, Free Blacks/Records/1833-37, RG 48, Box 1974, entry 757. See also E. Jordan, "'Just and True Account,'" 120–21 (Jordan transcribed both parish censuses).

65. ACDB No. 32, 412 (Sept. 7, 1835). The deed entered into the record that day in 1835 was signed by T. J. Randolph on Jan. 20, 1827.

66. ACWB No. 12, 95–96 (June 1, 1835).

67. ACMB 1834–36, 276 (Sept. 7, 1835).

68. ACWB No. 8, 248–50 (Aug. 7, 1826). For a discussion of Thomas Jefferson's paternity of Madison and Eston, see Gordon-Reed, *Hemingses of Monticello;* Foster et al., "Jefferson Fathered Slave's Last Child," 27–28; Nieman, "Coincidence or Causal Connection?" 198–210; Gordon-Reed, *Thomas Jefferson and Sally Hemings.*

69. This Critty (Hemings) Colbert (1783–1819) who married Burwell Colbert was the daughter of Nance Hemings, a sister of Critty (Hemings) Bowles (1769–1850). Nance and both Crittys were initially Thomas Jefferson's slaves.

70. ACWB No. 12, 95–86 (June 1, 1835). See also Critty Bowles's will, ACWB No. 20, 144 (Dec. 4, 1850), where she terms Martha Ann Colbert "a slave raised by me" owned by Lewis Randolph.

71. Stanton, *Free Some Day,* 116. Stanton also includes a quote from a letter written by Jefferson's granddaughter Ellen Coolidge in 1858, which states that it was Jefferson's "principle . . . to allow such of his slaves as were sufficiently white to pass for white men, to withdraw quietly from the plantation; it was called running away, but they were never reclaimed." Stanton further suggests that James Hemings was almost certainly one of the three young slaves Randolph referenced in the letter.

72. ACMB 1848–50, 246 (Sept. 4, 1849); ACMB 1850–54, 181 (Feb. 2, 1852); and ACMB 1856–59, 200 (Nov. 3, 1857). For information on Railey, Goodman, and the Carrs, see Woods, *Albemarle County,* 161, 210, 300.

73. Heinegg, *Free African Americans,* 1: 415. For more on how the issue of child support may have been far more important to county authorities than miscegenation, see Ely, *Israel on the Appommattox,* 305–6, 308–9, 574 n. 64.

74. Heinegg, *Free African Americans,* 1: 415–16; R. Davis, *Louisa County, Virginia;* Abercrombie, *Free Blacks of Louisa County;* Dorman, *Revolutionary Pension Applications,* 45: 11–12.

75. A.C. Fredericksville Parish Land Tax Books, 1782–87; Heinegg, *Free African Americans,* 1: 416; A.C. Fredericksville Parish Personal Property Tax Books, 1787–89.

76. Albemarle County Legislative Petitions 1776–1816, Box 3, Folder 74 (Nov. 14, 1789).

77. A.C. Fredericksville Parish Personal Property Tax Books, 1789–91; Albemarle County Record of Marriage Bonds 1780–1806 (June 5, 1791). William Simmons was a married white slaveholder with one white child. There are a number of free black Simmonses, all of whom are described as having a "very light complexion." Only Susannah Simmons can be directly linked to William Simmons.

78. A.C. Fredericksville Parish Land Tax Books, 1798–1805; ACDB No. 15, 135 (Apr. 15, 1805). For Goings's and Dunn's military service, see Woods, *Albemarle County,* 371. For Goings, see also Jackson, *Virginia Negro Soldiers and Sailors,* 35 (Jackson lists him as "Sherwood Going"). See also Virginia Land Office Military Certificates, Register and Entry 86 in the Virginia Land Office Inventory, Box 73, 22.

79. Albemarle County Marriage Register 1806–68, 9 (Jan. 3, 1810); A.C. Fredericksville Parish Land Tax Books, 1810–23; ACDB No. 23, 58–59 (June 1, 1822).

80. A.C. Fredericksville Parish Land Tax Books, 1823–29; A.C. Fredericksville Parish Personal Property Tax Books, 1823–29; Dorman, *Revolutionary Pension Applications,* 45: 11–12; Woods, *Albemarle County,* 364–71; Jackson, *Virginia Negro Soldiers and Sailors,* 35.

81. A.C. Fredericksville Parish Land Tax Books, 1829–37; E. Jordan, "'Just and True Account,'" 127–29.

82. Dorman, *Revolutionary Pension Applications,* 45: 11–12. The seven-year gap between Susannah's application and her receiving a continuation of the pension was caused by an unfortunate accident that slowed her paperwork. Albemarle resident Thomas Walker Gilmer was carrying her paperwork (and that of another free black pensioner) with him shortly after becoming secretary of the navy, but was accidentally killed in an explosion aboard the *Princeton,* a naval ship on which he was sailing to Washington. It took a few years to sort out the situation.

2. CHILDREN OF THE REVOLUTION

1. See Berlin, *Many Thousands Gone;* Berlin, *Slaves without Masters;* Kolchin, *American Slavery;* and Jackson, *Free Negro Labor.*

2. A.C. Record of Marriage Bonds, 1780–1806. See also Vogt and Kethley, *Albemarle County Marriages,* 1: 30.

3. A.C. Personal Property Tax Books, 1794–1820.

4. ACCOB 1795–98, 86 (May 5, 1796), 144 (Aug. 2, 1796).

5. Shepherd, *Statutes at Large,* 1: 238. See also Guild, *Black Laws of Virginia,* 95.

6. ACCOB 1803–4, 169 (July 4, 1803).

7. ACDB No. 22, 64–65 (Dec. 28, 1819). The land was on the south side of Three Notched Road between Charlottesville and the University of Virginia, adjoining the land of James Dinsmore.

8. For example, Robert Battles Sr. appears some years on the Fredericksville Parish tax lists, some years on the St. Anne's Parish tax lists; in some years his personal

property tax appears in one parish, his land tax in the other. This results both from the often informal documentation procedures in place in rural Virginia at the time and from the fact that Battles's property lay in the vicinity of the border between the two administrative districts.

9. A.C. Marriage Register 1806–68, 20 (Mar. 19, 1817).

10. A.C. Land Tax Book, 1820.

11. A.C. Fredericksville Parish Personal Property Tax Books, 1798 and 1805.

12. ACCOB 1806, 45 (Mar. 6, 1806); ACCOB 1806, 127–28 (May 6, 1806); *Patrick Johnson v. Robert Battles*, Albemarle County Judgments, Box 111, Mar. 1807.

13. Alexander Garrett Executor Accounts for Richard H. Allen estate, including estate sale accounts, ACWB No. 7, 195–200 (June 17, 1807). Accounts run through 1822 and include payments from Battles to the estate for the grindstone. The accounts also include payments from the estate to Robert Battles Sr. for his carpentry work on a school building on Allen's property.

14. Jane Lewis estate sale accounts, ACWB No. 5, 238 (Dec. 1, 1813).

15. ACDB No. 22, 486 (Feb. 5, 1822).

16. ACDB No. 25, 166–67 (Mar. 22, 1825).

17. Ibid.; and A.C. Land Tax Books, 1820–21.

18. ACDB No. 27, 197–98 (Apr. 30, 1825); von Daacke, "Slaves without Masters?" 39–60; and Woods, *Albemarle County*, 179.

19. ACCOB 1825, 70 (Mar. 9, 1825); and ACCOB 1826, 276 (Aug. 11, 1826).

20. A.C. Chancery Order Book No. 1, 1831–42, 30 (Oct. 11, 1832), 39 (Oct. 22, 1832).

21. Rawlings, *Early Charlottesville*, 92; U.S. Census for Virginia, 1820; ACWB No. 10, 262–64 (Aug. 4, 1831); *Robert Battles v. Charles Spencer's Heirs*, Albemarle County Chancery Causes (1843-029 CSC).

22. A.C. Marriage Register 1806–68, 51 (Aug. 6, 1832). The Presbyterian minister Francis Bowman conducted the service. See E. Jordan, "'Just and True Account,'" 134.

23. Woods, *Albemarle County*, 401; ACWB No. 11, 72–76 (July 15, 1831, Aug. 7, 1832).

24. See the details of Jesse Scott's life for more on Bishop. Bishop and Burton ran a tanyard that employed free blacks, hired slaves, and even laboring whites. All of these people commingled regularly on the south side of Charlottesville. In fact, Bishop was arrested at the home of the free man of color Jesse Scott. Both Scott and Bishop were charged with illegal gaming. Gaming locations, whether houses of entertainment or fields used for public gatherings, were often highly interracial settings.

25. ACWB No. 12, 152 (Nov. 2, 1835).

26. A.C. Fredericksville Parish Personal Property Tax Book, 1835 (Robert Battles Sr. is listed here as deceased, so he clearly died before Jan. of the following year); ACWB No. 12, 152 (Nov. 2, 1835); and ACWB No. 12, 178 (Mar. 7, 1836).

27. ACDB No. 35, 126 (May 3, 1837).

28. Ibid. The panel included William Garth, Isaac White, Joseph Watson, John Pollock, Thomas R. Bailey, Joshua Wheeler, John B. Perry, Claudius Mayo, Lewis Sowell, Benjamin Moore, and William Garland.

29. ACMB 1836–38, 484 (Dec. 10, 1838).

30. Ibid., 458 (Nov. 6, 1838).

31. ACDB No. 36, 500–501 (Dec. 3, 1838).

32. ACMB 1836–38, 458 (Nov. 6, 1838).

33. ACMB 1838–42, 18 (Mar. 4, 1839).

34. ACDB No. 37, 229–30 (May 3, 1839).

35. Ibid., 456–57 (July 18, 1839, Feb. 17, 1840).

36. ACWB No. 13, 114 (June 1, 1840); and E. Jordan, "'Just and True Account,'" 134. Even Robert Battles appears in Michael Johnson's administrator accounts, receiving payments for work completed and occasionally making payments to the estate. Julian Burruss (Burrows) was the nineteen-year-old seamstress living with the Battles family in 1833.

37. *Elijah Battles v. John T. Bishop,* Albemarle County Court Records, Judgments, 1823, Box 210. The court papers indicate that Battles first made a complaint in 1820. That complaint was set aside later the same year, but Battles renewed the charges, and the case continued until 1823.

38. ACCOB 1820–21, 237; *Elijah Battles v. John T. Bishop,* Albemarle County Court Records.

39. A.C. Marriage Register 1806–68, 27 (Apr. 25, 1821). James Farrar, father of the bride, gave bond, affirming that Nancy was over twenty-one years of age and providing surety of the lack of legal impediments to the marriage. *Elijah Battles v. John T. Bishop,* Albemarle County Court Records.

40. *Battles v. Bishop,* ACCOB 1822–23, 36 (Aug. 8, 1822); Woods, *Albemarle County,* 144. John Bishop's father was Joseph Bishop, a prominent property owner in town. He owned property on Main Street, Three Notched Road, Random Row, and Vinegar Hill. See also *Elijah Battles v. John T. Bishop,* Albemarle County Court Records.

41. A.C. St. Anne's Parish Personal Property Tax Books, 1816–20; ACDB No. 22, 64–65 (Dec. 28, 1819). Robert and Nancy had two other sons: Elijah and Wyatt Battles.

42. ACCOB 1820–21, 363 (Jan. 1, 1821); A.C. Marriage Register 1806–68, 27 (Jan. 4, 1821).

43. ACWB No. 77, 250 (Sept. 1, 1822). The will was recorded in Nov. 1822.

44. ACCOB 1822–23, 364 (July 7, 1823).

45. Ibid., 385, 472 (Aug. 4, 5, 1823). Apparently, the conflict was really between Wyatt Battles and William Spinner. Wyatt's brothers must have been there at the first argument and subsequent physical confrontation, but remained peripheral to the case. Elijah and Robert Jr. had their recognizances canceled, while Wyatt's remained in effect for the year. And this familial conflict continued beyond 1823. See also *Wyatt Battles v. William Spinner,* assault case, ACCOB 1825, 71 (Mar. 9, 1825); *William Spinner v. Robert Battles Jr.,* ACCOB 1826, 276 (Aug. 11, 1826). Both cases were dismissed in Aug. 1826.

46. ACCOB 1822–23, 364 (July 7, 1823). The Battles brothers appeared as defendants answering Spinner's charges. All three Battles men, along with Stephen Coram, filed fifty-dollar peace bonds ensuring their good behavior for a year. The case was dismissed on Aug. 5, 1823 (p. 472). William Spinner registered once, in 1812; Elijah Battles once,

in 1820; Robert Battles Jr. once, in 1821; and Wyatt Battles once, in 1825. All did so in preparation for marriage. None of these men ever ran afoul of the law as a result or ever felt the need to renew their registers, which by state law was supposed to happen once every three years.

47. ACDB No. 25, 435–36 (Feb. 6, 1826). For Martha H. Waltman's dower relinquishment, see ACDB No. 26, 297.

48. ACWB No. 8, 195 (Mar. 7, 1826); ACWB No. 10, 47–48 (Mar. 3, 1830); and ACWB No. 11, 31–33 (Mar. 9, 1832).

49. ACWB No. 8, 195 (Mar. 7, 1826); ACWB No. 10, 47–48 (Mar. 3, 1830); and ACWB No. 11, 31–33 (Mar. 9, 1832).

50. ACCOB 1830, 147 (Aug. 2, 4, 1830). See also ACMB 1830–31, 9, 21, 25 (Aug. 2–5, 1830), where the defendant George Spreigle is listed as both "Spriggle" and "Spriggles."

51. A.C. Fredericksville Parish Land Tax Books, 1829–31; ACWB No. 10, 304–6 (Nov. 7, 1831).

52. E. Jordan, "'Just and True Account,'" 134–35.

53. Robert Jr. lived with his wife, Mary, and their six children: Ellen (mulatto, age twelve), Martha (mulatto, age ten), Wyatt (mulatto, age eight), Susan (mulatto, age six), Robert III (mulatto, age four), and an as-yet-unnamed infant, a one-month-old baby boy. Listed as living with Elijah was his wife, Nancy, age thirty-five, a mulatto. Also listed were their children: Jepthah Battles (age ten), Nancy Battles (age eight, mulatto), and Sophia Battles (age six, mulatto).

54. The only people missing in 1833 were Wyatt Battles and Stephen and Keziah Coram. They may have moved out of the area. As recently as 1825, all three still resided on Three Notched Road. Unfortunately, no deeds exist that reveal where they might have gone. No census data suggests they were living on someone else's property.

55. ACDB No. 31, 132–33 (Oct. 9, 1833).

56. ACDB No. 41, 271–72 (Feb. 19, 1838). The original document, as recorded in the deed book, is dated 1838, but the document was not officially entered into the record until Dec. 23, 1843. No explanation exists for the discrepancy in dates.

57. E. Jordan, "'Just and True Account,'" 134; ACWB No. 12, 89–92 (June 1, 1835); ACWB No. 12, 152 (Nov. 2, 1835); ibid., 473–77 (Oct. 2, 1837); ACWB No. 13, 66–69 (Mar. 6, 1838); ibid., 307–8 (June 3, 1839), 460–63, (June 1, 1840); ACWB No. 14, 331–32 (Mar. 3, 1842); and ibid., 376–82 (June 6, 1842).

58. ACWB No. 12, 89–92 (June 1, 1835); ibid., 473–77 (Oct. 2, 1837); and ACWB No. 13, 121–24 (Aug. 6, 1838).

59. ACWB No. 12, 152 (Nov. 2, 1835).

60. ACCOB 1822–23, 36 (Aug. 8, 1822).

61. All the administrator accounts mentioned here also include payments to white artisans and workers. It would have been very likely that whites and free blacks had routine contact at these work sites. The accounts, however, do not specify whether white and free people of color worked together.

62. ACWB No. 15, 73–93 (Apr. 4, 1843).

63. Rawlings, *Early Charlottesville,* 55, 76.

64. Rawlings, *Albemarle of Other Days,* 76.

65. ACWB No. 15, 4 (Dec. 4, 1843).

66. A.C. Marriage Register 1806–68, 86 (Jan. 18, 1844).

67. ACWB No. 18, 141–45 (July 5, 1847); and A.C. Marriage Register 1806–68, 94 (Oct. 28, 1847).

68. ACDB No. 47, 236–37 (Apr. 17, 1849). Evelina Garrett's dower relinquishment is located on p. 437. She was examined by William F. Gooch and Alexander Pope Abell.

69. U.S. Census for Virginia, 1850. Dolly Cousins and Robert Battles Jr. and their families lived in the same dwelling house. Thomas Farrar's household included Jane C. Patterson, a fifty-year-old white woman.

70. ACWB No. 21, 259–96 (Mar. 1, 1852). Battles also shows up in another George Carr–administrated account: that of John H. Maddox in 1857. See ACWB No. 25, 235–43 (Oct. 6, 1857).

71. A.C. Marriage Register 1854–1903, 4 (Jan. 4, 1856). The register states: "They are free negroes, wedding at Elijah Battles' in Albemarle County."

72. Commonwealth Causes Box 38 (charges against Hatley Moss, dismissed), Box 39 (Rose Taylor, Joshua Craig, Eliza Garner, Maria Hatter, David Hite, Randolph Jones, Kitty Kean, Nancy Kinney, Woodson Marks, James Munroe), Box 40 (Randolph Jones, found guilty on Oct. 26, 1853). The court ordered that Jones "forfeit his freedom and be sold as a slave." No evidence exists of the court carrying out the sentence, and it appears as if Jones may have moved out of the area prior to the verdict.

73. See Free Negro Affidavits and Certificates, Albemarle County (Nov. 2, 1850); ACMB 1848–50, 412; ACMB 1850–54, 7–8, 15, 37, 40, 284, 360, 485; Albemarle County Free Negro and Slave Records, Box 2 and Box 3; Commonwealth Causes Box 38 (two residency complaints), Box 39 (thirteen residency complaints); Albemarle County Legislative Petitions (Dec. 12, 1850) (asking the legislature to reject free black residency applications); and Free Negro and Slave Records, Box 1, Petitions, 1851–52.

74. ACMB 1851–54, 10 (Dec. 3, 1850). The list here is substantial. Pp. 6–11 only contain short entries for free blacks proving their freedom and receiving certificates, and all were on Dec. 3, 1850. In total, eighty-seven free blacks either faced charges or received registers that day. A number of other Battleses (Elijah, Martha, Noah, Edward, Franklin), Farrars, Bowleses, Kenneys, Goingses, and Scotts all poured into town on that day for the same reason. See also ACMB 1848–50 for additional free black freedom certifications in late 1849 and into 1850 (starting on p. 279). The number of free people of color formally seeking free papers went up at this time and never returned to the pre-1850 low.

75. The court records concerning residency petitions and indictments of those violating the removal law indicate that a few other free people of color moved away at that time as well. See Commonwealth Causes, Box 39 (Jan. 28, 1852), summons for David Hite ("not found . . . lives in Washington"), and Box 39 (Jan. 28, 1852), summons for Kitty Kean ("defendant has left state . . . lives in Pennsylvania").

76. ACDB No. 50, 270–72 (Feb. 6, 1852).

77. ACDB No. 51, 496–97 (Mar. 13, 1853).

78. ACMB 1856–59, 188 (Oct. 6, 1857).

79. A.C. Marriage Register 1854–1903, 11 (Jan. 20, 1859).

80. U.S. Census for Virginia, 1860.

81. James A. Watson guardian accounts for deceased child Mary June Railey, ACWB No. 19, 396 (June 3, 1850) (includes payments to Robert Battles in 1847 and 1848).

82. Although many more free people of color sought free papers after 1849, and the county court appears to have pursued somewhat more assiduously those who violated the 1806 removal law, those same court documents evince the continuation of face-to-face relationships. See Commonwealth Causes, Box 39, 1851–52, where the free man of color James Munroe is summoned for remaining in the county without leave and is found guilty (Aug. 4, 1851), but almost a year later still resides in the county (when he, with the white lawyer Egbert R. Watson, files a peace bond in the amount of twenty-five dollars, guaranteeing his good behavior for a year); ACMB 1850–54, 360, (Mar. 8, 1852), where James B. Rogers appears in defense of the free woman of color Melissa Brock (lost free papers); ACMB 1848–50, 412, where Elizabeth Ailstock is charged with "going at large without her free papers" (she files recognizance with whites Chiles Brand and George Slaughter as security, two hundred dollars each, for her appearance in Dec. court [no ended papers are extant, but Elizabeth Ailstock registered her freedom in late 1852: ACMB 1850–54, 315]); ACMB 1850–54, 8, (Dec. 3, 1850), where Maria Hatter, charged with violating the 1806 removal law and not having her register, files a two-hundred-dollar bond with John T. Barksdale as security (see Commonwealth Causes, Box 39 [Aug. 4, 1852], case dismissed); ACMB 1850–54, 284 (Sept. 6, 1852), where the court grants Admiral Elias Elliott's residency request; and Free Negro & Slave Records, Box 3 (Mar. 23, 1853), where the free black Poindexter family, originally granted residency permission in Louisa County, is issued free papers.

3. GOOD BLACKS AND USEFUL MEN

1. Legislative Petitions, Hanover County, Nov. 16, 1784, Henrico County, Nov. 16, 1784, and King and Queen County, Dec. 2, 1800, at the *Digital Library on American Slavery* (http://library.uncg.edu/slavery/). Originals located at the Library of Virginia (LoV). See also Berlin, *Slaves without Masters*, 79–107; W. Jordan, *White over Black*, 406–22; Bogger, *Free Blacks in Norfolk*, 10–11; Quarles, *Negro in the American Revolution*, 185–95; Franklin, *Free Negro in North Carolina*, 10–13; Russell, *Free Negro in Virginia*, 62, 81; Jackson, *Free Negro Labor*, 172–75; Mullin, *Flight and Resistance*, 127; and Boles, *Black Southerners*, 58.

2. Shepherd, *Statutes at Large*, 1: 238. See Berlin, *Slaves without Masters*, 93, where Berlin argues that the 1793 law was passed at the urging of people living in urban areas, who were troubled by the growing presence both of free blacks and of slaves

passing as free in their midst. See also Bogger, *Free Blacks in Norfolk,* 29; and Jackson, *Free Negro Labor,* 172–75.

3. Berlin, *Slaves without Masters,* 82–84; Bogger, *Free Blacks in Norfolk,* 29; Russell, *Free Negro in Virginia,* 156; Shepherd, *Statutes at Large,* 3: 252. See also Guild, *Black Laws of Virginia,* 72. Guild counts sixty-one free people of color permitted by the legislature to remain in the state between 1810 and 1847.

4. See Berlin, *Many Thousands Gone,* 123–26; Berlin, *Slaves without Masters,* 145–49; Genovese, *Roll, Jordan, Roll,* 398–413; and Russell, *Free Negro in Virginia.*

5. ACWB No. 1, 25; ACDB No. 15, 465; ACWB No. 4, 255; ACDB No. 16, 418; ACDB No. 17, 17; and ACWB No. 6, Oct. 1, 1814.

6. For manumissions between 1816 and 1826, see ACDB No. 21, 416 (a free black man frees his wife and five children); ACDB No. 8, 248 (Thomas Jefferson frees five slaves); and ACWB No. 8, 256. See also Berlin, *Slaves without Masters,* 147. In 1837, the law would be amended again, giving local courts broader authority concerning free black residency. Starting in that year, the state assembly allowed courts to grant residency to any freed person of color who was of good character. See Wolf, *Race and Liberty,* chap. 4, for more on post-1806 manumissions and local practice concerning residency.

7. ACCOB 1816–18, 90–91. See also ibid., 466 (Jan. 5, 1817), when Quarles, for the first and only time in the next forty years, filed for his freedom certification. He was listed as "about thirty years, six feet one inch high yellow complexion black straight hair, second toe of the left foot cut off."

8. ACCOB 1818–19, 221 (Mar. 1, 1819).

9. Albemarle County Legislative Petitions 1817–36, Box 4, Folder 50.

10. Ibid. See also Wolf, *Race and Liberty,* 138: "A disjunction existed between white Virginians' views of free blacks generally, a view that held them as threatening and violent, and their ideas about the individual free black people whom they knew as members of their communities and whom they sometimes counted as friends."

11. Albemarle County Legislative Petitions 1817–36, Box 4, Folder 50.

12. I borrow the term from Whitman, *Price of Freedom,* an excellent examination of term slavery in the urban context.

13. ACDB No. 39, 98 (Oct. 18, 1841). Randolph Jones appears variously in the public record as Randol, Randal, Randall, and Randolph Jones. For the sake of continuity, I have chosen to use Randolph throughout. Both master and manumitted slave share the same surname (Jones). No other evidence exists, however, to suggest that Randolph was actually related to his former master.

14. See Douglass, *Narrative,* 105, for a description of a slave hiring his own time: "I sought my own employment, made my own contracts, and collected the money I earned."

15. ACDB No. 39, 98; ACMB 1838–42, 384 (Nov. 2, 1841).

16. A.C. Fredericksville Parish Personal Property Tax Books, 1841–43; ACDB No. 41, 232 (Nov. 27, 1843).

17. ACCCC, Box 33 (May 21, 1845). The ended papers refer to an earlier complaint by Woodley and Heiskell, but no records remain regarding that suit.

18. Ibid. Not much is known about Jesse Heiskell and Willis Woodley. Heiskell was connected at least by marriage to Albemarle elites, having married a Garth. In 1841, the court charged Heiskell and John S. Moon with attempting to fight a duel (see Wood, *Albemarle County,* 111). In 1846, Heiskell again appeared in court, this time to file a fifty-dollar bond for Peter Sneed after Sneed physically threatened the free black laborer Garrett Tyree. That same year, Willis Woodley had to file his own peace bond after an affray with Alexander Rives.

19. ACMB 1848–50, 71 (June 5, 1848); and ACCCC, Box 36 (May 21, 1849).

20. County Minute Books and County Court Order Books do not contain a register for Randolph Jones in 1850, but an 1851 criminal presentment mentions his Nov. 1850 registry, describing him as "age 37, free negro." See ACCCC, Box 40 (Oct. 26, 1853).

21. ACMB 1851–54, 37 (Mar. 3, 1851); and ACCCC, Box 38 (May 1, 1851). The relationship between Charles Jones and Randolph Jones is unclear. The only other time a "Charles Jones" appears in the public record is 1807–14, when a free mulatto named Charles Jones appears on tax rolls for the county. He may have been Randolph's father. This Charles Jones would have been over one hundred years old at the time of the summons in 1851. Thus, the Charles Jones in the summons was more likely a son of Randolph's.

22. ACCCC, Box 39 (June 10, 1851), Box 39 (Jan. 28, 1852), Box 40 (Oct. 26, 1853). Jones was jailed in Feb. 1852 and not found guilty until Oct. 1853. There is no extant evidence in the county records that Jones posted bail or pledged security for a court appearance. It seems highly likely that he remained in jail until that guilty verdict in 1853. However, there is also no extant evidence that Jones was actually sold back into slavery as the verdict had directed.

23. ACWB No. 14, 391 (June 6, 1842).

24. Slave marriages were not legally recognized but were often acknowledged by masters. In this case, James Munroe was involved in a type of abroad marriage, where the slave of one master was married to a slave owned by a different master. Munroe and Evelina, despite having different owners, probably lived together.

25. James Munroe appears variously in the public record as simply "James" or with the last name of Munroe or Monroe. For the sake of continuity and to avoid any confusion with the other James Monroe, the white Albemarle resident and the fifth president of the United States, I have used "Munroe" throughout.

26. ACDB No. 45, 364 (Sept. 28, 1847).

27. Albemarle County Legislative Petitions 1845–47, Box 5, Folder 74, LoV. Many university professors were slave owners, including Minor and McGuffey. Their support of Munroe likely had little to do with closeted abolitionist sentiments. Addison Maupin owned a dozen slaves. George Watson Carr was a member of a wealthy planter family that was connected through marriage to Thomas Jefferson.

28. Ibid.

29. Ibid.

30. Ibid.

31. Ibid.

32. Ibid.

33. Albemarle County Legislative Petitions, 1849–63, Box 6, Folder 15, LoV.

34. Albemarle County Legislative Petitions, 1849–63, Box 6, Folder 16, LoV.

35. *Southern Planter* 12 (Apr. 1852), 106–7, quoted in N. Jones, "Charlottesville and Albemarle County," 165–68.

36. *Review,* July 6, 13, Aug. 3, 1860, qtd. in N. Jones, "Charlottesville and Albemarle County," 167–68.

37. *Jeffersonian Republican,* Aug. 2, 1860, qtd. in N. Jones, "Charlottesville and Albemarle County," 167.

38. Albemarle County Legislative Petitions, 1849–63, Box 6, Folder 16, LoV.

39. Ibid.

40. ACMB 1850–54, 37 (Mar. 3, 1851). Also charged by that same grand jury were Maria Hatter, David Hite, Randolph Jones, Hatley Moss, Joshua Craig, Nancy Kinney, Woodson Marks, Eliza Garner, and Kitty Kean. ACCCC, Box 39.

41. ACCCC, Box 39.

42. ACDB No. 51, 80 (July 7, 1852).

43. ACDB No. 58, 296 (Jan. 21, 1860).

44. U.S. Census for Virginia, 1790–1860.

45. William Swingler's name appears variously in the public record as Swingler, Swinler, and Swindler. For the sake of continuity, I have chosen to use Swingler throughout.

46. Rawlings, *Albemarle of Other Days,* 126–29.

47. Hess, "Four Decades of Social Change," 1; A.C. Fredericksville Parish Personal Property Tax Books, 1841, 1842, 1846, 1848, 1850; and U.S. Census for Virginia, 1850.

48. ACCCC, Box 45; U.S. Census for Virginia, 1850 and 1860.

49. ACCCC, Box 45.

50. Ibid.

51. Ibid.

52. ACMB 1856–59, 81 (Apr. 6, 1857); ACCCC, Box 45; U.S. Census for Virginia, 1860.

53. Stephen's last name appears variously in the public record as Byars, Byers, Bias, Biars, and Brice. For the sake of continuity, I have chosen to use Byars throughout. Here the confusion over Stephen Byars's name appears to stem from inconsistent spelling only, not from any community confusion about his identity. Most versions of the name are roughly the same phonetically.

54. For more on the practice of slave hiring, see Martin, *Divided Mastery;* Lockley, *Lines in the Sand,* 64–66; Berlin, *Many Thousands Gone,* 156–57; Genovese, *Roll, Jordan, Roll,* 390–92; and U. B. Phillips, *American Negro Slavery.*

55. Albemarle County Legislative Petitions 1817–36, Box 4, Folder 53 (Dec. 11, 1835).

56. Ibid.; ACCCC, Box 16 (Oct. 21, 1831), indictment of Henry Wolfe for threatening to assault the patrol captain William Wertenbaker.

57. ACDB No. 35, 323 (Nov. 6, 1837); ACDB No. 35, 335 (Nov. 6, 1837); and ACMB 1836–38, 277 (Nov. 7, 1837).

58. Albemarle County Legislative Petitions 1837–48, Box 5, Folder 13 (Feb. 14, 1839).

59. Ibid. (Feb. 8, 1839).

60. ACMB 1838–42, 62 (June 4, 1839).

61. Ibid., 85 (Aug. 1839); ACMB 1838–42, 102 (Sept. 2, 1839); ACMB 1838–42, 109 (Oct. 7, 1839); and Albemarle County Legislative Petitions, Box 5, Folder 13 (Dec. 14, 1839).

62. ACDB No. 38, 104 (June 15, 1840). The lot adjoined the property of Clement McKennie and George Blaetterman. McKennie resided in a brick house on Main Street between the town and the university. Until 1827, he had edited and owned Charlottesville's first newspaper, the *Central Gazette.* At the time of this deed McKennie also ran a bookstore located near the university. This was the bookstore that was adjacent to the plot Stephen Byars was purchasing. George Blaetterman was a professor of modern languages at the university and lived in a residence adjacent to the Byars plot. See Rawlings, *Early Charlottesville,* 97; and J. Moore, *Albemarle,* 133. Interestingly, Professor Blaetterman failed to maintain his own respectable reputation. He was known to have a violent temper and be prone to angry outbursts, including publicly whipping his wife. He was subsequently dismissed from the university for such indiscreet and dishonorable actions.

63. ACDB No. 38, 105 (June 15, 1840).

64. U.S. Census for Virginia, 1840; A.C. St. Anne's Parish Personal Property Tax Book, 1841; A.C. St. Anne's Parish Land Tax Book, 1841. According to the 1806 removal law, any black freed after May 1806 had to seek official permission to remain in Virginia. Many free people of color chose instead to purchase family members without then filing a deed of manumission, thus avoiding the requirement for newly freed blacks to seek permission to remain.

65. ACMB 1838–42, 452 (May 2, 1842); ACCCC, Box 30 (Oct. 17, 1843); *Acts of Assembly,* 1838, 76. The law applied to free black children as well as adults. If they returned, children were to be separated from their parents and apprenticed until they turned twenty-one, then forcibly removed from the state. Free black adults were to be removed immediately.

66. ACMB 1838–42, 62 (June 4, 1839); ACCCC, Box 30. Albemarle County handled a total of six criminal presentments against free people of color in 1843 for violating the residency law (Reuben Lee, Nelson Roberts, Stephen Byars, Ginney Byars, Jerry Wood, Amy Wood).

67. ACDB No, 41. 113 (Dec. 22, 1843), 283 (Dec. 22, 1843).

68. ACCCC, Box 31.

69. Albemarle County Chancery Order Book No. 2, 295 (Jan. 1, 1846). After he lost that 1846 decision, Stephen Byars continued to be an active member of the community. See also ACWB No. 20, 235–56 (James Fry and Jesse Maury executor accounts for Jesse Lewis estate, which include income from and payments to Stephen Byars).

70. ACCCC, Box 53 (Sept. 29, 1866).

71. ACCCC, Box 53: *Commonwealth v. Stephen Byers* (Byars), and four separate cases titled *Commonwealth v. William Cole.*

72. The list here also includes the petitions and/or court cases for a number of other free blacks who are not discussed in detail in this chapter.

73. A.C. Fredericksville Parish Personal Property Tax Books, 1800–1820.

74. ACWB No. 7, 226 (June 3, 1822). Benjamin Goings's other children were Mary Brock, Agnes Hill, James, Susan, Jesse, Nelly, and Franky.

75. Ibid., 226–28.

76. Albemarle County Land Tax Lists for St. Anne's Parish, 1823–30; A.C. St. Anne's Parish Personal Property Tax Books, 1822–30.

77. E. Jordan, "'Just and True Account,'" 122, 128.

78. U.S. Census for Virginia, 1840.

79. A.C. St. Anne's Parish Land Tax Book, 1842; ACMB 1842–44, 143 (Mar. 7, 1843); ACWB No. 18, 172 (Jan. 24, 1846).

80. ACWB No. 18, 172.

81. Ibid. For the definition of *nuncupative will,* see Garner, *Black's Law Dictionary,* 666.

82. ACWB No. 18, 172.

83. ACMB 1845–47, 191 (Feb. 2, 1846); ibid., 203 (Apr. 5, 1846); ACWB No. 18, 172 (Aug. 2, 1847); ACMB 1845–47, 301 (Sept. 7, 1846); Ibid., 462 (Aug. 3, 1847).

4. "I'LL SHOW YOU WHAT A FREE NEGRO IS"

1. For more on free black property ownership, see Ely, *Israel on the Appomattox,* 95–100, chap. 8; Schweninger, *Black Property Owners;* Berlin, *Slaves without Masters,* 62–64, 244–49; Stevenson, *Life in Black and White,* 297–302; Franklin, *Free Negro in North Carolina,* 150–62; and Jackson, *Free Negro Labor.*

2. *Commonwealth v. John Goings,* ACCCC, Box 32 (Nov. 20, 1845).

3. ACCCC, Box 32 (Nov. 20, 1845); *Acts of the General Assembly,* Supplement, chap. 176, 234 (Feb. 21, 1823), with punishment by whipping and possibly banishment from the United States, chap. 183, 242 (Feb. 12, 1828), with mandatory life imprisonment, and chap. 187, 247 (Mar. 15, 1832), where after the Nat Turner Rebellion, punishment was increased to "death without benefit of clergy."

4. Hening, *Statutes at Large,* 12: 182.

5. ACCCC, Box 32 (Nov. 20, 1845), testimony of William Dowell.

6. Surprisingly little research and writing have been done concerning corn shuckings as sites of interracial contact. For the most extended discussion of slaves and corn shucking, see Genovese, *Roll, Jordan, Roll,* 315–19. For commentaries on their experiences as Virginia slaves participating in corn shuckings, see also Perdue, Barden, and Phillips, *Weevils in the Wheat,* 235, 278; and "Reminiscences of My Life and Work Among the Freedmen of Charlottesville, Virginia, from Mar. 1st 1866 to July 1st 1875," Philena Carkin Papers, 1866–75, University of Virginia Library, 105–6.

7. ACCCC, Box 32 (Nov. 20, 1845), testimony of Noah Tate and Colin, slave, the property of Elizabeth Salmon.

8. ACCCC, Box 32 (Nov. 20, 1845), testimony of Noah Tate.

9. ACCCC, Box 32 (Nov. 20, 1845), testimony of Paschal Gentry.

10. ACCCC, Box 32 (Nov. 20, 1854), testimony of Willis Dunn; Perdue, Barden, and Phillips, *Weevils in the Wheat*, 278–79; and Genovese, *Roll, Jordan, Roll*, 315, quoting former slave Sam Colquitt of Alabama.

11. ACCCC, Box 32 (Nov. 20, 1845), testimony of William Dowell.

12. For slave assaults of whites tried as cases of rebellion and/or involving death sentences, see *Commonwealth v. Isaac*, ACCCC, Box 14 (Oct. 21, 1825). Isaac, a ten-year-old slave boy owned by William Catterton, attacked the white girl Sally Catterton. He was convicted and sentenced to hang for the offense. The court papers do not indicate whether Isaac was actually hanged, but commutation of the sentence was common in cases involving young defendants (see Schwarz, *Twice Condemned*). See also *Commonwealth v. John*, Commonwealth Causes, Box 15 (1826). The slave John was charged with slave revolt, but the case was really an attempted poisoning of his master. See also *Commonwealth v. Lewis, Amanda, Edmund*, Commonwealth Causes, Box 42 (Dec. 3, 1855). Lewis and Amanda were slaves owned by Tandy Harris. Edmund was owned by Nancy Howard. They were charged with "feloniously plot[ting], conspir[ing], combin[ing], confederat[ing] and agree[ing] together to rebel and make insurrection." They had allegedly planned to murder Tandy Morris and run away and had attempted to get some other slaves to join them in fleeing. They were sentenced to receive thirty-nine lashes each at the public whipping post.

13. ACCCC, Box 32 (Nov. 20, 1845), testimony of slave Colin. The first name of the free black "Taylor" is illegible in the document, but this was most likely Fairfax Taylor, a vocal free man of color who had purchased his own freedom and became a local black political activist after the Civil War. See Vance, "Negro in the Reconstruction of Albemarle County," 19–22; Jackson, *Negro Office-Holders in Virginia*, 41; and J. Moore, *Albemarle*, 227–28. Fairfax Taylor as a slave lived in Clarke County. After purchasing his own freedom, Fairfax married Ellen Sammons. Their child, born in Clarke County but raised in Albemarle, was James T. S. Taylor, who fought in the Union army during the Civil War and returned after the war with over a thousand dollars. According to Jackson, Fairfax Taylor hired a white person to teach his son James "the fundamentals." Both worked as shoemakers in Albemarle. After the war, Fairfax was known locally as a black radical, pushing for the right to serve on juries and to attend the University of Virginia, who enjoyed majority support among the county's freedpeople.

14. ACCCC, Box 32 (May 20, 1846), Circuit Superior Court of Law and Chancery for Albemarle County.

15. For more on terrorist white vigilantism as a means of social control, see Berlin, *Slaves without Masters*, 336–39. Berlin argues that tight racial control did not require total enforcement, just occasional brutal repression. He feels that this repression was visited most frequently upon those who physically or verbally assaulted whites or who had any kind of regular contact with white women. Any visible and direct threat to white control, he adds, was met with great violence. Thomas Goings's case would seem a perfect fit, but no such violence occurred in Albemarle surrounding Goings's trial and acquittal. See also ACCCC, Box 32 (Nov. 20, 1845), testimony of Dr. Mallory.

16. ACCCC, Box 32 (Nov. 20, 1845), testimony of Dr. Mallory.

17. *Commonwealth v. William Goings,* ACCCC, Box 37 (July 5, 1850), testimony of Brightberry B. Gardner. See also ACMB 1848–50, 386, for Aug. 6, 1850, arraignment of Goings. Goings was charged and remanded to jail. See also ACMB 1851–54, 44 (Mar. 4, 1851), for Sheriff Thomas Brown's report to the court confirming the arrest and confinement of William Goings. No records remain verifying exactly what transpired between Aug. 1850 and Mar. 1851, but the existing evidence suggests that after being charged, William Goings posted bail and remained free on bond until Mar. 1851.

18. Testimony of Brightberry B. Gardner. The "coloured fellow named Spinner" was a local free black, Garland Spinner. The "Mr. Gentry" who helped with the search was either George Gentry or John Gentry Jr., both of whom, interestingly, appeared as witnesses for the free black William Goings.

19. Ibid.

20. Ibid.

21. Shepherd, *Statutes at Large,* 3: 274; and *Acts of the General Assembly,* Supplement, chap. 187, 246 (Mar. 15, 1832).

22. Shepherd, *Statutes at Large,* 3: 274; and *Acts of the General Assembly,* Supplement, chap. 187, 246 (Mar. 15, 1832).

23. ACCCC, Box 37 (July 5, 1850), testimony of John Goings. The court records display some confusion about Henderson Goings, referring to him as Henry Goings. But it was Henderson Goings who was married to Agnes Goings and owned a farm in the vicinity. Likewise, a Henry Goings did live in the area but was a teenager at the time, probably the brother of John Goings. The Mr. Davis referred to in the testimony was John Davis, a white neighbor.

24. Ibid.

25. Ibid.

26. Ibid.

27. Ibid.

28. ACCCC, Box 37 (July 5, 1850), testimony of slave Bob.

29. Ibid.

30. ACCCC, Box 37 (July 5, 1850), testimony of Mr. White.

31. Ibid., testimony of Willis Dunn. White's testimony suggests that Goings had more than one gun in his possession. White found no gun but did find buckshot, which was for a shotgun. But the murder weapon that several witnesses confirmed was the gun they saw Goings with was a pistol. Further, the bullets pulled from the body came from a pistol.

32. *William Goins v. Sherod Goins,* Albemarle County Chancery Causes (1850–001); ACMB 1848–50, 393.

33. ACCCC, Box 37 (July 5, 1850), testimony of John Goings; E. Jordan, "'Just and True Account,'" 127; N. Jones, "Charlottesville and Albemarle County," 237. Henderson Goings had an estate that in value was comparable to that which a free white farmer might own. Compare Goings with William C. Reynolds, Richard Pleasants, and Daniel Reg (N. Jones, "Charlottesville and Albemarle County," 227–36). One hundred dollars, for the years between 1830 and 1850, had the equivalent purchasing power in today's dollars of between $2,200 and $2,800.

34. ACDB No. 39, 479 (Aug. 5, 1842); testimony of Brightberry B. Gardner.

35. ACWB No. 20, 64 (Dec. 2, 1850), inventory and appraisal of Woodson K. Hall estate. See also Stony Point Store Ledger, 1856–59, for an example of a rural store extending lines of credit to white and black customers alike. This Albemarle County ledger contains lines of credit for both white and black customers but makes no mention of race. Customers are listed by name only.

36. ACWB No. 20, 64; A.C. Fredericksville Parish Personal Property Tax Books, 1814–36. The tax lists include two William Goingses: William the son of Sherod Goings and William the son of Sherod Goings's brother Jesse. This second "William Goings" in later tax lists is recorded as "Wilson" Goings. The first William Goings, the son of Sherod Sr., was the one charged with murdering Woodson K. Hall.

37. ACCOB 1828, 69 (Mar. 4, 1828); E. Jordan, "'Just and True Account,'" 127. Listed as living with William Goings are James Goings (mulatto, male, age twelve), Miley Goings (mulatto, male, age nine), Henry Goings (mulatto, male, age seven), Ira Goings (mulatto, male, age five), and Hardena Goings (mulatto, female, age nine months). The testimony of one witness in the murder trial, the white resident George Hall, referred to William's "wife" telling him he "was welcome to search the house," but she is never named and does not appear on census reports or tax lists. Likewise, no marriage certificate was ever recorded.

38. Rawlings, *Early Charlottesville,* 2.

39. Woods, *Albemarle County,* 39–43.

40. Woods, *Albemarle County,* 94; J. Moore, *Albemarle,* 141; Rawlings, *Early Charlottesville,* 71, 88; ACCCC, Boxes 27–55; and ACCCC, Box 36 (Oct. 3, 1847).

41. Testimony of Brightberry B. Gardner. The court papers do not clarify exactly which gun was the murder weapon, but do make it clear that Goings possessed more than one gun.

42. The commonwealth's witness list included Walker Frazier; Robert Johnson; Charles Dowell; Absolum Shiflett; Brightberry Gardner; Willis Dunn; Mr. White; George Hall; Robert Johnson; John Davis; Michael Catterton; the slave Bob; and the free men of color Zachariah Brock, John Roberts, Henderson Goings, John Goings, and Nelson Brock. Witnesses for William Goings included George Gentry, William Catterton, Tom Collins, Milton Wilhoit, Ezekiel Wilhoit, Warner Cox, Parrot Elliott, Joyce Shiflett, Henry Shiflett, John Gentry Jr., James Dunn, Nicholas H. Dunn, Joel Mason, Charles Dowell, Tandy Harris, and Fielding Rains Jr. (ACCCC, Box 37). Only George Gentry and John Gentry appear to have been men of more elite status. See Woods, *Albemarle County,* 205, 330, 371, 399.

43. No documents concerning William Goings's release from jail on bond after the initial arraignment in July 1850 exist. However, a sheriff's report dated Mar. 4, 1851, states that William Goings had been jailed and charged with murder. This report was filed at the beginning of the trial (ACMB 1851–54, 44).

44. ACCCC, Box 37, Box 38.

45. ACCCC, Box 29 (Jan. 10, 1842); Woods, *Albemarle County,* 336–37.

46. ACCCC, Box 29 (Jan. 10, 1842). For other examples of the court's handling of assault cases, see *Commonwealth v. Anderson Langford, Charles Allford, and Charles*

Barnett, ACCCC, Box 18.Two whites and a free black (Barnett) were charged with assaulting the white resident John Sprouse Jr. in 1830. Langford and Allford were arrested and charged; Barnett was not found at the time. All three were acquitted without serving any time in Mar. 1831. See also *Commonwealth v. James Hughes,* ACCCC, Box 36. James Hughes, a white laborer, was charged with assaulting the free black John Shelton in Aug. 1848. James Hughes was forced to file a two-hundred-dollar peace recognizance with an extra one hundred dollars in security pledged by Rice Bailey and John Craven. See also *Commonwealth v. John Shelton,* ACCCC, Box 41. The free black Shelton, charged with assaulting the white man Peter Sneed in May 1854, was ordered to file a one-hundred-dollar peace recognizance with another one-hundred-dollar surety provided by local whites Thomas Keller, John Wheat, and W. C. Walstrum.

47. *Commonwealth v. William Farrar et al.,* ACCCC, Box 44.

48. ACCCC, Box 44.

49. ACCOB 1806, 424 (Oct. 7, 1806); ACCOB 1829, 278, (Oct. 5, 1829). For land ownership, see Albemarle County Land Tax Lists for St. Anne's Parish, 1825–46.

50. A.C. St. Anne's Parish Land Tax Book, 1825.

51. E. Jordan, "'Just and True Account,'" 126; A.C. St. Anne's Parish Personal Property Tax Book, 1833; and A.C. Marriage Register 1806–68, 61 (July 22, 1835). Matilda Middlebrook may have been a cousin. A number of Middlebrooks in the county were also known as "Goings": A.C. St. Anne's Parish Personal Property Tax Books, 1830–40; A.C. St. Anne's Parish Land Tax Books, 1830–40; U.S. Census for Virginia, 1840; ACWB No. 18, 94–96 (June 7, 1847), settlement of Michael Catterton executor accounts for William Catterton Sr. estate.

52. ACWB No. 17, 459 (May 3, 1847); and ACWB No. 18, 276 (Jan. 3, 1848).

53. ACWB No. 18, 276 (Jan. 3, 1848).

54. I borrow the concept behind the phrase "propertied masters of lesser worlds" from Stephanie McCurry's *Masters of Small Worlds.*

5. BAWDY HOUSES AND WOMEN OF ILL FAME

1. ACCCC, Box 12, July 9, 1821.

2. U.S. Census for Virginia, 1820, 1830; ACWB No. 13, 44 (Feb. 5, 1838), will of Daniel Farley. Daniel Farley was the free black father of Betsy Ann Farley. His will states that his daughter was then living with Joshua Grady, a white blacksmith.

3. Albemarle County Legislative Petitions, Box 3, Folder 97 (Dec. 8, 1815). Andrew McKee, who in 1821 would assist several free people of color, was among the signers of the petition. See also ibid., Box 4, Folder 6 (Dec. 4, 1818).

4. ACCCC, Box 13 (Oct. 13, 1823).

5. Ibid. Prostitution and interracial activity have received relatively little coverage by historians. See Bynum, *Unruly Women,* for the most detailed discussion of prostitution. Bynum argues that law enforcement in the early nineteenth century sought merely to control prostitution. Authorities were not concerned with prostitu-

tion unless it crossed the color line. See also Rothman, *Notorious in the Neighborhood.* Rothman argues that populous urban areas provided a degree of anonymity essential to prostitution, suggesting that houses of prostitution were far less likely to operate in rural areas and far more likely to face great scrutiny (104). See also Lockley, *Lines in the Sand.* Lockley argues that prostitution and interracial houses of entertainment arose wherever African Americans and poor whites congregated but finds strict enforcement and harsh punishment of offenders the rule. All of these authors suggest that white elites were the most concerned with interracial activity. The 1821 presentment (Commonwealth Causes, Box 12) generally conforms to that assessment. In that document, the Albemarle residents David Fowler, George M. Kinsolving, William Huntington, Solomon Belew, and Valentine M. Southall all appear as witnesses for the commonwealth. Fowler was in the "cabinet and furniture business"; George W. Kinsolving until 1822 owned the Central Hotel in Charlottesville; William Huntington was a merchant who owned a general store on Random Row and was active in the Episcopal church; Solomon Belew (aka Ballou) owned considerable real estate in Albemarle and in the 1820s ran a carriage business between Charlottesville and Richmond whose terminus was the Central Hotel; and Valentine M. Southall was a lawyer and state legislator from the county. See Rawlings, *Early Charlottesville;* Woods, *Albemarle County;* and Rawlings, *Albemarle of Other Days.*

6. U.S. Census, 1820; ACCOB 1822–23, 24, 42; and Albemarle Old Papers Orphans' Indentures (Aug. 20, 1822, Nov. 5, 1822, Dec. 24, 1822). Fanny Barnett's exact age is difficult to determine. In 1806, she was listed as twenty-one (ACCOB 1806, 217); in 1833 she was listed as forty-seven years old (E. Jordan, "'Just and True Account,'" 121); in 1841 she was listed as forty-five years old (ACMB 1838–42, 260). Most likely, the age recorded in 1841 is wrong. All others seem to indicate that she was born circa 1785.

7. For the binding out of Fanny Barnett the elder's children, see ACCOB 1822–23, 24, 42; and Albemarle Old Papers Orphans' Indentures, 1822. See also U.S. Census for Virginia, 1830, where Fanny Barnett is listed as the free colored head of a household containing three free males under age ten, one free female under ten, one free female age ten to twenty-three, and two free females age thirty-six to fifty-four; Auditor of Public Accounts, Free Blacks/Records/1833-37, LoV (for 1833 colonization census), which is reprinted in E. Jordan, "'Just and True Account,'" 114–39.

8. U.S. Census for Virginia, 1840; ACCCC, Box 28 (Oct. 25, 1841). Betsy Randolph was married to Israel Jefferson, one of Thomas Jefferson's slaves. With the help of Betsy Randolph, he purchased himself from Thomas Walker Gilmer in 1838 for five hundred dollars. That same year, he and Betsy married. Israel was now technically owned by Randolph. In the 1841 affair with the Barnetts, the court summoned both Randolph women and Israel, "a servant of Betsy Randolph." For more on Israel Jefferson and Betsy Randolph, see Stanton, *Free Some Day,* 95–96.

9. ACMB 1838–42, 386 (Nov. 2, 1841); Rawlings, *Early Charlottesville,* 98; and Albemarle County Marriage Register 1806–68, Folders 68 and 75.

10. ACCCC, Box 32 (July 5, 1845). The two cases are located in separate folders, both with the same date. Both are signed by Hawkins but only "marked" by Fanny and Septimia Barnett.

11. A.C. Fredericksville Parish Personal Property Tax Books, 1845–47; ACDB No. 42, 188.

12. ACDB No. 42, 188.

13. ACCOB 1806, 217; E. Jordan, "'Just and True Account,'" 121; ACMB 1834–36, 197; ACMB 1838–42, 260; ACMB 1848–50, 413; ACMB 1850–54, 316; and ACMB 1856–59, 184.

14. Rawlings, *Early Charlottesville,* 98; ACCCC, Box 25.

15. ACMB 1842–4, 224 (Aug. 8, 1843).

16. ACMB 1838–42, 373 (Nov. 1, 1841); ACMB 1842–44, 216 (Aug. 8, 1843); A.C. Marriage Register 1806–68, 77 (Apr. 20, 1840); and ACMB 1842–44, 20 (June 7, 1842). One free black in the indictment, a Reuben Lee, "admitted the truth of the charge" that he was residing in the commonwealth in violation of the 1806 removal law, but nonetheless was allowed at the time to remain; see ACDB No. 49, 229 (Jan. 6, 1845).

17. ACCCC, Box 34, Box 35.

18. Ibid.

19. ACCCC, Box 35 (May 5, 1847).

20. Ibid.; and ACMB 1845–47, 412.

21. ACMB 1845–47, 412; and ACMB 1848–50, 413 (Nov. 4, 1850), when most of the above women appeared at the court together to register for their freedom certificates.

22. U.S. Census for Virginia, 1850.

23. U.S. Census for Virginia, 1860. Septimia Barnett occupied dwelling house no. 57.

24. Ibid., which indicates that Samuel Leitch Jr. was sixty and owned six thousand dollars in real property and thirty-five hundred dollars in personal property.

25. According to Loren Schweninger, approximately half of all free women of color worked as laundresses or seamstresses, and a few "controlled a substantial proportion of the total black wealth." See Schweninger, *Black Property Owners,* 85–86. See also M. Ely, *Israel on the Appomattox,* 138–43. Those accounts contradict Brenda Stevenson, who argues that laundresses toiled desperately for "a few cents a day." See Stevenson, *Life in Black and White,* 294.

26. ACWB No. 25, 461. The will was written on Nov. 19, 1856, and first brought to the courthouse on June 8, 1859, shortly after Dawson's death. On July 4, 1859, James P. Robinson, Churchill Richardson, and the attorney Thomas Parr dropped their opposition to the will, and it was entered into the record for probate. For evidence of Roderick's race, see U.S. Census for Virginia, 1860, where he is described as a three-year-old mulatto boy.

27. Berlin, *Many Thousands Gone,* 269–70.

28. U.S. Census for Virginia, 1850, 1860; *Commonwealth v. Marinda French,* ACCCC, Box 47.

29. *Commonwealth v. Marinda French,* ACCCC, Box 47. Bibb was a merchant in town and the first cashier of the Charlottesville Savings Bank. He owned a brick

house located on Ridge Street, a short distance from the Random Row area, where Marinda French resided. Bibb's business was located on Main Street, between the town and the university. Woods, *Albemarle County,* 143. See also Rawlings, *Early Charlottesville,* 20, 74, 106–7.

30. ACCCC, Box 47; and ACMB 1856–59, 400. John T. Barksdale was a member of a prominent Albemarle family. He was the son of John H. Barksdale. Much of the family resided a few miles north of town. French's connection with this family suggests that the connections forged on a few streets in the village of Charlottesville actually linked people to a much wider geographic area. John T. Barksdale, in addition to continuing to farm the family plantation north of town, also owned the Eagle Tavern in Charlottesville, adjacent to the court square. Barksdale purchased the tavern in 1842. Woods, *Albemarle County,* 142; and Rawlings, *Early Charlottesville,* 27.

31. U.S. Census for Virginia, 1850; ACMB 1856–59, 187 (Oct. 6, 1857); and ACMB 1848–50, 413 (Nov. 4, 1850).

32. ACMB 1848–50, 413 (Nov. 4, 1850). For other registrants on that day, see also p. 414.

33. Ibid., 413 (Nov. 4, 1850); A.C. Fredericksville Parish Personal Property Tax Book, 1848; ACMB 1851–54, 10 (Dec. 3, 1850). There is no way to tell for certain, but it seems possible that Hite and French were involved in 1850 and had been for some time. All of French's younger children were significantly darker than her oldest daughter and darker than Marinda herself. Hite was relatively close in age to French, and French clearly interacted regularly with the many slaves going at large in the area. Hite, prior to his manumission in 1839, may have been one such slave.

34. Shepherd, *Statutes at Large,* 3: 252. The 1806 law provided: "If any slave hereafter emancipated shall remain within this Commonwealth for more than twelve months after his freedom, he shall forfeit such right, and may be sold by the overseers for the benefit of the poor." ACMB 1848–50, 413 (Nov. 4, 1850); and ACMB 1851–54, 10 (Dec. 3, 1850).

35. There is no evidence in Albemarle of an 1839 manumission—no deeds and no wills—that could be for David Hite. He may well have been freed in another county and later moved to Albemarle.

36. ACMB 1851–54, 37 (Mar. 3, 1851); ACCCC, Box 39, which includes a June 10, 1851, summons and a Jan. 28, 1852, summons. One of the sheriffs, either George Slaughter or Charles Cocke, has written a note on the back of the Jan. summons stating that Hite had left the county and moved to Washington, D.C. Also charged on those same days were the free blacks Joshua Craig, Rose Taylor, Eliza Garner, Maria Hatter, Randolph Jones, Kitty Kean, Nancy Kinney, Woodson Marks, James Munroe, and Hatly Moss.

37. U.S. Census for Virginia, 1850, 1860.

38. ACDB No. 42, 188 (Oct. 18, 1845); and ACDB No. 69, 43 (Aug. 7, 1874).

39. ACWB No. 19, 132 (June 4, 1849). Thomas Fry at his death owned no slaves and possessed an estate worth $685.87. That total included a list of bonds due to him, including the nine dollars for firewood from Fanny Barnett.

40. Her actions demonstrated some concern, however, as she and her family renewed their registers in Nov. 1850. None of the Barnetts had registered in at least a decade at that point, despite the legal requirement to renew the certificate every three years. David Hite, freed in 1839 but never having registered, came in that same day and registered, but would later be formally charged. It appears that ten free people of color who had been born before 1806 or born to free parents in Virginia were initially charged with violating the removal law. See ACMB 1850–54, 5 (Dec. 2, 1850); and ibid., 7 (Dec. 4, 1850).

41. ACDB No. 49, 230 (Jan. 1, 1851). The land was originally conveyed by deed from Hawkins and his wife to Louisa Goings on Jan. 6, 1845.

42. Ohio was a common choice for Albemarle residents, white and black, who sought to move to a free state. A number of local manumissions included details for sending the freed slaves away from Virginia. See ACWB No. 4, 255, will of John White; ACDB No. 58, 98, 192, Martha L. Crank's deeds of manumission for her slaves; ACWB No. 22, 247, Mildred Lewis freeing slaves and providing for transport to Liberia or Ohio. For whites moving to Ohio, see ACWB No. 8, 254; ACWB No. 10, 310; ACWB No. 13, 321–324; ACWB No. 21, 386; and ACWB No. 22, 202. For free blacks who removed to Ohio, see ACDB No. 35, 219; ACDB No. 37, 449; ACDB No. 41, 515; ACDB No. 49, 229; ACWB No. 18, 172; ACDB No. 45, 364; ACDB No. 47, 351; ACDB No. 49, 230; ACDB No. 50, 270; ACDB No. 51, 80, 496; ACDB No. 53, 260; ACWB No. 25, 156; and ACDB No. 58, 296.

43. ACCCC, Box 41 (Apr. 1, 1851, May 15, 1854).

44. ACDB No. 51, 193 (Nov. 29, 1852).

45. ACDB No. 53, 431. Moore conveyed the land in trust to John Collier on Jan. 7, 1854, as part of an arrangement intended to satisfy the creditors John S. Saunders and Thomas R. Bailey. Collier advertised the public auction in early Nov. and held the sale at the end of that month. The lot bordered Peter Harman's stable and the land of Rice G. Bailey, Fontaine Brockman, and Andrew Sample.

46. Ibid., 432.

47. ACCCC, Box 42 (May 9, 1855).

48. ACCCC, Box 33; E. Jordan, "'Just and True Account,'" 130; and ACMB 1854–47, 22.

49. U.S. Census for Virginia, 1840.

50. ACMB 1845–47, 22 (Mar. 3, 1845). The three white men were Peter Heiskell, Elijah Dunkum, and Walter Perry. Heiskell was a physician who lived in the immediate vicinity of the Kinneys. The Heiskells at the time were a young family of modest means. They lived next door to Clement P. McKennie, a wealthy white merchant, and McKenzie Fortune, a dark-skinned free black man. Dunkum was a dry-goods purveyor who lived in a large house on Ridge Street. Perry remains a little harder to track. There was a W. Perry, who owned a butcher shop on Main Street (Rawlings, *Early Charlottesville,* 90), and a W. D. Perry, who advertised, "Let the World Say What They Can, for selling fine Liquors—Perry's the Man!" (J. Moore, *Albemarle,* 172).

51. Ibid., 40 (Apr. 7, 1845).

52. Ibid., 63 (June 2, 1845). The extant records do not state who testified.

53. U.S. Census for Virginia, 1850.

54. ACCCC, Box 44 (July 6, 1857). Chiles Brand had complained to the court on July 3 about the June 30 assault. On July 6, Ailstock was tried and sentenced.

55. ACCCC, Box 44; and ACMB 1856–59, 127 (July 6, 1857).

56. ACCCC, Box 44.

57. Old Papers, Orphans' Indentures, Oct. 12, 1840; ACMB 1848–50, 413 (Nov. 4, 1850).

58. Shepherd, *Supplement to the Revised Code,* 246.

59. ACMB 1859–62, 453 (June 3, 1862). Septimia Barnett as recently as Oct. 1857 had renewed her freedom certificate, which described her as a free mulatto, age twenty-nine, of light complexion (ACMB 1856–59, 185 [Oct. 6, 1857]).

60. ACDB No. 60, 58 (Dec. 16, 1862), 127 (Jan. 15, 1863).

61. ACDB No. 61, 107 (Dec. 25, 1863). Betsy Barnett at the time of the sale lived just a few doors down from Septimia. The census lists her as age forty-one, a free colored clothes washer with a thirty-dollar personal estate. See also ACMB 1863–66, 178 (Mar. 8, 1864), where Betsy Barnett successfully applies to the county court and is recognized as a "free person of mixed blood, daughter of free woman of color Fanny Barnett, and Not a Negro." In 1864, all three daughters of Fanny Barnett had achieved a legally recognized social whiteness. In the eyes of the community and in the eyes of local authorities, they were no longer free blacks.

62. ACDB No. 64, 521. According to this complicated deed of sale, the Pelter Property originally contained 337 acres of land. At the time of Barnett's purchase, however, 37 acres had already been sold out of the original plot. Barnett thus purchased a 300-acre plot of land.

63. Ibid., 521; Woods, *Albemarle County,* 278.

64. ACDB No. 64, 521.

65. ACDB No. 67, 104 (Apr. 13, 1872).

66. ACDB No. 69, 43 (Aug. 7, 1874); U.S. Census for Virginia, 1860.

67. For freedom registration, see ACCOB 1806, 217; ACMB 1834–36, 197; ACMB 1838–42, 260; ACMB 1845–47, 514; ACMB 1848–50, 413; ACMB 1850–54, 316; and ACMB 1856–59, 184–85. For seeking and achieving legal recognition of their non-black status, see ACMB 1859–62, 453; and ACMB 1863–66, 178.

6. AN EASY MORALITY

1. Recollections of Richard Thomas Walker Duke, Jr., 4 vols.

2. E. Jordan, "'Just and True Account,'" 118.

3. Recollections of Richard Thomas Walker Duke, Jr., 1: 21.

4. Perdue, Barden, and Phillips, *Weevils in the Wheat,* 9, 25, 67, 84, 143. The memoirs of ex-slaves are filled with references to interracial sex, ranging from white masters raping their slaves to more consensual relationships. The relationships referred to in these documents were most often between white men and black women.

See also pp. 81, 86, 90, 108, 146, 157, 174 (white woman), 201–2, 224, 245, 255, 293, 300, 331–32. See also Ely, *Israel on the Appomattox,* 305–7; Hodes, *White Women, Black Men,* 1–122; Stevenson, *Life in Black and White,* 137–38, 180–81, 236–38, 304–5; Berlin, *Slaves without Masters,* 6–7, 265–68; and Johnston, *Race Relations in Virginia,* 217–36.

5. Perdue, Barden, and Phillips, *Weevils in the Wheat,* 91, 117, 250.

6. Recollections of Richard Thomas Walker Duke, Jr., 3: 220–24.

7. Stanton, *Free Some Day,* 132; Stanton, "Monticello to Main Street," 94–126; Rawlings, *Early Charlottesville,* 84. For the deed of sale, see ACDB No. 9, 36–37.

8. Stanton, "Monticello to Main Street," 97–100; Recollections of Richard Thomas Walker Duke, Jr., 3: 223; Rawlings, *Early Charlottesville,* 63.

9. Stanton, "Monticello to Main Street," 97–100; Recollections of Richard Thomas Walker Duke, Jr., 3: 223–24. No deed of manumission remains for Mary Hemings. Whether this is the result of poor recordkeeping by the county clerk at the time or stems from the fact that Bell never entered one, the community saw her as a free woman. Her free status was clearly connected both to her own reputation and to that of her common-law husband. Likewise, no deed of manumission exists for her son, Robert Washington Bell, but he, too, was seen as free. Almost four decades after marrying, her daughter, Sarah Jefferson Bell, was freed by her son in 1838 (ACMB 1836–38, 467). However, since at least the turn of the century, the community had considered her free.

10. ACWB No. 4, 59–60 (May 9, 1797). In the will, Bell continued linking himself through the children to his common-law wife: "in order to enable Mary Wells [Hemings] the mother of said Robert and Sally to support and maintain the said Children Robert & Sally until they arive at the age of maturity She the said Mary is to have free and full possession of all my houses and Lotts in the Towns of Charlottesville and Milton and all my household and kitchen furniture during her natural life."

11. Ibid. The will was drawn up on May 9, 1797, but Bell did not die until sometime in 1800. The county clerk recorded the will in Dec. of that year.

12. Recollections of Richard Thomas Walker Duke, Jr., 3: 223–24, 4: 1; Albemarle County Personal Property Tax Books, 1797–1813; A.C. Land Tax Books, 1797–1813; U.S. Census for Virginia, 1810.

13. Vogt and Kethley, *Albemarle County Marriages,* 1: 278 (Thomas Bell's white nephew William Love served as the bondsman at the wedding); Recollections of Richard Thomas Walker Duke, Jr., 3: 220–24; Rawlings, *Early Charlottesville,* 84; and O. Langhorne, *Southern Sketches,* 82.

14. O. Langhorne, *Southern Sketches,* 82–83.

15. ACCOB 1813–15, 263 (Nov. 3, 1813). For Love's deed of trust, see ACDB No. 15, 13–14 (Sept. 4, 1804), where Jesse Scott purchased what had originally been William Love's interest in the estate from the creditor Cornelius Schenck for $202.

16. ACCOB 1813–15, 263; Recollections of Richard Thomas Walker Duke, Jr., 3: 224. Robert Washington Bell after 1813 disappears from the documentary record in Albemarle.

17. ACDB No. 15, 13–14 (Sept. 4, 1804); A.C. Fredericksville Parish Personal Property Tax Books, 1805–10.

18. A.C. Fredericksville Parish Personal Property Tax Books, 1804–11; ACLOB 1809–21, 47 (May 7, 1810), 58–59 (May 9, 1810), 84 (May 8, 1811).

19. A.C. Fredericksville Parish Personal Property Tax Books, 1812, 1815.

20. ACDB No. 18, 479–81 (July 13, 1813).

21. ACDB No. 18, 479–81; ACDB No. 22, 356 (Apr. 13, 1821); and ACDB No. 22, 404 (Aug. 13, 1821).

22. U.S. Census for Virginia, 1820; A.C. Fredericksville Parish Personal Property Tax Books, 1820–26; A.C. St. Anne's Parish Land Tax Books, 1820–26; ACCOB 1822–23, 163 (Nov. 9, 1822); ACWB No. 8, 195 (Mar. 7, 1826); ACDB No. 29, 313–14 (June 7, 1826); ACWB No. 9, 328–40 (Jan. 5, 1829).

23. Gordon-Reed, *Hemingses of Monticello,* 115. Thomas Jefferson only legally freed Robert and James Hemings during his lifetime.

24. The particulars of how the Fossett family and the extended Hemings family became free have been extensively covered by other historians. I am more concerned here with Jesse Scott's involvement, because he neatly links the white, free black, and slave communities in the county. For more on the Hemings-Fossett story, see Gordon-Reed, *Hemingses of Monticello;* Stanton, *Free Some Day;* Stanton, "Monticello to Main Street"; Lewis and Onuf, *Sally Hemings and Thomas Jefferson;* Gordon-Reed, *Thomas Jefferson and Sally Hemings;* and Onuf, *Jeffersonian Legacies.*

25. U.S. Census for Virginia, 1830, 1840; E. Jordan, "'Just and True Account,'" 114–39.

26. U.S. Census for Virginia, 1830; ACWB No. 10, 75–77 (July 5, 1830); U.S. Census for Virginia, 1840; Shepherd, *Supplement to the Revised Code,* 246–48. For Jesse Scott's land ownership, see A.C. Land Tax Books, 1825–32.

27. ACDB No. 29, 544 (Mar. 20, 1832); ACDB No. 31, 442 (June 27, 1834); ibid., 444–45 (June 27, 1834); and Woods, *Albemarle County,* 136.

28. ACDB No. 32, 198–200 (June 27, 1834).

29. A.C. Marriage Register 1806–58, 59 (Jan. 1, 1835); Delaney and Rhodes, *Free Blacks of Lynchburg,* 143–44. Christopher M. Smith and Sarah Foster each make only one appearance in the Albemarle public record—the register of their marriage. Fifteen years later, a Christopher M. Smith and a Susan Smith were registered in the city of Lynchburg. Lynchburg and Charlottesville had free black populations that shared a number of surnames, including Scott, Smith, Goings, Barnett, Battles, Bowles, Cousins, Evans, and Farrar. In some cases, such as that of the Smiths, there was a direct link between the two communities. See also p. 144, where the free black Norman Scott is listed as having been born in Albemarle County in 1828.

30. ACWB No. 12, 398–401 (Apr. 14, 1837).

31. Albemarle County Marriage Register, 1780–1805, 219 (Oct. 10, 1802); ACDB No. 36, 469 (Nov. 1, 1838); and ACMB 1836–38, 467 (Nov. 7, 1838).

32. ACDB No. 38, 88 (May 29, 1840).

33. ACMB 1838–42, 183 (June 1, 1840). For an examination of the relationship of towns to the rural agricultural areas that surrounded them, see Tolbert, *Constructing Townscapes.*

34. U.S. Census for Virginia, 1840; ACWB No. 15, 486–99 (Sept. 2, 1844); ACWB No. 14, 282–86 (Jan. 3, 1842); ACWB No. 19, 34–85 (Feb. 5, 1849); ACWB No. 19, 351–53 (Feb. 4, 1850); ACDB No. 38, 303–4 (Dec. 26, 1840); and U.S. Census for Virginia, 1850.

35. U.S. Census for Virginia, 1850; J. Moore, *Albemarle,* 173; Rawlings, *Early Charlottesville,* 6, 71, 78–79; and Woods, *Albemarle County,* 87.

36. Shepherd, *Statutes at Large,* 3: 252; ACMB 1856–59, 203 (Nov. 3, 1857); and Lipscomb, *Writings of Thomas Jefferson,* 14: 261–71, letter dated Mar. 4, 1815, to Francis C. Gray, Esq. Although himself a public foe of miscegenation, Jefferson nonetheless implied that racial amalgamation would likely fit mulattoes for full membership in society. Thomas Jefferson Randolph testified on behalf of James and Robert Scott, the children of Sarah J. Scott and Jesse Scott, and Susan Catherine Foster and Clayton Randolph Foster, the children of Ann Foster. A month before the court decision, Ann Foster had registered her freedom for the first and only time. The clerk described her as a twenty-six-year-old woman of light complexion (ACMB 1856–59, 188 [Oct. 6, 1857]). Foster, like Jesse and Sarah J. Scott, was very nearly white. Foster's children surely had a white man for a father.

37. Hening, *Statutes at Large,* 12: 184; and Shepherd, *Supplement to the Revised Code,* 246–48. For a compilation of Virginia laws, see Guild, *Black Laws of Virginia,* 29, 30, 33, 108–9 (for laws dealing with racial classification).

38. U.S. Census for Virginia, 1860.

39. Woods, *Albemarle County,* 232, 270, 342, 364–66; A.C. Land Tax Book, 1782; and ACWB No. 3, 203–5, 212–13. The 1793 inventory of Stephen Hughes Sr.'s estate listed fourteen named slaves. His will bequeathed to heirs thirteen additional named slaves. His neighbors Peter Marks and Thomas West also signed the county declaration of independence. Thomas West also had a sexual relationship with a slave woman.

40. A.C. Fredericksville Parish Land Tax Book, 1788. Stephen Hughes Jr. purchased two lots that were a couple of blocks west of Thomas Bell's place. Bell was a friend of Stephen Sr.; see ACWB No. 3, 203 (Oct. 1793) 212–213 (estate inventory and appraisal).

41. ACDB No. 12, 504 (Sept. 1, 1798). The clerk recorded "Elijah," but the name he should have recorded was Eliza Hastings.

42. Woods, *Albemarle County,* 232, 262–63; and A.C. Land Tax Books, 1782–95.

43. It was not common for blacks freed by their masters to take the last names of their masters. See Berlin, *Slaves without Masters,* 51–52. It was also not common for the clerk recording the deed of manumission to assign them the last name of their master or to call a surname provided by the freedperson an alias. Interestingly, the children whom Stephen freed in 1798 were most likely his own, but all had been born while the mother was still enslaved by Peter Marks. Three of the children had first names that were common in the Marks family (Hastings, Sophia, Johanna). Daughter Mary would go on to marry Thomas Jefferson's son Madison Hemings, whom Jefferson freed through his will. See Justus, *Down from the Mountain,* 78. Justus incorrectly identifies Mary Hughes as Mary McCoy, whom Justus claims was the daughter of a Ghana Huse and Ghana's master, Stephen Hughes. Justus again mistakenly identifies Chancy Hughes as Ghana and terms Chancy a slave at the time of Mary's birth. For the list of property transac-

tions with neighbors John Pollock, John Wheeler, and James Lewis that remains suggestive of the visible nature of Stephen and Chancy's relationship, see ACDB no. 14, 209–10 (Jan. 7, 1803); ACDB No. 19, 124 (Sept. 19, 1814); ibid., 515 (Dec. 4, 1815); ACDB No. 20, 200 (Oct. 9, 1816); ibid., 286 (July 30, 1816); and ibid., 287 (Mar. 20, 1817).

44. ACCCC, Box 11 (Apr. 27, 1817).

45. Ibid. Joshua Grady posted surety for Hughes's keeping of the peace.

46. ACDB No. 23, 321–23 (May 18, 1820).

47. ACDB No. 24, 133 (Dec. 13, 1823). Stephen Hughes died sometime between 1822 and 1827. No records exist that state when he died, but 1823 seems highly likely. His and Chancy's youngest child had reached adulthood by 1823, and Stephen was nearly eighty years old. By 1827, Chancy had clearly taken possession of Stephen's farm. Hastings's decision to sell his interest in the Pollock mill may well have been connected to Stephen Hughes's death.

48. ACDB No. 28, 168 (Oct. 1, 1827). The deed of sale lists the nineteen-and-one-half-acre property as bordering property owned by Chancy Hughes, John Pollock, and others.

49. ACCOB 1829, 285–286 (Nov. 2, 1829). For more on the infrequency of free black registration, see Berlin, *Slaves without Masters,* 327–29; and Ely, *Israel on the Appomattox,* 251–54.

50. ACCOB 1830, 167 (Aug. 5, 1830); Albemarle County Court Judgments, Jan.–Mar. 1830, Box 254; ACWB No. 18, 141–45 (1845).

51. Stanton, "Monticello to Main Street," 109–12; Woods, *Albemarle County,* 110.

52. *Commonwealth v. Joshua Grady,* ACCCC, Box 7 (June 10, 1811); *Commonwealth v. Peter Barnett* Box 7 (Oct. 26, 1811); *Commonwealth v. Peter Barnett,* Box 8 (Nov. 4, 1811); *Commonwealth v. Joshua Grady,* Box 10, two folders regarding separate illegal gaming charges in 1817 and 1818.

53. ACCCC, Box 12 (July 9, 1821).

54. The only extant reference to this presentment is found in ACLOB 1822–31, 246 (May 8, 1827), where *Commonwealth v. David Isaacs and Nancy West, Commonwealth v. Andrew McKee and Matsy Cannon,* and *Commonwealth v. Betsy Ann Farley* are all dismissed. See also Rothman, *Notorious in the Neighborhood,* 65, 261 n. 27. Rothman there cites ACLOB 1822–31, 131 (May 13, 1824) as the source in which "the grand jury also presented two other couples for fornication." P. 131, however, only makes brief reference to *Commonwealth v. David Isaacs and Nancy West* and not to the other two cases. Likewise, that page does not indicate what they were accused of.

55. ACCCC, Box 20 (Sept. 20, 1833), testimony of Daniel Farley and Joshua Grady. See also ACMB 1832–34, 287.

56. Testimony of Daniel Farley and Joseph Fossett.

57. ACCCC, Box 20 (Sept. 20, 1833), testimony of Daniel Farley, Joshua Grady, Joseph Fossett, and Elijah Battles.

58. *Commonwealth v. Elijah Farrer* (assault), ACCCC, Box 20 (Oct. 19, 1833). This folder contains the judgments for both the attempted murder charge and the unlawful stabbing charge.

59. ACCCC, Box 20 (Oct. 19, 1833), both folders; ACMB 1832–34, 287; E. Jordan, "'Just and True Account,'" 114–39; ACWB No. 12, 486–92 (Oct. 2, 1837); and ACWB No. 13, 44 (Feb. 5, 1838). Elijah Farrar would return to Charlottesville and continue his violent ways. In Aug. 1835, just back from his prison stay, Elijah Farrar ran into Benjamin Ficklin, one of the justices who had passed judgment in his assault case. The two exchanged words, and Farrar allegedly "menaced and threatened" Ficklin. Farrar's confrontation occurred in front of Constable William Summerson and someone named John Major, who was in Summerson's custody at the time. In addition to threatening Ficklin, Farrar told Major to "escape and go at large." He was charged separately for both incidents, but not jailed. Both cases were dismissed in 1837 (ACCCC, Box 24 [Mar. 7, 1837]). In 1839, Farrar was involved in another assault and had to file a peace recognizance (ACCCC, Box 24 [July 4, 1839]). Farrar would be the victim of an assault in 1851 (ACCCC, Box 38 [Feb. 7, 1851]).

60. Berkeley, "Prophet without Honor," 180–90. I offer only a quick summary on McPherson's life here. The Berkeley article remains the authoritative source on McPherson.

61. Ibid., 181–85.

62. For more on Thomas West and family, see Buckley, "Unfixing Race," 349–80. For more on Nancy West, see Rothman, *Notorious in the Neighborhood*, 57–91; Stanton, "Monticello to Main Street," 94–126; and Ely, Hantman, and Leffler, *To Seek the Peace of the City.* Thomas West was a friend of William Taliaferro, who was a neighbor and friend of Stephen Hughes. Stephen Hughes knew Joshua Grady. West was also well acquainted with Thomas Bell, who knew Thomas Jefferson. All of these men had long-term sexual relationships with mulatto women.

63. See Rothman, *Notorious in the Neighborhood*, 65, 261–62 n. 28. Rothman cites ACLOB 1822–31, 131 (May 13, 1824), for the charges against all three couples. However, p. 131 only includes a brief mention of *Commonwealth v. David Isaacs and Nancy West* and does not address the nature of the charges. See also ACLOB 1822–31, 172, 190, 208, for *Commonwealth v. Joshua Grady.* That case was a trespass case. Grady was presented on May 12, 1825 (172), the case continued on Oct. 12, 1825 (190), and the guilty verdict was returned on May 10, 1826 (208). Grady was fined forty dollars. The only mention of Joshua Grady/Betsy Ann Farley and Andrew McKee/Matsy Cannon occurs on May 8, 1827 (246), where the prosecutions of both those cases and that of David Isaacs/Nancy West are dismissed. As Rothman indicates, Matsy Cannon simply does not appear elsewhere in the documents (262 n. 28). I found a Mary Cannon in 1857 who was charged with running a house of prostitution (*Commonwealth v. Mary Cannon,* Albemarle County Commonwealth Causes, Box 44), but the court papers make no indication of Mary's race or age. The commonwealth's attorney declined to prosecute. See also E. Jordan, "'Just and True Account,'" 135, for descriptions of Polly Cowan (age twenty-two, Negro) and Margarett Cowan (age four, Negro, daughter of Benjamin and Polly) in 1833; Free Negro and Slave Records, Box 2, free papers for Mary Cowan (age eighteen, yellow complexion, papers dated 1847 from Goochland County), who renewed her papers in Albemarle on June 2, 1851; and ACMB 1856–59, 202 (Nov. 3, 1857) for

registration of Mary S. Cowen (age seventeen, dark mulatto). It is unlikely that any of these women could have been the "Matsy Cannon" recorded in ACLOB in 1827.

64. Rothman, *Notorious in the Neighborhood,* 59–64. Even in more clear-cut cases, where a married man had sexual relations with a woman married to someone else, prosecutions were rare and convictions even rarer in Albemarle. Francis Birckhead in 1847 was charged with "unlawfully and scandalously living in a state of open, notorious fornication and concubinage with a certain mulatto woman named Dolly Evans." Birckhead posted a two-hundred-dollar recognizance guaranteeing his appearance in court, but Mary Ann Birckhead and Samuel Birckhead, who were called as witnesses for the commonwealth, failed to appear. The charges were ultimately dropped (ACCCC, Box 34 [June 1846]). The married white woman Nancy Kirby (along with her two male partners) was charged in Albemarle County with two separate counts of adultery and fornication in 1859. The commonwealth's attorney declined to continue prosecution of all of the cases (Albemarle County Court Commonwealth Causes, Box 47 [Feb. 3, 1859]). No other criminal indictments for fornication of interracial cohabitation appear in ACCCC, 1789–1867.

CONCLUSION

1. Jefferson, *Thomas Jefferson: Writings,* 266–70. In the same query, Jefferson also disparages black looks and compares alleged black lust for whites to that of the orangutan, which Jefferson believed lusted after black women instead of female orangutans when given the choice. See also Russell, *Free Negro in Virginia,* 75.

2. ACDB No. 9, 177 (Nov. 9, 1785). Thomas West was also the father of the free mulatto Nancy West (see chap. 6). Interestingly, James Henry West's sister Nancy West was always considered a person of color by the Albemarle County community.

3. A.C. Fredericksville Parish Land Tax Book, 1793; ACWB No. 3, 302–3 (Sept. 6, 1796); ACCOB 1795–98, 216 (Dec. 5, 1796); ACWB No. 4, 18–19 (Dec. 6, 1798); and Rothman, *Notorious in the Neighborhood,* 55–56.

4. Testimony of Benjamin Wheeler (Albemarle County Ended Chancery Causes, Circuit Superior Court, case no. 354, *Hays v. Hays*), qtd. in Rothman, *Notorious in the Neighborhood,* 69; Albemarle County Record of Marriage Bonds, 1780–1806 (Aug. 29, 1794). James Henry West ultimately settled in Amherst County, where he lived as a white property owner.

5. O. Langhorne, *Southern Sketches,* 82.

6. *Virginia Advocate,* Aug. 6, 1830, reprinted from the *New Haven Register* (microfilm, University of Virginia Alderman Library).

7. O. Langhorne, *Southern Sketches,* 82–83.

8. Rawlings, *Early Charlottesville,* 73, 79.

9. Ibid.; J. Moore, *Albemarle,* 491. No other mentions of this paper exist. Nor is there any other account of a fire that destroyed the newspaper office.

10. ACMB 1848–50, 308 (Feb. 5, 1850); ACCCC, Box 37 (Feb. 6, 1850), *Commonwealth v. Isaacs;* and Rawlings, *Early Charlottesville,* 79.

Bibliography

MANUSCRIPTS AND UNPUBLISHED PRIMARY SOURCES

Albemarle County Courthouse, Charlottesville, Va.

Chancery Order Books
Deed Books
Law Order Books
Marriage Registers
Minute Books
Order Books
Record of Marriage Bonds
Surveyor's Books
Will Books

Alderman Library, University of Virginia, Charlottesville

Ballenger Creek Baptist Church Papers
Central Gazette (Charlottesville newspaper)
Chestnut Grove Baptist Church Minute Book
Jeffersonian Republican (Charlottesville newspaper)
Memoirs of Thomas J. C. Fagg
Mountain Plain Baptist Church, Record of the Church Minister
Mount Edd Baptist Church Minute Book
Papers of John Kelly, 1812–1838
Philena Carkin Papers, 1866–1902
Recollections of Richard Thomas Walker Duke, Jr.
Stony Point Store Ledger
United States Population Census—Virginia, 1790, 1810–1860
Virginia Advocate (Charlottesville newspaper)

Library of Virginia, Richmond

Albemarle County, Auditor of Public Accounts Records
Albemarle County Chancery Causes
Albemarle County Court Commonwealth Causes
Albemarle County Court Records, Claims and Accounts
Albemarle County Court Records, Military and Pension, 1785–1919
Albemarle County, Delinquent Free Negroes

Albemarle County, Ended Chancery Causes—Circuit Superior Court
Albemarle County Judgments
Albemarle County Land Tax Books
Albemarle County, Legislative Petitions
Albemarle County—Old Papers, Orphans' Indentures
Albemarle County Personal Property Tax Books
Albemarle County, Registration and Certificates of Free Negroes

Virginia Baptist Historical Society, Richmond

Hardware Baptist Church Minute Book
Spring Hill Baptist Church Record
Sharon Baptist Church Record

Other Unpublished Materials

Vernon, Robert. "The Free Black Population of Albemarle County, Virginia, 1744–1865." Unpublished partial draft guide to county records concerning free blacks, 1995.

OTHER PRIMARY AND SECONDARY SOURCES

Abercrombie, Janice L. *Free Blacks of Louisa County, Virginia*. Athens, Ga.: Iberian Publishing Co., 1994.

Alexander, Adele Logan. *Ambiguous Lives: Free Women of Color in Rural Georgia, 1789–1879*. Fayetteville: University of Arkansas Press, 1991.

Allen, Theodore W. *The Invention of the White Race, Volume 1: Racial Oppression and Social Control*. London: Verso, 1994.

———. *The Invention of the White Race, Volume 2: The Origin of Racial Oppression in Anglo-America*. London: Verso, 1997.

Aptheker, Herbert. *American Negro Slave Revolts*. New York, 1943.

Babcock, Theodore Stoddard. "Manumission in Virginia, 1782–1806." Master's thesis, University of Virginia, 1974.

Bardaglio, Peter. *Reconstructing the Household: Families, Sex, and the Law in the Nineteenth-Century South*. Chapel Hill: University of North Carolina Press, 1995.

Barden, John Randolph. "'Flushed with Notions of Freedom': The Growth and Emancipation of a Virginia Slave Community, 1732–1812." PhD dissertation, Duke University, 1993.

Bay, Mia. *The White Image in the Black Mind: African-American Ideas about White People, 1830–1925*. New York: Oxford University Press, 2000.

Bear, James A. "The Hemings Family at Monticello." *Virginia Cavalcade* 29 (Autumn 1979): 78–87.

Berlin, Ira. *Many Thousands Gone: The First Two Centuries of Slavery in North America*. Cambridge: Belknap Press, 1998.

———. *Slaves without Masters: The Free Negro in the Antebellum South*. New York: The New Press, 1974.

———. "Time, Space, and the Evolution of Afro-American Society on British Mainland North America." *American Historical Review* 85 (1980): 44–78.

Berlin, Ira, Marc Favreau, and Steven F. Miller, eds. *Remembering Slavery: African Americans Talk about Their Personal Experiences of Slavery and Emancipation.* New York: The New Press, 1998.

Berlin, Ira, and Ronald Hoffman, eds. *Slavery and Freedom in the Age of the American Revolution.* Urbana: University of Illinois Press, 1983.

Berthoff, Rowland. "Conventional Mentality: Free Blacks, Women, and Business Corporations as Unequal Persons, 1820–1870." *Journal of American History* 76 (December 1989): 753–84.

Berkeley, Edmund, Jr. "Prophet without Honor: Christopher McPherson, Free Person of Color." *Virginia Magazine of History and Biography* 77 (April 1969): 180–90.

Bethel, Elizabeth Rauh. *The Roots of African-American Identity: Memory and History in Antebellum Free Communities.* New York: St. Martin's Press, 1997.

Bleser, Carol, ed. *In Joy and in Sorrow: Women, Family, and Marriage in the Victorian South, 1830–1900.* New York: Oxford University Press, 1991.

Bodenhorn, Howard. "The Mulatto Advantage: The Biological Consequences of Complexion in Rural Antebellum Virginia." *Journal of Interdisciplinary History* 33 (Summer 2002): 21–46.

Bogger, Tommy L. *Free Blacks in Norfolk, Virginia, 1790–1860: The Darker Side of Freedom.* Charlottesville: University Press of Virginia, 1997.

Boles, John B. *Black Southerners, 1619–1869.* Lexington: University Press of Kentucky, 1983.

Boles, John B., and Evelyn Thomas Nolen, eds. *Interpreting Southern History: Historiographical Essays in Honor of Sanford W. Higginbotham.* Baton Rouge: Louisiana State University Press, 1987.

Bolster, W. Jeffrey. *Black Jacks: African American Seaman in the Age of Sail.* Cambridge: Harvard University Press, 1997.

Boulton, Alexander O. "The American Paradox: Jeffersonian Equality and Racial Science." *American Quarterly* 47 (September 1995): 467–92.

Breen, T. H., and Stephen Innes. *"Myne Owne Ground": Race and Freedom on Virginia's Eastern Shore, 1640–1676.* New York: Oxford University Press, 1980.

Brodie, Fawn M. *Thomas Jefferson: An Intimate History.* New York: W. W. Norton, 1974.

Brown, Kathleen M. *Good Wives, Nasty Wenches, and Anxious Patriarchs: Gender, Race, and Power in Colonial Virginia.* Chapel Hill: University of North Carolina Press, 1996.

Brown, Letitia Woods. *Free Negroes in the District of Columbia, 1790–1846.* New York: Oxford University Press, 1972.

Brown, Phil. "Black-White Interracial Marriages: A Historical Analysis." *Journal of Intergroup Relations* 16 (Autumn–Winter 1989–1990): 26–36.

Brown, Thomas. "The Miscegenation of Richard Mentor Johnson as an Issue in the National Election Campaign of 1835–1836." *Civil War History* 39 (1993): 5–30.

Buckley, Thomas E. "Unfixing Race: Class, Power, and Identity in an Interracial Family." *Virginia Magazine of History and Biography* 102 (July 1994): 349–80.

Burckin, Alexander I. "A 'Spirit of Perserverance': Free African-Americans in Late Antebellum Louisville." *Filson Club History Quarterly* 70 (January 1996): 61–81.

Burg, B. R. "The Rhetoric of Miscegenation: Thomas Jefferson, Sally Hemings, and Their Historians." *Phylon* 47 (June 1986): 128–38.

Burton, Orville. *In My Father's House Are Many Mansions: Family and Community in Edgefield, South Carolina.* Chapel Hill: University of North Carolina Press, 1985.

Burton, Orville, and Robert C. McMath Jr., eds. *Class, Conflict, and Consensus: Antebellum Southern Community Studies.* Westport, Conn.: Greenwood Press, 1982.

Bushman, Katherine G., ed. *The Registers of Free Blacks 1810–1864, Augusta County, Virginia and Staunton, Virginia.* Verona, Va.: Mid-Valley Press, 1989.

Butler, Reginald Dennin. "Evolution of a Rural Free Black Community: Goochland County, Virginia, 1728–1832." PhD dissertation, Johns Hopkins University, 1989.

Bynum, Victoria. *Unruly Women: The Politics of Social and Sexual Control in the Old South.* Chapel Hill: University of North Carolina Press, 1992.

———. "'White Negroes' in Segregated Mississippi: Miscegenation, Racial Identity, and the Law." *Journal of Southern History* 64 (May 1998): 247–76.

Campbell, James M. *Slavery on Trial: Race, Class, and Criminal Justice in Antebellum Richmond, Virginia.* Gainesville: University Press of Florida, 2007.

Catterall, Helen Tunncliff, ed. *Judicial Cases Concerning American Slavery and the Negro.* 5 volumes. Washington, D.C.: Carnegie Institution, 1927–37.

Cecil-Fronsman, Bill. *Common Whites: Class and Culture in Antebellum North Carolina.* Lexington: University Press of Kentucky, 1992.

Clinton, Catherine, and Michelle Gillespie, eds. *The Devil's Lane: Sex and Race in the Early South.* New York: Oxford University Press, 1997.

———. "'With a Whip in His Hand': Rape, Memory, and African-American Women." In *History and Memory in African-American Culture,* ed. Genevieve Fabre and Robert O'Meally, 205–18. New York: Oxford University Press, 1994.

Cohen, David W., and Jack P. Greene, eds. *Neither Slave nor Free: The Freedmen of African Descent in the Slave Societies of the New World.* Baltimore: Johns Hopkins University Press, 1972.

Condon, John Joseph, Jr. "Manumission, Slavery and Family in the Post-Revolutionary Rural Chesapeake: Anne Arundel County, Maryland, 1781–1831." PhD dissertation, University of Minnesota, 2001.

Curry, Leonard P. *The Free Black in Urban America 1800–1850: The Shadow of a Dream.* Chicago: University of Chicago Press, 1981.

Dabney, William Minor. "Jefferson's Albemarle: History of Albemarle County, Virginia, 1727–1819." PhD dissertation, University of Virginia, 1951.

Davis, Adrienne D. "The Private Law of Race and Sex: An Antebellum Perspective." *Stanford Law Review* 51 (January 1999): 221–88.

Davis, Angela Y. *Women, Race, and Class.* New York: Random House, 1981.

Davis, David Brion. *The Problem of Slavery in the Age of Revolution, 1770–1823*. Ithaca, N.Y.: Cornell University Press, 1975.

Davis, Rosalie Edith. *Louisa County, Virginia, Tithables and Census, 1743–1785*. Manchester, Mo.: R. E. Davis, 1988.

Deal, J. Douglas. "A Constricted World: Free Blacks on Virginia's Eastern Shore, 1680–1750." In *Colonial Chesapeake Society*, ed Lois Green Carr, Philip D. Morgan, and Jean B. Russo, 275–305. Chapel Hill: University of North Carolina Press, 1988.

———. *Race and Class in Colonial Virginia: Indians, Englishmen, and Africans on the Eastern Shore During the Seventeenth Century*. New York: Garland Publishing, 1993.

Delaney, Ted, and Phillip Wayne Rhodes. *Free Blacks of Lynchburg, Virginia, 1805–1865*. Lynchburg: Warwick House, 2001.

Dew, Charles B. *Bond of Iron: Master and Slave at Buffalo Forge*. New York: W. W. Norton, 1994.

Dominguez, Virginia R. *White by Definition: Social Classification in Creole Louisiana*. New Brunswick: Rutgers University Press, 1986.

Dorman, John Frederick. *Virginia Revolutionary Pension Applications*. 52 volumes. Fredericksburg, Va.: J. F. Dorman, 1996.

Douglass, Frederick. *Narrative of the Life of Frederick Douglass, an American Slave, Written by Himself*. Ed. David W. Blight. 2nd edition. Boston: Bedford/St. Martin's, 2003.

Dykstra, Robert R., and William Silag. "Doing Local History: Monographic Approaches to the Smaller Community." *American Quarterly* 37 (1985): 411–25.

Edwards, Laura F. *The People and Their Peace: Legal Culture and the Transformation of Inequality in the Post-Revolutionary South*. Chapel Hill: University of North Carolina Press, 2009.

Egerton, Douglas R. *Gabriel's Rebellion: The Virginia Slave Conspiracies of 1800 and 1802*. Chapel Hill: University of North Carolina Press, 1993.

Ellefson, C. Ashley. "Free Jupiter and the Rest of the World: The Problems of a Free Negro in Colonial Maryland." *Maryland Historical Magazine* 66 (1971): 1–13.

Ellis, Joseph J. *American Sphinx: The Character of Thomas Jefferson*. New York: Alfred A. Knopf, 1997.

Ely, Carol, Jeffrey Hantman, and Phyllis Leffler. *To Seek the Peace of the City: Jewish Life in Charlottesville*. Charlottesville: Hillel Jewish Center, 1994.

Ely, Melvin Patrick. *Israel on the Appomattox: A Southern Experiment in Black Freedom from the 1790s Through the Civil War*. New York: Alfred A. Knopf, 2004.

Fields, Barbara Jeanne. "Ideology and Race in American History." In *Region, Race, and Reconstruction: Essays in Honor of C. Vann Woodward*, ed. J. Morgan Kousser and James M. McPherson, 143–77. New York: Oxford University Press, 1982.

———. *Slavery and Freedom on the Middle Ground: Maryland During the Nineteenth Century*. New Haven, Conn.: Yale University Press, 1985.

———. "Slavery, Race, and Ideology in the United States of America." *New Left Review* 181 (May–June 1990): 95–118.

Finkelman, Paul. *Slavery and the Founders: Race and Liberty in the Age of Jefferson.* Armonk, N.Y.: M. E. Sharpe, 1996.

Foner, Eric. *The Story of American Freedom.* New York: W. W. Norton, 1998.

Forbes, Jack D. "The Evolution of the Term Mulatto: A Chapter in Black-Native American Relations." *Journal of Ethnic Studies* 10 (1982): 45–66.

Foster, Eugene, et al. "Jefferson Fathered Slave's Last Child." *Nature* 396 (November 5, 1998): 27–28.

Fox-Genovese, Elizabeth. *Within the Plantation Household: Black and White Women of the Old South.* Chapel Hill: University of North Carolina Press, 1988.

Franklin, John Hope. *The Free Negro in North Carolina, 1790–1860.* Chapel Hill: University of North Carolina Press, 1943.

———. *Race and History: Selected Essays, 1938–1988.* Baton Rouge: Louisiana State University Press, 1989.

Franklin, John Hope, and Loren Schweninger. *Runaway Slaves: Rebels on the Plantation.* New York: Oxford University Press, 1999.

Frederickson, George. *The Arrogance of Race: Historical Perspectives on Slavery, Racism, and Social Inequality.* Middletown, Conn.: Wesleyan University Press, 1988.

———. *The Black Image in the White Mind: The Debate on Afro-American Character and Destiny, 1817–1914.* Middletown, Conn.: Wesleyan University Press, 1971.

———. *White Supremacy: A Comparative Study in American and South African History.* New York: Oxford University Press, 1981.

Garner, Bryan A., ed. *Black's Law Dictionary.* 3rd ed. Eagan, Minn.: Thomson-West, 2006.

Genovese, Eugene. *Roll, Jordan, Roll: The World the Slaves Made.* New York: Random House, 1972.

Getman, Karen A. "Sexual Control in the Slaveholding South: The Implementation and Maintenance of a Racial Caste System." *Harvard Women's Law Journal* 7 (1984): 115–52.

Goldfield, David R. "Urban-Rural Relations in the Old South: The Example of Virginia." *Journal of Urban History* 2 (February 1976): 146–68.

Gomez, Michael. *Exchanging Our Country Marks: The Transformation of African Identities in the Colonial and Antebellum South.* Chapel Hill: University of North Carolina Press, 1998.

Gordon-Reed, Annette. *The Hemingses of Monticello.* New York: W. W. Norton, 2008.

———. *Thomas Jefferson and Sally Hemings: An American Controversy.* Charlottesville: University Press of Virginia, 1997.

Gould, Virginia Meacham, ed. *Chained to the Rock of Adversity: To Be Free, Black, and Female in the Old South.* Athens: University of Georgia Press, 1998.

Gross, Ariela J. "Litigating Whiteness: Trials of Racial Determination in the Nineteenth Century South." *Yale Law Journal* 108 (October 1998): 109–88.

Grossberg, Michael. *Governing the Hearth: Law and Family in Nineteenth-Century America.* Chapel Hill: University of North Carolina Press, 1985.

Guild, June Purcell. *Black Laws of Virginia: A Summary of the Legislative Acts of Virginia Concerning Negroes From Earliest Times to the Present.* 1936. New York: Negro Universities Press, 1969.

Haney Lopez, Ian F. *White by Law: The Legal Construction of Race.* New York: New York University Press, 1996.

Hanger, Kimberly S. *Bounded Lives, Bounded Places: Free Black Society in Colonial New Orleans, 1769–1803.* Durham, N.C.: Duke University Press, 1997.

Harris, J. William. *Plain Folk and Gentry in a Slave Society.* Middletown, Conn.: Wesleyan University Press, 1985.

Harrison, Susan. "Black Women in the Nineteenth-Century South." *Mississippi Quarterly* 46 (Spring 1993): 284–90.

Heinegg, Paul. *Free African Americans of North Carolina, Virginia, and South Carolina From the Colonial Period to about 1820.* 2 volumes. Baltimore: Clearfield Publishing, 2001.

Hening, William Waller, ed. *The Statutes at Large, Being a Collection of All the Laws of Virginia from the First Session of the Legislature in 1619.* 13 volumes. New York, Richmond, and Philadelphia, 1809–1823.

Hess, Karl IV. "Four Decades of Social Change: Scottsville, Virginia, 1820–1860." Master's thesis, University of Virginia, 1973.

Higginbotham, A. Leon, Jr. *In the Matter of Color: Race and the American Legal Process.* New York: Oxford University Press, 1978.

Higginbotham, A. Leon, Jr., and Greer C. Bosworth. "'Rather Than the Free': Free Blacks in Colonial and Antebellum Virginia." *Harvard Civil Rights-Civil Liberties Law Review* 26 (Winter 1991): 17–66.

Higginbotham, A. Leon, Jr., and Anne F. Jacobs. "The 'Law Only as an Enemy': The Legitimization of Racial Powerlessness Through the Colonial and Antebellum Criminal Laws of Virginia." *North Carolina Law Review* 70 (April 1992): 969–1070.

Higginbotham, A. Leon, Jr., and Barbara K. Kopytoff. "Racial Purity and Interracial Sex in the Law of Colonial and Antebellum Virginia." *Georgetown Law Journal* 77 (1989): 1967–2029.

Hindus, Michael S. "Black Justice under White Law: Criminal Prosecutions of Blacks in Antebellum South Carolina." *Journal of American History* 63 (December 1976): 575–99.

Hobson, Barbara Meil. *Uneasy Virtue: The Politics of Prostitution and the American Reform Tradition.* New York: Basic Books, 1987.

Hodes, Martha, ed. *Sex, Love, Race: Crossing Boundaries in North American History.* New York: New York University Press, 1999.

———. *White Women, Black Men: Illicit Sex in the Nineteenth-Century South.* New Haven, Conn.: Yale University Press, 1997.

Hoffman, Ronald, Mechal Sobel, and Fredrika J. Teute, eds. *Through a Glass Darkly: Reflections on Personal Identity in Early America.* Chapel Hill: University of North Carolina Press, 1997.

Hogan, William Ransom, and Edwin Adams Davis, eds. *William Johnson's Natchez: The Ante-Bellum Diary of a Free Negro.* Baton Rouge: Louisiana State University Press, 1951.

Howington, Arthur F. *What Sayeth the Law: The Treatment of Slaves and Free Blacks in the State and Local Courts of Tennessee.* New York: Garland Publishing, 1986.

Hudson, Larry E., Jr., ed. *Working toward Freedom: Slave Society and Domestic Economy in the American South.* Rochester, N.Y.: University of Rochester Press, 1994.

Hughes, Louis. *Thirty Years a Slave: From Bondage to Freedom.* Milwaukee: South Side Printing, 1897.

Hunter, Tera W. *To 'Joy My Freedom: Southern Black Women's Lives and Labors after the Civil War.* Cambridge: Harvard University Press, 1997.

Ireland, Robert M. "Frenzied and Fallen Females: Women and Sexual Dishonor in the Nineteenth-Century United States." *Journal of Women's History* 3 (Winter 1992): 27–44.

Isaac, Rhys. *The Transformation of Virginia, 1740–1790.* New York: W. W. Norton, 1982.

Jackson, Luther Porter. *Free Negro Labor and Property Holding in Virginia, 1830–1860.* New York: Atheneum, 1942.

———. *Negro Office-Holders in Virginia, 1865–1895.* Norfolk: Guide Quality Press, 1945.

———."Virginia Negroes and Seamen in the American Revolution," *Journal of Negro History* 26 (July 1942): 247–87.

———. *Virginia Negro Soldiers and Seamen in the Revolutionary War.* Norfolk: Guide Quality Press, 1944.

Jacobs, Harriet. *Incidents in the Life of a Slave Girl.* Ed. Jean Fagan Yellin. Cambrdige: Harvard University Press, 1987.

Jefferson, Thomas. *Papers of Thomas Jefferson.* Ed. Julian Boyd. 20 volumes. Princeton, N.J.: Princeton University Press, 1950–82.

———. *Papers of Thomas Jefferson.* Ed. Charles T. Cullen. 7 volumes to date. Princeton, N.J.: Princeton University Press, 1982- .

———. *Thomas Jefferson: Writings.* Ed. Merrill D. Peterson. New York: Literary Classics of the United States, 1984.

———. *The Writings of Thomas Jefferson.* Ed. Paul Leicester. Ford. 12 volumes. New York: G. P. Putnam and Sons, 1892–99.

———. *The Writings of Thomas Jefferson.* Ed. Andrew A. Lipscomb. 20 vols. Washington, D.C.: Issued under the auspices of the Thomas Jefferson Memorial Association of the United States, 1904–5.

Johnson, Michael P., and James L. Roark. *Black Masters: A Free Family of Color in the Old South.* New York: W. W. Norton, 1984.

———. *No Chariot Let Down: Charleston's Free People of Color on the Eve of the Civil War.* Chapel Hill: University of North Carolina Press, 1984.

Johnson, Walter. *Soul by Soul: Life inside the Antebellum Slave Market.* Cambridge: Harvard University Press, 1999.

Johnson, Whittington B. "Free African-American Women in Savannah, Georgia, 1800–1860: Affluence and Autonomy Amid Adversity." *Georgia Historical Quarterly* 76 (Summer 1992): 260–83.

Johnston, James Hugo. *Race Relations in Virginia and Miscegenation in the South, 1776–1860.* Amherst: University of Massachusetts Press, 1970.

Jones, Jacqueline. *Labor of Love, Labor of Sorrow: Black Women, Work, and the Family from Slavery to the Present.* New York: Basic Books, 1985.

Jones, Newton Bond. "Charlottesville and Albemarle County, Virginia, 1819–1860." PhD dissertation, University of Virginia, 1950.

Jordan, Ervin L., Jr. "'A Just and True Account': Two Parish Censuses of Albemarle County Free Blacks," *Magazine of Albemarle County History* 53 (1995): 114–39.

Jordan, Winthrop D. *White over Black: American Attitudes toward the Negro, 1550–1812.* Chapel Hill: University of North Carolina Press, 1968.

Jordan, Winthrop D., and Sheila L. Skemp, eds. *Race and Family in the Colonial South.* Jackson: University Press of Mississippi, 1987.

Justus, Judith P. *Down from the Mountain: The Oral History of the Hemings Family.* Perrysburg, Ohio: Lesher Printers, 1990.

Kennedy-Haflett, Cynthia. "'Moral Marriage': A Mixed-Race Relationship in Nineteenth-Century Charleston, South Carolina." *South Carolina Historical Magazine* 97 (July 1996): 206–26.

Kenzer, Robert C. *Kinship and Neighborhood in a Southern Community: Orange County, North Carolina, 1849–1881.* Knoxville: University of Tennessee Press, 1987.

Kerr-Ritchie, Jeffrey R. *Freedpeople in the Tobacco South.* Chapel Hill: University of North Carolina Press, 1999.

Koger, Larry. *Black Slaveowners: Free Black Slave Masters in South Carolina, 1790–1860.* Columbia: University of South Carolina Press, 1985.

Kolchin, Peter. *American Slavery, 1619–1877.* New York: Hill and Wang, 1993.

Koons, Kenneth E., and Warren R. Hofstra. *After the Backcountry: Rural Life in the Great Valley of Virginia, 1800–1900.* Knoxville: University of Tennessee Press, 2000.

Landers, Jane, ed. *Against All Odds: Free Blacks in the Slave Societies of the Americas.* London: Frank Cass, 1996.

Langhorne, Elizabeth. "A Black Family at Monticello." *Magazine of Albemarle County History* 43 (1985): 1–16.

Langhorne, Orra. *Southern Sketches from Virginia.* Charlottesville: University Press of Virginia, 1964.

Langston, John Mercer. *From the Virginia Plantation to the National Capitol, or the First and Only Negro Representative in Congress from the Old Dominion.* Hartford, 1894.

Lebsock, Suzanne. *The Free Women of Petersburg: Status and Culture in a Southern Town, 1784–1860.* New York: W. W. Norton, 1984.

Leslie, Kent Anderson. *Woman of Color, Daughter of Privilege: Amanda America Dickson, 1849–1893.* Athens: University of Georgia Press, 1995.

Lewis, Jan Ellen, and Peter S. Onuf, eds. *Sally Hemings and Thomas Jefferson: History, Memory, and Civic Culture.* Charlottesville: University Press of Virginia, 1999.

Lockley, Timothy James. *Lines in the Sand: Race and Class in Lowcountry Georgia, 1750–1860.* Athens: University of Georgia Press, 2001.

Logan, Rayford W., ed. *Memoirs of a Monticello Slave, as Dictated to Charles Campbell in the 1840s by Isaac, One of Thomas Jefferson's Slaves.* Charlottesville: University Press of Virginia, 1951.

Lowman, David St. Clair. "Unwanted Residents: The Plight of the Emancipated Slave in Virginia, 1806–1835." Master's thesis, College of William and Mary, 1977.

Madden, T. O., Jr. *We Were Always Free: The Maddens of Culpeper County, Virginia, a 200-year Family History.* New York: W. W. Norton, 1992.

Martin, Byron Curti. "Racism in the United States: A History of the Anti-Miscegenation Legislation and Litigation." PhD dissertation, University of Southern California, 1979.

Martin, Jonathan D. *Divided Mastery: Slave Hiring in the American South.* Cambridge: Harvard University Press, 2004.

Mathews, Jean. "Race, Sex, and the Dimensions of Liberty in Antebellum America," *Journal of the Early Republic* 6 (Autumn 1986): 275–92.

Matison, Sumner Eliot. "Manumission by Purchase." *Journal of Negro History* 33 (April 1948): 146–67.

McColley, Robert. *Slavery and Jeffersonian Virginia.* Urbana: University of Illinois Press, 1964.

McCurry, Stephanie. *Masters of Small Worlds: Yeoman Households, Gender Relations, and the Political Culture of the Antebellum South Carolina Low Country.* New York: Oxford University Press, 1995.

McDonald, Robert M. S. "Race, Sex, and Reputation: Thomas Jefferson and the Sally Hemings Story." *Southern Cultures* 4 (Summer 1998): 46–64.

McLeod, Norman C., Jr. "Free Labor in a Slave Society: Richmond, Virginia, 1820–1860." PhD dissertation, Howard University, 1991.

McLeRoy, Sherrie S., and William R. McLeRoy. *Strangers in Their Midst: The Free Black Population of Amherst County, Virginia.* Bowie, Md.: Heritage Books, 1993.

Mead, Edward C. *Historic Homes of the South-West Mountains Virginia.* Philadelphia: J. B. Lippincott, 1899.

Medford, Edna Greene. "'I Was Always a Union Man': The Dilemma of Free Blacks in Confederate Virginia." *Slavery and Abolition* 15 (December 1994): 1–21.

Miller, John Chester. *The Wolf by the Ears: Thomas Jefferson and Slavery.* New York: Free Press, 1977.

Mills, Gary B. "Miscegenation and the Free Negro in Antebellum 'Anglo' Alabama: A Reexamination of Southern Race Relations." *Journal of American History* 68 (June 1981): 16–34.

———. "Tracing Free People of Color in the Antebellum South: Methods, Sources, and Perspectives." *National Genealogical Society Quarterly* 78 (1990): 262–78.

Moore, John Hammond. *Albemarle: Jefferson's County, 1727–1976.* Charlottesville: Albemarle County Historical Society, 1976.

Moore, Sally Falk. *Law as Process: An Anthropological Approach.* London: Routledge and Kegan Paul, 1978.

Morgan, Edmund. *American Slavery, American Freedom: The Ordeal of Colonial Virginia.* New York: W. W. Norton, 1975.

Morgan, Philip D., ed. *"Don't Grieve after Me," The Black Experience in Virginia, 1619–1986.* Hampton: Hampton University, 1986.

———. "Interracial Sex in the Chesapeake." In Lewis and Onuf, *Sally Hemings and Thomas Jefferson,* 52–86.

———. *Slave Counterpoint: Black Culture in the Eighteenth-Century Chesapeake and Lowcountry.* Chapel Hill: University of North Carolina Press, 1998.

Mullin, Gerald W. *Flight and Rebellion: Slave Resistance in Eighteenth-Century Virginia.* New York: Oxford University Press, 1972.

Nash, A. E. Keir. "Fairness and Formalism in the Trials of Blacks in the State Supreme Courts of the Old South." *Virginia Law Review* 56 (1970): 64–100.

Nash, Gary B. *Forging Freedom: The Formation of Philadelphia's Black Community, 1720–1840.* Cambridge: Harvard University Press, 1988.

———. *Race and Revolution.* Madison: Madison House, 1990.

Nash, Gary B., and Jean R. Soderlund. *Freedom by Degrees: Emancipation in Pennsylvania and Its Aftermath.* New York: Oxford University Press, 1991.

Nicholls, Michael L. "Passing through This Troublesome World: Free Blacks in the Early Southside." *Virginia Magazine of History and Biography* 92 (1984): 50–70.

Nieman, Fraser D. "Coincidence or Causal Connection? The Relationship between Thomas Jefferson's Visits to Monticello and Sally Hemings's Conceptions." *William and Mary Quarterly* 56 (1): 198–210.

Olwell, Robert. "Becoming Free: Manumission and the Genesis of a Free Black Community in South Carolina, 1740–1790." *Slavery and Abolition* 17 (April 1996): 1–19.

Onuf, Peter S., ed. *Jeffersonian Legacies.* Charlottesville: University Press of Virginia, 1993.

Patterson, Orlando. *Freedom.* Volume 1, *Freedom in the Making of Western Culture.* New York: Basic Books, 1991.

———. *Slavery and Social Death: A Comparative Study.* Cambridge: Harvard University Press, 1982.

Perdue, Charles L., Jr., Thomas E. Barden, and Robert K. Phillips, eds. *Weevils in the Wheat: Interviews with Virginia Ex-Slaves.* Charlottesville: University Press of Virginia, 1976.

Phillips, Christopher. *Freedom's Port: The African-American Community of Baltimore, 1790–1860.* Urbana: University of Illinois Press, 1997.

Phillips, Ulrich B. *American Negro Slavery.* New York: D. Appleton, 1918.

Quarles, Benjamin. *The Negro in the American Revolution.* Chapel Hill: University of North Carolina Press, 1961.

Rawick, George P., ed. *The American Slave: A Composite Autobiography.* 17 volumes: supplement 1, 12 volumes; supplement 2, 10 volumes. Westport, Conn.: Greenwood Press, 1972–79.

Rawlings, Mary. *The Albemarle of Other Days*. Charlottesville: Michie Company, 1925.

———. *Antebellum Albemarle*. Charlottesville: Michie Company, 1935.

———, ed. *Early Charlottesville: Recollections of James Alexander, 1828–1874*. Charlottesville: Albemarle County Historical Society, 1942.

Rothman, Joshua D. *Notorious in the Neighborhood: Sex and Families across the Color Line in Virginia, 1787–1861*. Chapel Hill: University of North Carolina Press, 2003.

Russell, John Henderson. "Colored Freemen as Slave Owners in Virginia." *Journal of Negro History* 1 (July 1916): 233–42.

———. *The Free Negro in Virginia, 1619–1865*. Johns Hopkins University Studies in Historical and Political Science, vol. 21, no. 3. Baltimore: Johns Hopkins Press, 1913.

Saks, Eva. "Representing Miscegenation Law." *Raritan* 8 (Autumn 1988): 39–69.

Saunders, Robert M. "Crime and Punishment in Early National America: Richmond, Virginia, 1784–1820." *Virginia Magazine of History and Biography* 86 (January 1978): 33–44.

Schmidt, Fredrika Teute, and Barbara Ripel Wilhelm. "Early Proslavery Petitions in Virginia." *William and Mary Quarterly*, 3rd series, 30 (January 1973): 133–46.

Schwalm, Leslie A. *A Hard Fight for We: Women's Transition from Slavery to Freedom in South Carolina*. Urbana: University of Illinois Press, 1997.

Schwarz, Philip J. "Emancipators, Protectors, and Anomalies: Free Black Slaveowners in Virginia." *Virginia Magazine of History and Biography* 95 (July 1987): 317–38.

———. *Twice Condemned: Slaves and the Criminal Laws of Virginia, 1705–1865*. Baton Rouge: Louisiana State University Press, 1988.

Schweninger, Loren. *Black Property Owners in the South, 1790–1915*. Urbana: University of Illinois Press, 1990.

———. "Property-Owning Free African-American Women in the South, 1800–1870." *Journal of Women's History* 1 (Winter 1990): 13–44.

Scott, James C. *Domination and the Arts of Resistance: Hidden Transcripts*. New Haven: Yale University Press, 1990.

Scott, John Anthony. "Segregation: A Fundamental Aspect of Southern Race Relations, 1800–1860." *Journal of the Early Republic* 4 (Winter 1984): 421–41.

Sensbach, Jon F. *A Separate Canaan: The Making of an Afro-Moravian World in North Carolina, 1763–1840*. Chapel Hill: University of North Carolina Press, 1998.

Sheldon, Marianne Buroff. "Black-White Relations in Richmond, Virginia, 1782–1820." *Journal of Southern History* 45 (February 1979): 27–44.

Shepherd, Samuel, ed. *The Statues at Large, Being a Collection of All the Laws of Virginia from the First Session of the Legislature in 1619*. New series. 3 volumes. Richmond, 1835.

———. *Supplement to the Revised Code of the Laws of Virginia*. Richmond: Samuel Shepherd and Co., 1833.

Shifflett, Crandall A. *Patronage and Poverty in the Tobacco South: Louisa County, Virginia, 1860–1900*. Knoxville: University of Tennessee Press, 1982.

Sidbury, James. *Ploughshares into Swords: Race, Rebellion, and Identity in Gabriel's Virginia, 1783–1810.* Cambridge: Cambridge University Press, 1997.

Siegel, Frederick F. *The Roots of Southern Distinctiveness: Tobacco and Society in Danville, Virginia, 1780–1865.* Chapel Hill: University of North Carolina Press, 1987.

Smith, Glenn Curtis. "Newspapers of Albemarle County, Virginia." *Papers of the Albemarle County Historical Society* 1 (1940–41): 36–37.

Sobel, Mechal. *The World They Made Together: Black and White Values in Eighteenth-Century Virginia.* Princeton, N.J.: Princeton University Press, 1987.

Stanton, Lucia. *Free Some Day: The African-American Families of Monticello.* Charlottesville: Thomas Jefferson Foundation, 2000.

———. "Monticello to Main Street: The Hemings Family and Charlottesville." *Magazine of Albemarle County History* 55 (1997): 95–126.

Stauffenberg, Ann Lenore. "Albemarle County, Virginia, 1850–1870." Master's thesis, University of Virginia, 1973.

Steckel, Richard H. "Miscegenation and the American Slave Schedules." *Journal of Interdisciplinary History* 11 (Autumn 1980): 251–63.

Stevenson, Brenda E. *Life in Black and White: Family and Community in the Slave South.* New York: Oxford University Press, 1996.

Takagi, Midori. *"Rearing Wolves to Our Own Destruction": Slavery in Richmond, Virginia, 1782–1865.* Charlottesville: University Press of Virginia, 1999.

Tolbert, Lisa C. *Constructing Townscapes: Space and Society in Antebellum Tennessee.* Chapel Hill: University of North Carolina Press, 1999.

Toplin, Robert Brent. "Between Black and White: Attitudes Towards Southern Mulattoes, 1830–1861." *Journal of Southern History* 45 (May 1979): 185–200.

Towler, Sam. "The West Family." *Central Virginia Heritage* 10 (Summer 1993): 55.

Trotter, Joe William, Jr. *River Jordan: African American Urban Life in the Ohio Valley.* Lexington: University Press of Kentucky, 1998.

Tushnet, Mark V. *The American Law of Slavery, 1810–1860: Considerations of Humanity and Justice.* Princeton, N.J.: Princeton University Press, 1981.

Tyler-McGraw, Marie. "Richmond Free Blacks and African Colonization, 1816–1832." *Journal of American Studies* 21 (August 1987): 207–24.

Tyler-McGraw, Marie, and Gregg D. Kimball. *In Bondage and Freedom: Antebellum Black Life in Richmond, Virginia.* Richmond: Valentine Museum, 1988.

Vance, Joseph Carroll. "The Negro in the Reconstruction of Albemarle County, Virginia." Master's thesis, University of Virginia, 1953.

Virginia Writers' Project. *The Negro in Virginia, Compiled by Workers of the Writers' Program of the Works Project Administration in the State of Virginia.* New York: Hastings House, 1940.

Vogt, John, and T. William Kethley Jr. *Albemarle County Marriages, 1780–1853.* 3 volumes. Athens, Ga.: Iberian Publishing, 1991.

von Daacke, Kirt. "Free Black Families and Freedom in Albemarle County, Virginia, 1787–1860." Unpublished paper, Johns Hopkins University, 1998.

———. "Slaves without Masters? The Butler Family of Albemarle County, 1780–1860." *Magazine of Albemarle County History* 55 (1997): 38–59.

Waldrep, Christopher, and Donald G. Nieman, eds. *Local Matters: Race, Crime, and Justice in the Nineteenth Century South.* Athens: University of Georgia Press, 2001.

Wallenstein, Peter. *Tell the Court I Love My Wife: Race, Marriage, and Law—An American History.* New York: Palgrave MacMillan, 2002.

Warner, Lee H. *Free Men in an Age of Servitude: Three Generations of a Black Family.* Lexington: University Press of Kentucky, 1992.

Webb, William Edward. "Charlottesville and Albemarle County, Virginia, 1865–1900." PhD dissertation, University of Virginia, 1955.

Weeks, Stephen B. *Southern Quakers and Slavery.* Baltimore: Johns Hopkins Press, 1896.

Whitman, T. Stephen. *The Price of Freedom: Slavery and Manumission in Baltimore and Early National Maryland.* Lexington: University Press of Kentucky, 1997.

Williamson, Joel. *New People: Miscegenation and Mulattoes in the United States.* New York: Free Press, 1980.

Wolf, Eva Sheppard. *Race and Liberty in the New Nation: Emancipation in Virginia from the Revolution to Nat Turner's Rebellion.* Baton Rouge: Louisiana State University Press, 2006.

Woods, Edgar. *Albemarle County in Virginia.* Charlottesville: Michie Company, 1901.

Woodson, Carter G. "The Beginnings of the Miscegenation of the Whites and Blacks," *Journal of Negro History* 3 (October 1918): 335–53.

———. "Free Negro Owners of Slaves in the United States in 1830." *Journal of Negro History* 9 (January 1924): 48–85.

Woolfolk, George R. "Turner's Safety Valve and Free Negro Westward Migration." *Journal of Negro History* 50 (July 1965): 185–97.

Worrall, Jay, Jr. *The Friendly Virginians: America's First Quakers.* Athens, Ga.: Iberian Publishing, 1994.

Wright, James M. *The Free Negro in Maryland, 1634–1860.* New York: Columbia University Press, 1921.

Wyatt-Brown, Bertram. *Southern Honor: Ethics and Behavior in the Old South.* New York: Oxford University Press, 1982.

Zaborney, John Joseph. "Slaves for Rent: Slave Hiring in Virginia." PhD dissertation, University of Maine, 1997.

Zack, Naomi. *Race and Mixed Race.* Philadelphia: Temple University Press, 1993.

Zackodnik, Teresa. "Fixing the Color Line: The Mulatto, Southern Courts, and Racial Identity." *American Quarterly* 53 (September 2001): 420–51.

Index

Carter G. Woodson Institute Series

Michael Plunkett, *Afro-American Sources in Virginia: A Guide to Manuscripts*

Sally Belfrage, *Freedom Summer*

Armstead L. Robinson and Patricia Sullivan, eds., *New Directions in Civil Rights Studies*

Leroy Vail and Landeg White, *Power and the Praise Poem: Southern African Voices in History*

Robert A. Pratt, *The Color of Their Skin: Education and Race in Richmond, Virginia, 1954–89*

Ira Berlin and Philip D. Morgan, eds., *Cultivation and Culture: Labor and the Shaping of Slave Life in the Americas*

Gerald Horne, *Fire This Time: The Watts Uprising and the 1960s*

Sam C. Nolutshungu, *Limits of Anarchy: Intervention and State Formation in Chad*

Jeannie M. Whayne, *A New Plantation South: Land, Labor, and Federal Favor in Twentieth-Century Arkansas*

Patience Essah, *A House Divided: Slavery and Emancipation in Delaware, 1638–1865*

Tommy L. Bogger, *Free Blacks in Norfolk, Virginia, 1790–1860: The Darker Side of Freedom*

Robert C. Kenzer, *Enterprising Southerners: Black Economic Success in North Carolina, 1865–1915*

Midori Takagi, *"Rearing Wolves to Our Own Destruction": Slavery in Richmond, Virginia, 1782–1865*

Alessandra Lorini, *Rituals of Race: American Public Culture and the Search for Racial Democracy*

Mary Ellen Curtin, *Black Prisoners and Their World, Alabama, 1865–1900*

Philip J. Schwarz, *Migrants against Slavery: Virginians and the Nation*

Armstead L. Robinson, *Bitter Fruits of Bondage: The Demise of Slavery and the Collapse of the Confederacy, 1861–1865*

Francille Rusan Wilson, *The Segregated Scholars: Black Social Scientists and the Creation of Black Labor Studies, 1890–1950*

Gregory Michael Dorr, *Segregation's Science: Eugenics and Society in Virginia*

Glenn McNair, *Criminal Injustice: Slaves and Free Blacks in Georgia's Criminal Justice System*

William Dusinberre, *Strategies for Survival: Recollections of Bondage in Antebellum Virginia*

Valerie C. Cooper, *Word, Like Fire: Maria Stewart, the Bible, and the Rights of African Americans*

Michael L. Nicholls, *Whispers of Rebellion: Narrating Gabriel's Conspiracy*

Henry Goings, *Rambles of a Runaway from Southern Slavery,* edited by Calvin Schermerhorn, Michael Plunkett, and Edward Gaynor

Philip J. Schwarz, ed., *Gabriel's Conspiracy: A Documentary History*

Kirt von Daacke, *Freedom Has a Face: Race, Identity, and Community in Jefferson's Virginia*